# THE POCKET GUIDE TO WINE

As a freelance wine journalist, Barbara Ensrud writes a weekly column for the New York *Daily News* and regular columns for *Vogue*, *The Wine Spectator*, and many other newspapers and magazines. She has also contributed to several best-selling wine books, including *The Joys of Wine* and *The New York Times Wine Book*. A member of the New York Wine Writers Circle and the International Wine and Food Society, Ms. Ensrud has traveled extensively in many vineyard regions of the world and frequently lectures on wine.

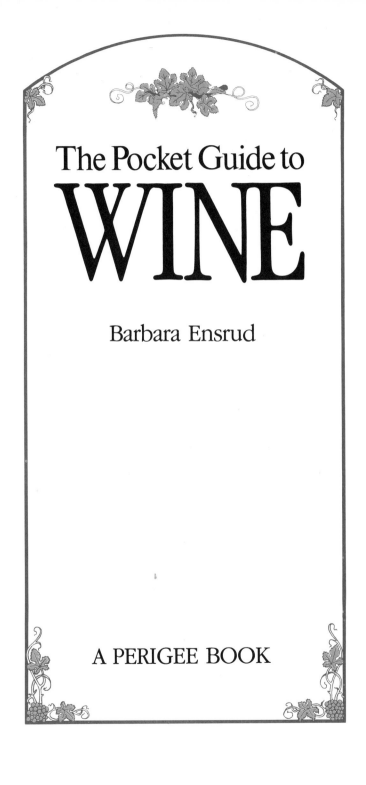

# The Pocket Guide to
# WINE

Barbara Ensrud

A PERIGEE BOOK

To Alec Waugh
who first excited my interest in wine
and to Hella
for her generous encouragement and support

**Perigee Books**
are published by
**G. P. Putnam's Sons**
200 Madison Avenue
New York, New York 10016

Published simultaneously in Canada by
Academic Press Canada Limited, Toronto.

Library of Congress Catalog Card Number: 80-80950
ISBN: 0-399-50483-4
First Perigee Printing, 1980


The Pocket Guide to Wine was produced and prepared by
**Quarto Marketing, Ltd.**
**212 Fifth Avenue, New York, New York 10010**

Editors: John Smallwood and Wendy L. Ruoff
Designer: Mary Tiegreen
Production: Millie Falcaro
Maps by Randall Lieu
Illustrations by Mary Tiegreen

Printed and bound in the United States of America by
**Maple-Vail Group**

# CONTENTS

# INTRODUCTION

For some years now I have heard friends and others plead for a practical, down-to-earth wine book that didn't tell them more than they wanted to know or had time to absorb. When I was approached to do this little book, it seemed the perfect answer to such a need. Mostly it is for those who already enjoy wine, who do not profess to know a great deal but want ready access to the kind of serviceable information that will aid them in choosing the right wine for the moment. It makes no pretense of being complete or encyclopedic—that job has been superbly done by several others on large scale and small. This is a more selective guide, geared to the wine labels we are most likely to encounter in trying to select wine.

As a sort of "field guide" to the principal wines from some 20 countries, this book can be used on several different levels. Beginners, for example, can dip into its various sections and explore the wines described with some guidance to the level of quality they are getting for their money. Even the most knowledgeable consumer will find it a useful reference on occasion—in a wine shop, confronted with the myriad of wine labels from all over the world, or perhaps abroad, winding along the slopes of Burgundy, through the hills of northern Italy, or the valleys of California or the Rhineland.

The guide includes thumbnail sketches of more than 1,500 wines—including quality ratings for the majority of them. While it does not include, by any means, all the wines made in each country, it does cover a broad range of those most commonly seen in wine shops and restaurants of the world's leading wine markets, with enough indication of style, quality, and value to enable you to choose intelligently.

Another reason for doing yet another wine book is the effort to keep pace with the exciting changes that are going on in the world of wine. The tremendous surge of interest in wine moved from a brisk trot in the late sixties to a lively canter by the close of the seventies, and shows no signs of breaking stride, especially in places like California, Italy, Australia, and even France. Winelovers of the eighties can look ahead to greater variety than ever before: Increased demand for wines at every level of quality and price has ushered in an abundance of wines new to many markets. As prices for the best and rarest escalate, wines from other and newer regions come into their own. One has only to take a look at chapters such as Australia, the United States, Italy, and France to get some idea of what I mean.

Wine, in all its facets, from vineyard to barrel to bottle and glass, fascinates me endlessly. One of the things I love most about wine is the interesting variety of people involved with growing, making, and selling it. Nature, of course, assures that each vintage will be different, and the greatness of any wine must begin in the grape, but it is the human element at each step along the way that determines the ultimate outcome, whether modest or grand. The simple but sound wine for everyday use is as important as the great wine saved for rare moments. Indeed, how could we so thoroughly appreciate the latter without some casual experience of the former?

Wine is a very sociable substance. It requires cooperative efforts among those who make it available—the growers, the winemakers, the tradesmen—and promotes conviviality among those who share it when it is poured. And wine, most definitely, is a thing to be shared. In the company of others, be they friends or strangers, wine is a common language, and the easy flow and exchange of opinion provides one of the best and most pleasurable ways to learn; hence, the proliferation of wine clubs and tasting groups. Many a friendship is born through a kindred love of the grape.

The forbidding "mystique" that surrounded wine until recently has begun to subside as more and more people enjoy wine for themselves. But there is still, and always will be, a certain mystery as to how the juice of crushed grapes becomes in some instances a sublime and exalted beverage—whose experience, though it has incited poets to rhyme, is quite beyond anything the mere printed word can evoke. It is something you must taste and experience for yourself to understand why that is so. It is my hope that this little book will prove not only a useful companion at moments of need but a stimulus to delve more deeply into a subject—and substance—that offers some of life's most rewarding experiences.

# HOW TO USE THIS BOOK

To make this book as simple and quick to use as possible, it has been geared primarily to interpreting the information given on the labels themselves. Each of the major wine-producing countries has been given a separate chapter, the main part of which is composed of a Wine Guide—an alphabetical listing of wines, grape varieties in instances where useful, and some specific wine-growing regions. The important wine-growing regions are listed (keyed to maps for the largest producers) at the start of each chapter and, where necessary, a Glossary of Wine Terms is given.

Wines from the leading producers, such as California, France, Italy, and Germany, are rated. I have not rated wines I have not personally tasted, except in a few instances when the evaluation has been based on discussions with members of the trade whose opinions I respect. Nor have I rated wines that are only just beginning to appear on the world's markets or those from regions that are still in the process of establishing an identity, such as the wines from New York State, for example. To some extent, this is true for California, but a great deal more has been achieved there; present ratings could change in the next few years and future editions will be revised accordingly.

# HOW TO READ AN ENTRY

For easier reading, as few symbols and abbreviations as possible are used. Sweet and sparkling wines (and a few fortified wines) are identified as such within their entries. In all other instances, the wine may be assumed to be dry table wine (the fortified wines of Spain and Portugal have a chapter of their own).

Each Wine Guide entry is listed under the principal name that appears on the label (whether place name, grape variety, or producer) and gives all or most of the following information:

1. **Wine Colors.** At the left of each entry, the color or colors of the wine.

   (R)    red wine
   (W)    white wine
   (RO)    rosé wine
   (3)    red, white, and rosé wines

   **Note:** If the principal wine is red, however, and only a little white or rosé is produced under the same name or vice versa, that information is indicated within the text entry rather than in the symbol at the left.

2. **Wine Regions.** The region of origin or where the wine comes from. Most regions are given in abbreviated form; the full terms are given under Principal Wine Region listings.

3. **Vintage Years.** Good to excellent vintage years (where useful).

   **Note:** Only those years that were good to excellent, and still drinkable, are cited; few are noted beyond the early 1960s; vintages for port include the 1950s.

4. **Wine Ratings.** Ratings of one to four stars in ascending order of quality.

   ★    acceptable, everyday quality
   ★★    good, above average
   ★★★    very good, notable, distinctive
   ★★★★    very finest, outstanding, expensive

   **Note:** A "+" sign indicates a wine that is a little above its rating but not quite up to the next level. A range of quality among the various wines produced in a given region is indicated thusly: ★ / ★★★★ (acceptable to outstanding), ★★ / ★★★ (above average to very good).

5. **Cross References** to glossary entries in each chapter are in SMALL CAPS.

# THE WINES OF
# FRANCE

**F**rance is the world's premier wine-producing nation. Not in terms of quantity, where she is now surpassed by Italy, but rather for the quality and variety of her best wines. Bordeaux, Burgundy (the red and white wines of both), Champagne—these are the famous wine-producing areas against whose products most of the world's wines are judged. They, as well as the best from other regions—the Rhône, the Loire, and Alsace—are the prototypes for most of the wines we consume, no matter where they are made. Yet they are a mere 10 percent of France's total production of 25 million gallons, the average annual yield from her 3 million acres of vineyards. Eighty percent are sold in bulk or as *vin ordinaire*, which is the lowest level of French wines.

French wines are the most strictly regulated in the world. All the best and most famous wines are covered by *Appellation Contrôlée* laws. These laws do not rate the wines qualitatively, as in Germany; primarily, they are the government's guarantee that the wine in the bottle corresponds precisely to what the label says it is. They guarantee denomination of origin, determine grape variety, yield per acre, and alcoholic strength and regulate vinification techniques and vineyard practices. The laws cover appellations as broad as the whole of Bordeaux or as minute as a 2-acre vineyard in Burgundy, with a staggering range of regions and vineyards in between. Eighty-five percent of French wines imported to this country are Appellation Contrôlée wines.

Below this level there are three others:

*Vins Délimités de Qualité Supérieur* (VDQS), a secondary level that includes many creditable wines of sound regional character, mostly for everyday use.

*Vins de Pays*, wines that may come from 44 specified regions. Much experimentation is going on at this level, introducing grape varieties to regions where they were not grown before. Some authorities feel this will eventually result in a good quantity of fresh, young table wines suitable for immediate consumption. As yet, very little is available outside France.

*Vins de Marque*, proprietary brands or trademarks, usually blends of different grape varieties and from various regions. Some are better than others, depending on the firm that makes them, but they are usually a better grade than vin ordinaire.

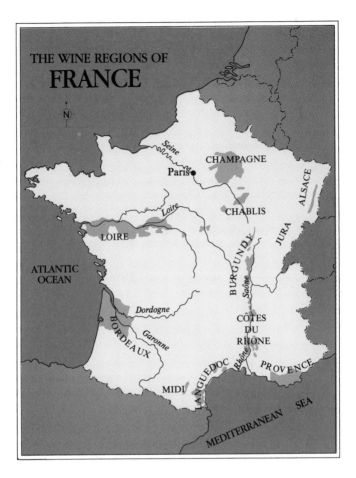

THE WINE REGIONS OF
**FRANCE**

N

Seine
CHAMPAGNE
Paris
Loire
CHABLIS
LOIRE
ALSACE
JURA
BURGUNDY
ATLANTIC
OCEAN
Saône
Dordogne
CÔTES
DU
RHÔNE
BORDEAUX
Garonne
Rhône
PROVENCE
LANGUEDOC
MIDI
MEDITERRANEAN SEA

# PRINCIPAL WINE REGIONS

**Alsace** (Als.)    Province in northeastern France with vineyards on lower slopes of the Vosges Mountains west of the Rhine producing mostly dry, rather full-bodied white wines named for their grape varieties—Riesling, Gewürztraminer, Sylvaner, Pinot Gris, Pinot Blanc.

**Bordeaux** (Bord.)    City and region in southwestern France straddling the estuary of the Gironde and extending along the slopes and plains of the Dordogne and Garonne river valleys. Subdivided into several delimited areas, the best of which are the Médoc, Haut-Médoc (which includes the communes of Saint-Estèphe, Pauillac, Saint-Julien, and Margaux), Graves, Saint-Émilion, and Pomerol. Principal grape varieties are Cabernet Sauvignon, Merlot, and Cabernet Franc. Red wines noted for intense fruit, harsh with tannins in youth but classically structured and capable of maturing into elegant, long-lived wines. Average to good dry whites from Graves and adjacent areas, exquisite sweet whites from Sauternes and Barsac. See map on page 10.

**Burgundy** (Burg.)    France's other world-famous wine region, renowned for its full-bodied, intensely fragrant reds and whites along the Côte d'Or (see maps on pages 15 and 16) and the light fruity reds of Beaujolais. Also Chablis to the north between Paris and Dijon.

**Champagne** (Cham.)   France's northernmost wine region, about 90 miles east of Paris. Producer of the world's first and best sparkling wines at principal cities of Reims and Épernay. Chardonnay and Pinot Noir grapes do well in the chalky limestone soil and cool climate.

**Côtes de Provence** (Prov.)   Hilly region between Marseilles and Nice producing red, white, and rosé. Popular locally and on the Riviera, the wines are light, fresh, and pleasant but not distinguished. Some better known names are Bandol, Cassis, and Bellet.

**Jura** (Ju.)   Very small region near Swiss border with vineyards along the foothills of the Jura Mountains. Average reds and whites, a good rosé called Arbois, and some sparkling wine.

**Languedoc** (Lang.)   One of France's oldest wine regions, producing mostly VIN ORDINAIRE but also several recently upgraded appellations such as Côtes de Rousillon, Corbières, and Fitou.

**Loire Valley** (L.V.)   Vineyards follow the long, sinuous course of the Loire for most of its 600 miles until it empties into the Atlantic at Nantes. Mostly whites of fresh, flowery character are produced along its banks; the names Muscadet, Sancerre, Vouvray, and Pouilly-Fumé are well known. See map on page 18.

**Rhône Valley** (R.V.)   Region in southeastern France below Burgundy known mostly for ripe, stalwart reds such as Hermitage and Château-neuf-du-Pape and a few similarly full-bodied whites. See map on page 23.

# WINE GUIDE

Ⓡ **d'Agassac Ch.** Bord. 79 78 76 75 73 71 ★★
Property at Ludon near Margaux owned by same owners of the fifth-growth Calon-Ségur, with well-made wines, getting better.

**Aligoté.** Grape variety used for the lesser white wines of Burgundy; yields large quantities of dry, drinkable wines; best when young. Usually seen as Bourgogne Aligoté.

Ⓡ🅦 **Aloxe-Corton.** Burg. 78 76 73 72 71 69 ★★/★★★★
Northernmost town on Côte de Beaune with fine, long-lived reds, elegant full-bodied whites, including top white Corton-Charlemagne. Reds: Corton, also Bressandes, Clos du Roi, Rénardes.

**Alsace.** See Principal Wine Regions or grape names, such as Riesling, Gewürztraminer.

Ⓡ **l'Angelus, Ch.** Bord. 78 76 75 71 ★★
Classed growth of Saint-Émilion, generally softer wines that mature early and agreeably.

Ⓡ **d'Angludet, Ch.** Bord. 79 78 77 76 75 71 70 ★★+
Good CRU EXCEPTIONNEL property near Margaux, often ranks with higher classed growths. Good value.

**Anjou.** Province along the Loire producing light fruity wines, mostly from Chenin Blanc, some rosé, around towns of Angers and Saumur. Both sweet and dry. See Coteaux du Lyon, de la Loire, Saumur.

**Appellation Contrôlée.** See Introduction.

③ **Arbois.** Ju. ★★
Light, fruity wines of varying quality but generally agreeable from this village near Swiss border. Some pleasant sparkling wines also. Best when young.

Ⓦ **d'Arche, Ch.** Bord. 75 71 70 67 ★★+
Good-sized estate in Sauternes producing fine sweet wines, often good value. Second wine under Ch. d'Arche-Lafaurie label.

(R) **Ausone Ch.** Bord. 79 78 77 76 75 71 70 66 ★★★★
Top-ranked growth of Saint-Émilion; slipped in stature for a time, but seems again to be moving toward excellent wines, especially since 1975.

(RW) **Auxey-Duresses.** Burg. 79 78 76 74 73 71 ★★+
Village on the Côte de Beaune producing quality reds and whites of second degree and generally lighter, less distinguished but quite pleasant. Good value.

(R) **Balestard-la-Tonnelle, Ch.** Bord. 79 78 76 75 71 70 ★★+
Very old, good estate among classed growths of Saint-Émilion, immortalized by the poet François Villon.

(3) **Bandol.** Prov. ★★
Village on western edge of Côtes de Provence producing light wines from lesser grape varieties; red rather better than white or rosé. Drink young.

**Banyuls.** Coastal village in the foothills of the Pyrénées above Spain's Costa Brava, producing France's portlike fortified wine, Banyuls.

(RW) **Baret, Ch.** Bord. 79 78 77 76 75 71 70 ★★
Good reds, better whites from small estate in Graves near city of Bordeaux. Good value.

(W) **Barsac.** Bord. 76 75 73 71 70 67 ★★/★★★
Town and region near Sauternes producing similarly luscious sweet wines. Best vineyards: Climens, Coutet, also Doisy-Daëne.

**Barton-Guestier** B&G. Large, well-known shipping firm of Bordeaux, average to good wines.

(R) **Batailley, Ch.** Bord. 79 78 77 76 75 73 71 70 66 64 61 ★★★
Excellent fifth growth of Pauillac (adjacent to Haut-Batailley), some 20,000 cases deep, firm long-lived wines.

(W) **Bâtard-Montrachet.** Burg. 79 78 77 76 73 71 ★★★
One of the finest whites of the Côte de Beaune, ranks with Chevalier and just under Le Montrachet itself. Expensive.

(R) **Beaujolais.** Burg. 79 78 76 ★★★
France's most delightful light red—full flavored, berryish fruit, lively charm. Best value: Beaujolais-Villages. Best when young and slightly cooled. See also CRUS such as Brouilly, Fleurie, Morgon.

(R) **Beaujolais nouveau, primeur.** The earliest Beaujolais available, bottled within a few days of fermentation and shipped as of November 15 (PRIMEUR) or December 15 (NOUVEAU). Fragile, drink by spring following harvest.

(R) **Beaujolais Supérieur.** A grade higher than simple Beaujolais but not in the class of Villages or the CRUS.

(RW) **Beaumes-de-Venise.** R.V. ★★
Sweet Muscat dessert wine made in the Rhône Valley, beguilingly delicious flavors and aroma. Good value.

(R) **Beaumont, Ch.** Bord. 79 78 77 76 75 71 70 ★★
Generally good and consistent CRU BOURGEOIS, between Saint-Julien and Margaux communes. Good value.

(RW) **Beaune.** Burg. 79 78 76 74 73 72 71 69 ★★/★★★
Major wine center of the Côte d'Or, as well as appellation for some very fine PREMIER CRU wines from several top-rated vineyards: Clos des Mouches, Gréves, Féves, Marconnets, Cras, among others.

(R) **Beauregard, Ch.** Bord. 79 78 77 76 75 71 70 ★★
One of the better properties of Pomerol (and not to be confused with lesser estates of same name in other parts of Bordeaux); round, graceful wines. Good value.

(R) **Beauséjour, Ch.** Bord. 79 78 77 76 75 71 70 ★★+
Several châteaux of this name in Bordeaux but not of this Saint-Émilion class. Property now divided, other half known as Beauséjour-Duffau-Lagarosse; both very good. Good value.

(R) **Beau-Site, Ch.** Bord. 79 78 76 75 ★★
CRU BOURGEOIS vineyard in Saint-Estèphe making agreeable wines in better vintages.

Ⓡ **Belair, Ch.** Bord. 79 78 76 75 70 ★★
Classed growth of Saint-Émilion and under same ownership as Ausone. Good value.

Ⓡ **de Bel-Air.** Bord. 79 78 76 75 71 70
Two properties with this name, one also in Lalande-Pomerol. Both
agreeable wines, often good value. Also the name of a CRU
EXCEPTIONNEL in the Haut-Médoc (Marquis d'Aligre) that is steadily
worthwhile. Good value.

Ⓡ **Belgrave, Ch.** Bord. 79 78 76 75 ★★
Minor classified growth near Saint-Julien; variable but better of late,
with firm, fullish wines.

Ⓢ **Bellet.** Prov. ★★
Small production near Nice, popular on the Riviera and quite pleasant.
Good value.

Ⓡ **Bellevue, Ch.** Bord. 79 76 75 71 ★★+
Best of numerous properties of the name, round and agreeable wines
from this GRAND CRU CLASSÉ of Saint-Émilion.

Ⓡ **Bel-Orme-Tronquoy-Lalande, Ch.** Bord. 79 78 76 75 ★★
Agreeable CRU BOURGEOIS above Saint-Estèphe but lacks the latter's
sturdy density.

# GLOSSARY OF WINE TERMS

**Appellation Contrôlée.** *Highest level of French wine laws guaranteeing origin and authenticity of label information. These words appear on labels of all France's best wines.*

**Blanc de Blancs.** *White wine from all white grapes.*

**Blanc de Noir(s).** *White wine made from black-skinned grapes.*

**Botrytis cinerea.** *Mold that grows on grapeskins, desirable for varieties like Sémillon and Sauvignon Blanc where it concentrates sugars and results in the luscious sweet wines of Sauternes.*

**Brut.** *Dry.*

**Caves.** *Cellar. (Mise en bouteilles dans no caves means "bottled in
our cellars" and is no guarantee of anything.)*

**Chai.** *Storage shed for maturing wine.*

**Chambre.** *Room temperature; in old days rooms were much cooler
than the 68° to 78°F (20° to 22°C) they are today.*

**Chateau.** *Term used in Bordeaux for the manor house of a property.
Some are grand, but others are little more than modest country
homes.*

**Chateau-bottled.** *Term indicating wines grown, produced and bottled on the property. Formerly a strong indication of quality;
somewhat less so today.*

**Claret.** *English term for red Bordeaux.*

**Clos.** *Enclosed vineyard, or property.*

**Classé.** *Classified.*

**Commune.** *Vineyard area surrounding a town. A commune is specifically delimited.*

**Côte.** *Hillside.*

**Cru.** *"Growth," used to designate a specific property or vineyard.*

**Cru Bourgeois.** *A large classification of Médocs not included in the
1855 classification.*

**Cru Classés.** *The classified growths of the Médoc, Saint-Émilion,
Graves, and Sauternes. Pomerol has no official classification.*

**Cru Exceptionnel.** *A grade higher than CRU BOURGEOIS.*

(RW) **Bergerac.** Bord. 79 78 76 75 ★/★★
Town on the Dordogne river east of Bordeaux; some drinkable reds and an interesting sweet white, Monbazillac.

(R) **Beychevelle, Ch.** Bord. 79 78 77 76 75 72 71 70 66 64 61 ★★★
Superior classed growth of Saint-Julien, known for its splendid texture, elegance, and breed.

**Beyer, Leon.** Respectable producer in Alsace, good Riesling, Gewürztraminer, Sylvaner.

(W) **Blanquette de Limoux.** Lang. ★
Sparkling wine produced near the city of Carcassone in southern France. Dry version fresh and agreeable.

(RW) **Blaye.** Bord. 79 78 77 76 75 ★/★★
Good-sized region opposite the Médoc producing average reds and whites, the best entitled to name Premières Côte de Blaye.

**Blanc-Fumé.** Local name for the Sauvignon Blanc along the Loire at Pouilly-sur-Loire.

(W) **Bollinger.** One of the leading Champagne houses, producing full-bodied classic-style champagnes. Top of the line: Tradition R.D., deluxe Champagne. This Champagne spends several years on yeast before disgorgement.

---

Cuvée. *In Champagne, a blend.*

Demi-sec. *Half-dry (quite sweet for Champagne).*

Domaine. *An estate, or single holding; equivalent to château in Burgundy and the Rhône.*

Doux. *Sweet.*

Grand Cru. *Great growth, the rank awarded by French wine authorities to the best vineyards of Burgundy and Chablis, also Saint-Émilion in Bordeaux.*

Premier Cru. *First growth, but actually the second (and quite good) level of wines in Burgundy and Chablis.*

Méthode champenoise. *Original method of putting the sparkle in wines by refermenting in the original bottle and other specialized techniques.*

Mise en bouteilles au château. *Château-bottled, that is, wine bottled on the property where grown; once a definite sign of quality but now commonly used and not necessarily a mark of distinction.*

Mise en bouteilles á la proprieté, Mise au domaine. *Estate-bottled, same as above but used in Burgundy, the Rhône, and elsewhere outside Bordeaux.*

Monopole. *Vineyard with single owner.*

Mousseux. *Sparkling, term used for all French sparkling wines outside the district of Champagne.*

Négociant. *Merchant who buys directly from growers, often bottling the wine at his own firm.*

Pétillant. *Lightly sparkling.*

Récolte. *Harvest.*

Sec. *Dry.*

Sur lie. *Wine left on its lees, or yeast sediments, after fermentation, until bottling. In some cases, such as Muscadet, this gives it an appealing freshness. Recent laws have altered the term somewhat to mean the wine must be bottled before June after the harvest.*

Vin ordinaire. *Table wine of ordinary, everyday level.*

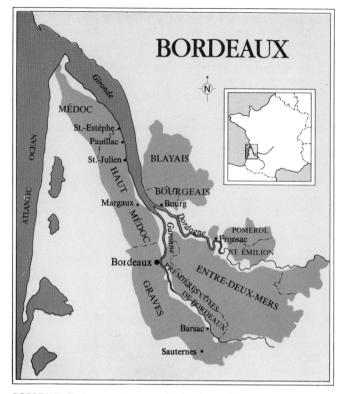

BORDEAUX. Bordeaux produces nearly a hundred million gallons of wine a year. Some of France's finest wines come from its best districts—Haut-Médoc, Graves, Pomerol, and Saint-Émilion for elegant, long-lived reds; Sauternes and Barsac for sweet whites and Graves for dry, full-bodied whites. Attractive wines are also produced in such lesser regions as the Médoc, Entre-Deux-Mers, Bourg, Blayais, and Canon Fronsac, and they are often very good value.

Ⓡ **Bonnes-Mare.** Burg. 78 77 76 73 72 71 69 66 ★★★★
GRAND CRU vineyard between Chambolle-Musigny and Morey-Saint-Denis; powerful as Chambertin but rather more refined, one of the top dozen reds of the Côte-d'Or.

**Bordeaux, Bordeaux Supérieur.** Broadest and lowest appellations for Bordeaux. Supérieur is slightly higher in alcohol. Usually blended wines that cannot use a more specific place-name.

**Bouchard Aîné.** Long-established shipping firm based in Beaune, owners of several average-to-good properties along the Côte de Beaune.

**Bouchard Pére et Fils.** Very old, distinguished Burgundy shippers, with considerable (and venerable) vineyards on the Côtes de Beaune.

Ⓡ **Bourg, Côtes de.** Bord. 79 78 76 75 ★/★★
Good to average reds, some whites from region on the Gironde opposite the lower Médoc. Occasionally full-bodied and good value in strong vintages.

ⓇⓌ **Bourgogne.** Burg. 79 78 77 76 73 72 71 ★★
Basic appellation for wines of Burgundy, some pleasant, round, and fruity but lacking the distinction of more specific appellations of the region that include village or vineyard names. See also Aligoté.

(R) **Bourgogne Passe-tout-grain.** Burg. ★
Lesser red Burgundy blended from half Gamay and half Pinot Noir. Somewhere between Burgundy and Beaujolais but lacking the personality of either, though sometimes agreeable.

(R) **Bourgueil.** L.V. 79 78 76 ★★+
A light, good Cabernet from the Touraine.

(RW) **Bouscaut, Ch.** Bord. 79 78 77 76 75 71 70 ★★+
Good quality reds and dry white Graves at property south of Bordeaux, formerly owned by Americans, now sold back to French.

**Bouzy.** Important village in Champagne with the best of Pinot Noir vineyards; also a still red, Bouzy Rouge, delightful but limited production, occasionally available in Paris.

(R) **Boyd-Cantenac.** Bord. 79 78 77 76 75 73 71 70 66 ★★★
Classed growth of Margaux; under consultant Emile Peynaud, wines have improved considerably in the last decade.

(R) **Branaire-Ducru, Ch.** Bord. 79 78 76 75 73 71 70 66 61 ★★★
Fourth-growth Saint-Julien, with typical round elegant fruit and Saint-Julien finesse.

(R) **Brane-Cantenac, Ch.** Bord. 79 78 77 76 75 74 71 70 66 61 ★★★
Reliably good second growth of Margaux, fragrant, supple, sound wines, often good value; large estate of 180 acres. Good value.

(R) **Brouilly.** Burg. 79 78 ★★★
One of the nine GRANDS CRUS of Beaujolais, characterized by round, full lively fruit, though not long-lived. Best: Château de la Chaize, Château Thivin.

(RO) **Cabernet d'Anjou.** L.V. ★★
Light, fruity, off-dry rosé made around Saumur from Cabernet Franc. Usually better, drier than Rosé d'Anjou.

**Cabernet Sauvignon.** Principal red wine grape of Bordeaux, mostly Médoc.

(R) **Cahors.** South West France 79 75 70 ★★
Once a hard, dark wine mostly from Malbec grape but vinified in lighter style today with addition of Merlot and other grapes. Still capable of aging well into interesting but not extraordinary wine.

(W) **Caillou, Ch.** Bord. 79 76 75 73 71 70 67 ★★★
Excellent sweet wines from this old property in Barsac. Good value.

(R) **Calon-Ségur, Ch.** Bord. 79 78 77 76 75 71 70 67 66 61 ★★★
One of the best classified growths of Saint-Estèphe, with typical heartiness and body; among the longest-lived of Saint-Estèphe wines.

(R) **de Camensac, Ch.** Bord. 79 78 76 75 71 70 ★★+
Minor Haut-Médoc classified growth, lackluster for years but expanded vineyards and modern techniques have resulted in much improvement in recent years; big, good depth, powerful aromas. Good value.

(R) **Canon, Ch.** Bord. 79 78 77 76 75 71 70 66 ★★★
Fine, generous full-bodied wines from this classed growth of Saint-Émilion.

(R) **Canon-La Gaffelière, Ch.** Bord. 79 78 76 75 ★★
Second-level growth on western slopes, generally typical Saint-Émilion; earthy, full-bodied, quick-maturing. Good value.

(R) **Cantemerle, Ch.** Bord. 79 78 76 75 71 70 ★★★
Fifth growth of the 1855 Haut-Médoc classification but better than its level. Well-balanced, supple wines of great finesse. Good value.

(R) **Cantenac-Brown, Ch.** Bord. 79 78 77 76 75 73 71 70 66 62 61 ★★★
Third-growth Margaux (Cantenac) showing breed and elegance typical of the commune but generally fuller-bodied than other Margaux.

(R) **Capbern, Ch.** Bord. 79 78 76 75 ★★
Full-bodied Saint-Estèphe, same owners as Calon-Ségur.

(RW) **Carbonnieux, Ch.** Bord. 79 78 77 76 75 74 71 70 ★★★
Vigorous reds, fine dry whites from old property in Léognan, Graves.

Ⓡ **Cardonne, La.** Bord. ★★
Recently purchased by the Lafite branch of Rothschilds, this CRU BOUR-GEOIS in the northern Médoc has produced variable quality wines so far, but a good firm 1975.

**Carraudes de Lafite.** Wine of Chateau Lafite, from younger vines; less depth and class but still very good; not produced since 1967, when new plantings reached maturity. See Moulin de Carruades.

③ **Cassis.** Prov. ★★
Village on the Riviera producing light, agreeable reds, rosés, and dry whites (best) for drinking young. Cassis is also the name of a black currant liqueur made in Dijon.

Ⓦ **Cerons.** Bord. 79 77 75 ★/★★
Medium sweet or off-dry whites from this region between Graves and Sauternes. Not widely known but can be quite pleasant.

Ⓡ **Certan-de-May.** Bord. 79 78 77 76 75 71 70 ★★★
One of the smallest vineyards in Pomerol producing big, long-lived wines, often firmer than most Pomerols.

Ⓦ **Chablis.** Burg. 78 76 75 71 70 ★★★
Famous white Burgundy quite different from southern Burgundy whites, though also made entirely from Chardonnay. Flinty, dry, full-bodied whites, somewhat austere but with classic elegance in good years; thin and acidic in poor years. Classic with shellfish, especially oysters.

**Chablis Grand Cru.** The finest Chablis, consisting of seven vine-yards—Vaudésir, Les Clos, Grenouilles, Blanchots, Preuses, Bougros, Valmur. Elegant richness in great years like 1978, 1976, 1975.

**Chablis Premier Cru.** The second level of vineyards ranking just be-low GRAND CRU, often quite superb. Best vineyards: Les Fôrets, Four-châume, Montée de Tonnere, Monts-du-Milieu, Vaulorent.

Ⓡ **Chambertin.** Burg. 79 78 77 76 73 72 71 70 69 66 61 ★★★★
The most famous red Burgundy, and deservedly for its sturdy vigor and splendid proportions, heady perfumed aroma, and durability.

Ⓡ **Chambertin-Clos de Bèze.** Burg. 79 78 77 76 73 72 71 70 69 66 ★★★★
Estate adjoining Chambertin, the wines virtually indistinguishable in some years of, at least equal greatness.

Ⓡ **Chambolle-Musigny.** Burg. 79 78 77 76 73 71 69 ★★/★★★★
A top commune on the Côte de Nuits. Village wines of supple elegance: GRAND CRU: Le Musigny; PREMIERS CRUS: Amoureuses, Les Charmes.

Ⓦ **Champagne.** World's best sparkling wine from delimited region east of Paris, made solely by special method known as MÉTHODE CHAM-PENOISE.

Ⓡ **Champigny.** L.V. 79 78 ★★+
Very pleasant fruity, light red from the Loire Valley around Saumur, somewhat Beaujolais-like in style.

Ⓡ **Chapelle-Chambertin.** Burg. 79 78 77 76 73 71 70 69 66 ★★★
Ranked a GRAND CRU but rather less grand than Chambertin, though still impressive.

**Chardonnay** (sometimes Pinot Chardonnay). Noble white grape used exclusively for white Burgundy, Chablis, Macon, BLANC DE BLANCS Champagne.

Ⓡ **Charmes-Chambertin.** Burg. 79 78 77 76 73 71 70 69 66 ★★★
Lighter than most of the Chambertins but shows similar finesse and nobility.

Ⓡ Ⓦ **Chassagne-Montrachet.** Burg. 79 78 76 74 73 72 71 70 69 ★★★
Important commune on the Côte de Beaune with several superlative white wine vineyards, including Montrachet, Bâtard-Montrachet, Criots-Bâtard-Montrachet, Ruchottes, followed by (and including good reds) Boudriotte, Caillerets, Morgeot.

(R) **Chasse-Spleen, Ch.** Bord. 79 78 77 76 75 71 70 ★★+
Estate at Moulis, Haut-Médoc, ranked as CRU EXCEPTIONNEL. Round, full wines of depth and breed. Good value.

(W) **Chateau-Chalon.** Ju. ★★★
Unusual dry white wine with character of a dry sherry due to formation of flor yeast on the surface of fermenting wine. Limited production but worth trying.

(R) **Chateau de la Chaize.** Burg. 79 78 76 ★★★
Best-known estate of Beaujolais; full, fruity charm. Good value.

(W) **Chateau Grillet.** R.V. 79 78 76 72 71 70 ★★★
France's smallest appellation covering a single vineyard (3.5 acres) on the northern Rhône; rich golden dry wines, spicy aromas.

(R) **Châteauneuf-du-Pape.** R.V. 78 77 76 74 72 71 70 69 67 ★★/★★★
Popular and widely known sturdy red from southern Rhône Valley made mostly from Syrah and Grenache. Widely variable quality, at best has soft, round richness that is most appealing.

(R) **Chénas.** Burg. 79 78 76 ★★★
One of the nine GRAND CRUS of Beaujolais, fuller-bodied, sturdier than most.

**Chenin Blanc.** Fruity white grape planted mostly along the Loire.

(R) **Cheval-Blanc, Ch.** Bord. 79 78 77 76 75 74 73 71 66 64 62 61 ★★★★
Top-ranked growth of Saint-Émilion, superbly rich, round wines of great depth and long life, though generally drinkable sooner than comparable Médocs.

(W) **Chevalier-Montrachet.** Burg. 78 76 74 73 71 70 ★★★+
The "rightful son" of Montrachet (see Bâtard-Montrachet), almost as rich and beautiful, though less powerful; only 17 acres and expensive.

(R) **Chinon.** L.V. 78 76 75 ★★+
A light cabernet from the Touraine; sound little red that used to be a good value but now somewhat overpriced.

(R) **Chiroubles.** Burg. 79 78 ★★★
One of the loveliest, fruitiest of the nine Beaujolais CRUS; early maturing, soft, and fragrant.

**Cissac.** Commune in the Haut-Médoc near Saint-Estèphe with several good CRUS BOURGEOIS growths.

(R) **Citran, Ch.** Bord. 79 78 76 75 73 71 ★★
Sound, Haut-Médoc solid wines from one of the best CRUS BOURGEOIS. Good value.

**Clairet.** Light red wine, though not quite rosé.

(W) **Clairette de Die.** R.V. ★★
Sparkling wine popular in southern France, made from Clairette and Muscat grapes; sweet, with Muscat aromas.

(R) **Clerc-Milon, Ch.** Bord. 79 78 77 76 75 71 70 ★★★
Fifth-growth Pauillac of Haut-Médoc now owned by Baron Philippe de Rothschild; well-made wines with typical Pauillac depth and character.

(W) **Climens.** Bord. 79 78 76 75 73 71 70 67 ★★★
Superb sweet whites from commune of Barsac, possibly its best.

(R) **Clinet, Ch.** Bord. 79 78 76 75 71 70 ★★+
Small but quite good Pomerol, classic light Bordeaux. Good value.

(R) **Clos de la Roche.** Burg. 79 78 77 76 73 71 70 69 ★★★+
GRAND CRU at Morey-Saint-Denis on the Côte de Nuits with almost the grandeur of Chambertin, but a shade less majestic. Good value.

(R) **Clos des Lambrays.** Burg. 79 78 77 76 73 71 70 69 ★★★
Excellent PREMIER CRU vineyard on the Côte de Nuits at Morey-Saint-Denis; powerful and long-lived.

(RW) **Clos des Mouches.** Burg. 79 78 76 74 73 71 70 69 ★★★
Full-bodied red and distinguished white from PREMIER CRU vineyard near Beaune. One of the Beaune's best vineyards.

(R) **Clos de Tart.** Burg. 78 76 73 72 71 70 69 ★★★+
  GRAND CRU at Morey-Saint-Denis; gentler, more subtle than the sturdier wines nearby, but prized for its richness and lovely bouquet.

(R) **Clos de Vougeot.** Burg. 79 78 77 76 74 73 72 71 70 69 66 ★★★/★★★★★
  Magisterial chateau on the Côte de Nuits, 124-acre vineyard with numerous owners, and thus wines of variable quality; at its best generously full-flavored, with intense, lingering bouquet. A small quantity of white, Clos Blanc de Vougeot, also quite fine.

(R) **Clos l'Église.** Bord. 79 78 76 75 71 70 ★★★
  Polished, graceful Pomerol, one of its best vineyards. Good value.

(R) **Clos Fourtet.** Bord. 79 78 77 76 75 71 70 ★★★
  A great growth of Saint-Émilion, but less impressive of late.

(R) **Clos des Jacobins.** Bord. 79 78 76 75 71 70 ★★+
  Classed growth of Saint-Émilion, same owners as Talbot, Gruaud-Larose in Médoc. Modest, pleasant wine.

(R) **Clos du Roi.** Burg. 79 78 76 73 72 71 70 69 ★★★
  Two excellent PREMIER CRU vineyards on the Côte de Beaune, one at Beaune, the other at Corton-Clos du Roi richer and more distinctive.

(R) **Clos René.** Bord. 79 78 76 75 71 70 66 61 ★★★
  Good Pomerol classed growth of second level, mature wines often lush and highly perfumed after 8 to 12 years.

(R) **Clos St. Denis.** Burg. 79 78 77 76 73 72 71 70 69 ★★★
  Excellent GRAND CRU of Chambertin-like constitution; complex, long-lived. Good value.

(R) **Clos St. Jacques.** Burg. 79 78 77 76 73 72 71 70 69 66 ★★★+
  PREMIER CRU at Gevrey-Chambertin, probably tops on the Côte d'Or in that class. Rich, full, substantial, very near to Chambertin itself.

(R) **Clos St. Jean.** Burg. 79 78 77 76 73 72 71 69 ★★★
  Best PREMIER CRU vineyard for red wine from Chassagne-Montrachet on the Côte de Beaune; sound value.

(W) **Condrieu.** R.V. ★★+
  Interesting Rhône Valley white, mostly dry but some semisweet, unusual fragrance; most consumed locally and worth looking for.

(R) **La Conseillante, Ch.** Bord. 79 78 76 75 71 70 66 ★★★
  Among the top properties of Pomerol, often rich, plush-textured wines, but may need at least a decade to show it.

(R) **Corbières.** Lang. 79 78 76 ★★
  A sturdy, medium-bodied red of VDQS level; Corbières du Rousillon also good, a bit coarser. Some lesser white and rosé also made.

(R) **Cornas.** R.V. 79 78 76 75 72 71 70 69 67 ★★+
  Robust, attractive red from the northern Rhône that ages quite well in strong vintages.

**Corsica.** Island in the Mediterranean belonging to France, lately expanded production of robust, mostly average-quality wine. Best are A. C. Patrimonio and Ajaccio.

(R) **Corton.** Burg. 79 78 77 76 73 71 70 69 66 ★★★★
  Top red of the Côte de Beaune at Aloxe-Corton and a GRAND CRU that can stand with the best reds of the Côte-de Nuits. Staunch, rich, and long-lived.

(W) **Corton-Charlemagne.** Burg. 79 78 76 74 73 71 70 69 ★★★★
  Superb white Corton from celebrated vineyard named for Charlemagne who once owned vineyards in the region in the eighth century (though may not have been these). Steely elegance, rich fruit.

(R) **Cos d'Estournel, Ch.** Bord. 79 78 77 76 75 71 70 67 66 64 62 61 ★★★
  Outstanding second growth in Saint-Estèphe now owned by Prats family; rich, sturdy wines that mature with considerable finesse of flavor and bouquet. Good value.

(R) **Cos Labory, Ch.** Bord. 79 78 76 75 71 ★★
  Good, robust Saint-Estèphe with reputable though not especially distinguished wines.

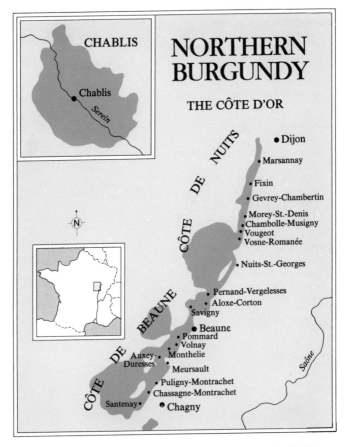

NORTHERN BURGUNDY. Burgundy's wine regions are among the oldest in France but produce only a third as much wine as Bordeaux. The Côte d'Or of northern Burgundy is subdivided into the Côte de Nuits—known for its famous red wines from the communes of Fixin to Nuits-St.-Georges—and the Côte de Beaune—known for both reds and whites from Beaune, center of Burgundy's wine trade—to Santenay. Chablis lies north and west of the Côte d'Or.

Ⓦ **Coteaux Champenois.** Cham. ★★★
The still dry white wine of Champagne, made from Chardonnay. Often quite good but expensive; best within two or three years.

Ⓦ **Coteaux de la Loire.** 79 78 76 75 ★★★
Fragrant, full-flavored whites made from Chenin Blanc in Anjou. Best appellation: Savennières. Good value.

Ⓦ **Coteaux du Layon.** L.V. 79 78 76 75 ★★+
Sweet whites with appealing fruit and fragrance from Chenin Blanc grape; among the best are Bonnezeaux, Quarts de Chaume. Also some rosé. Angers is center of the region.

③ **Coteaux du Loir.** L.V. ★★
The Loir is a tributary of the Loire near Tours; a lesser region for mild reds, whites, rosés, best of which is Jasnières.

Ⓡ **Coteaux du Tricastin.** R.V. 79 78
Area around Valence in the northern Rhône, recently elevated to APPEL-LATION CONTRÔLÉE. Often better than Cotes du Rhône. Good value.

**Côte de Beaune.** Southern half of Burgundy (see map, page 16), known for softer reds (except Corton) and exquisite whites such as

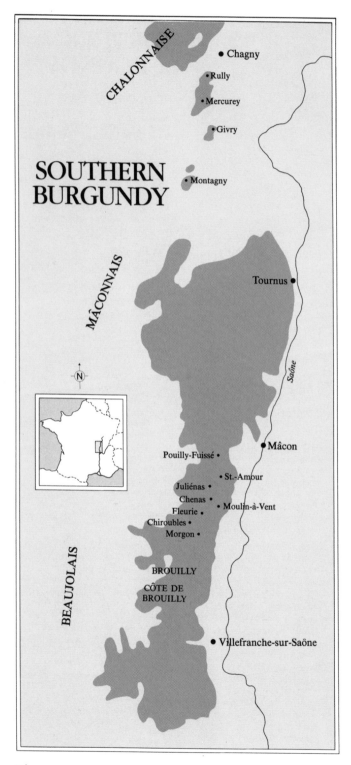

**SOUTHERN BURGUNDY.** The wines of southern Burgundy are not as illustrious as those of the north, but the dry white wines of Mâcon and the fruity reds of Beaujolais offer excellent value and delightful drinking. Along the Côte Chalonnaise, Givry and Mercurey are best known for fullish reds and Montagny and Rully mainly for dry whites that are increasingly better known.

Meursault, Corton-Charlemagne, and Montrachet. Also an appellation for lesser reds and whites from vineyards around Beaune; Côte de Beaune-Villages is of similar rank and, unless a town name is attached, covers the general region.

(R) **Côte de Brouilly.** Burg. 79 78 77 ★★★
Excellent GRAND CRU of Beaujolais, from the upper slopes of the Mont du Brouilly, generally more substantial fruit than Brouilly with a bit more finesse. Look for Chateau Thivin.

**Côte de Nuits.** The northern half of Burgundy's Côte d'Or, taking its name from the commune of Nuits-Saint-Georges. As a regional appellation, covers blended wines that are little seen outside France or Burgundy itself.

**Côte d'Or.** Literally, "golden slope," the name for the strip of vineyards between Dijon and Santenay that produces Burgundy's finest wines (see map, page 15).

(R) **Côte Rotie.** R.V. 79 78 76 71 70 69 67 66 ★★★
One of the northern Rhône's best wines, tough and tannic in youth but becomes mellow, rich, and smooth-textured with age. Good value.

(R) **Côtes Canon-Fronsac.** Bord. 79 78 76 75 ★★
Small area west of Pomerol and Saint-Émilion; robust little wines best after four years or so of aging, generally age better than Côtes de Fronsac; both, however, good value.

(3) **Côtes de Provence.** ★/★★
Elevated in 1977 from VDQS to APPELLATION CONTRÔLÉE. Light, unassuming reds, whites, rosés, best consumed young and along the Riviera or hilly country back of it where they are made. Better value there.

(3) **Côtes du Rhône.** R.V. 79 78 76 ★/★★
Light, agreeable wines, mostly red and rosé from the southern Rhône Valley. Côtes du Rhône-Villages more substantial.

(3) **Côtes du Rousillon.** Lang. 79 78 76 ★★
Red, white, and rosé from the foothills of the Pyrénées near Perpignan; the medium-character, full-bodied reds are good everyday wines.

(3) **Côtes du Ventoux.** R.V. 79 78 76 ★+
Light wines of a portion of the southern Rhône, similar to Côtes du Rhône; recently elevated from VDQS to APPELLATION CONTRÔLÉE.

(W) **Couhins.** Bord. 79 78 ★★
Well-made dry white from Graves; insignificant amount of red also. Good value.

(R) **La Couronne.** Bord. 79 78 77 76 75 71 70 ★★
Fine CRU EXCEPTIONNEL at Pauillac made by owners of Ducru-Beaucaillou and Haut-Batailley; good depth, well-balanced. Good value.

(RW) **La Cour Pavillon.** Bord. 79 78 76 ★★
Red and white proprietary brands marketed by Gilbey, reds from northern Médoc more consistently attractive.

(W) **Coutet, Ch.** Bord. 79 76 75 73 71 70 67 62 ★★★+
Top vineyard at Barsac producing luscious golden sweet wines remarkable for breed and bouquet. Good value.

(W) **Criots-Bâtard-Montrachet.** Burg. 79 78 76 74 73 71 70 69 ★★★
Superb dry white, almost indistinguishable from neighboring Bâtard-Montrachet, generous fruit, body, and bouquet.

(RW) **Crozes-Hermitage.** R.V. 79 78 76 74 72 70 ★★/★★★
Sturdy Rhône reds of lesser distinction than Hermitage but often as attractively full-flavored. Whites okay but less interesting. Good value.

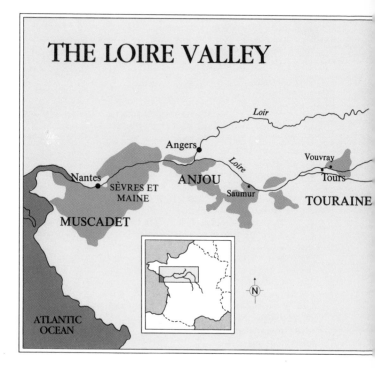

# THE LOIRE VALLEY

- Loir
- Angers
- Loire
- Vouvray
- Nantes
- SÈVRES ET MAINE
- ANJOU
- Saumur
- Tours
- TOURAINE
- MUSCADET
- ATLANTIC OCEAN
- N

**Deutz & Geldermann.** Cham. ★★★
One of the top, though lesser known Champagne houses; classic full-bodied style. Deluxe CUVÉE: William Deutz.

**Doisy-Daëne.** Bord. 76 75 71 70 ★★★
Full, opulent, sweet white wines near Sauternes; consistently first rate, well-balanced wines. Good value.

**Doisy-Védrines.** Bord. 79 75 71 70 ★★★
Older Barsac name, originally included Doisy-Daëne; also rich and full.

**Dom Pérignon.** Cham. 75 71 70 69 ★★★★
The deluxe CUVÉE of Moët et Chandon in Champagne; excellent classic, full-bodied, elegant wine.

**Domaine de Chevalier.** Bord. 79 78 77 76 75 72 71 70 66 ★★★+
Superb, firm, full-bodied red, richly textured with age and equal to second-growth Médocs. The dry white is one of the best white Graves but very little is made.

**Domaine Dujac.** One of the best and newer shippers of the Côte de Nuits with several excellent vineyards in Chambolle-Musigny, Morey-Saint-Denis, and Gevrey.

**Dopff & Irion.** Leading producer in Alsace with good Riesling, Gewürztraminer.

**Ducru-Beaucaillou, Ch.** Bord. 79 78 77 76 75 73 72 71 70 66 64 61 ★★★
One of the top two or three châteaux of Saint-Julien; beguiling fruit, elegance, and bouquet, yet very long-lived. Good value.

**Duhart-Milon-Rothschild, Ch.** Bord. 79 78 76 75 71 70 66 ★★★
Fourth growth of Pauillac now owned by the Rothschilds of Lafite, which it is near. Firm, powerful wines though not yet in the class with other Pauillacs.

**Durfort-Vivens, Ch.** Bord. 78 76 75 70 66 ★★★
Second-growth property of Margaux that languished for a while but is coming on strong again with fine, elegant wines of breed and alluring bouquet.

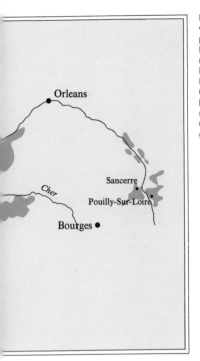

**LOIRE VALLEY.** Large quantities of white, rosé, and red wines are produced along the winding course of France's longest river, the Loire. The most famous wines are white: Pouilly-Fumé, Sancerre, Vouvray, and Muscadet. Good light reds such as Chinon, Bourgueil, and Champigny, based on Cabernet varieties, are also made but in much smaller quantities. Chenin Blanc and Sauvignon Blanc grapes predominate for white wines.

(Map labels: Orleans, Cher, Sancerre, Pouilly-Sur-Loire, Bourges)

ⓡ **Échézeaux.** Burg. 79 78 76 73 72 71 70 69 ★★★+
GRAND CRU at Flagey-Echézeaux on the Côte de Nuits; opulent fruit and bouquet but rather less density than the bigger Burgundies.

ⓦ **Entre-deux-Mers.** Bord. 79 78 77 ★★
Dry white of average to good quality from a large area between the Dordogne and Garonne rivers, best when young and fresh.

ⓡ **L'Évangile, Ch.** Bord. 79 78 76 75 74 71 70 ★★★
Full-bodied Pomerol of good repute; youthful hardness becomes delicate and very pretty with age.

ⓦ **de Fargues, Ch.** Bord. 76 75 ★★+
Notable, well-balanced Sauternes, not the richness and depth of top growths but quite good. Same owners as Chateau Yquem. Good value.

ⓇⓌ **Fieuzal, Ch.** Bord. 79 78 76 75 71 70 ★★+
Sound, generous red from Graves, increasingly attractive in last decade. Dry white also good, but both made in relatively small quantities.

ⓡ **Figeac, Ch.** Bord. 79 78 77 76 75 73 71 70 66 64 62 61 ★★★+
Exceedingly fine classified growth of Saint-Émilion and one of the most popular for its lusty warmth in youth; can be quite long-lived with full-bodied roundness throughout.

ⓦ **Filhot.** Bord. 79 76 75 72 71 70 67 ★★★
Lovely sweet wines from this second-growth Sauternes, occasionally somewhat drier but noted for classic balance, breed.

ⓡ **Fitou.** Lang. 79 78 76 ★★
Hearty red of some depth with good aging potential. Good value.

ⓡ **Fixin.** Burg. 79 78 76 73 71 70 69 ★★/★★★
Lesser commune at northern end of Côte de Nuits. Not as generously endowed as bigger reds to the south but well structured and among the best values in quality. Best vineyards: Clos de la Perrière, Clos du Chapitre, Hervelets. Good value.

ⓡ **Fleurie.** Burg. 79 78 ★★★
Beaujolais GRAND CRU, generously fruity and joyous wine, noted for flowery bouquet.

Ⓡ **Les Forts de Latour.** Bord. 78 76 75 70 66 ★★★
Second wine of Château Latour; very high-class Pauillac, with strength, depth, and distinctive aroma; ready much sooner than Latour.

Ⓡ **Fourcas-Hosten, Ch.** Bord. 78 76 75 71 ★★+
Superior CRU BOURGEOIS at Listrac in central Médoc. Good value.

Ⓡ **la Gaffelières, Ch.** Bord. 79 78 77 76 75 71 70 ★★★
Formerly known as La Gaffelière-Naudes; very strong comeback in recent years, situated near slopes of Chateau Ausone, Saint-Émilion.

**Gamay.** Grape variety best known for the fruity wines of Beaujolais.

Ⓡ **le Gay, Ch.** Bord. 79 78 76 75 74 71 70 ★★+
One of the better second-level Pomerols, warm, full-bodied, generally early maturing.

Ⓡ **Gazin, Ch.** Bord. 78 76 75 71 70 66 ★★★
One of Pomerol's largest estates; good, robust wines though not quite top level.

Ⓡ **Gevrey-Chambertin.** Burg. 78 76 73 72 71 70 69 66 ★★/★★★
Important commune of the Côte d'Or, site of Chambertin vineyards. Wines with the village name can be quite good; PREMIERS CRUS even better from vineyards like Clos Saint-Jacques, Varoilles Aux Combottes.

Ⓦ **Gewürztraminer.** Als. 79 78 77 76 75 71 ★★★
Dry, full-bodied whites with enticing spice aromas, rather austere fruit. Often age well; reserve wines intense and rich.

Ⓡ **Gigondas.** R.V. 79 78 76 71 70 67 ★★+
Variable quality reds that can be sturdy, full-bodied, warmly attractive—good value when they are.

Ⓡ **Giscours, Ch.** Bord. 79 78 77 76 75 71 70 67 66 61
Large, well-run estate at Labarde, Margaux, owned by Gilbey; highly perfumed, consistently fine wines, very long-lived.

ⓇⓌ **Givry.** Burg. 79 78 76 73 72 71 ★★+
Light reds and whites of the Côte Chalonnaise; sound, if not impressive Burgundian character. Good value.

Ⓡ **Gloria, Ch.** Bord. 79 78 77 76 75 71 70 67 66 61 ★★★
A CRU BOURGEOIS but portions of vineyards were part of other famous Saint-Julien vineyards, so wines show typical fullness and a certain dash. Good value.

Ⓡ **Grancey, Ch.** Burg. 79 78 76 73 72 71 70 69 66 ★★★
Well-known shipper Louis Latour's Corton; big and long-lived.

Ⓡ **Grand-Barrail-Lamarzelle-Figeac.** Bord. 78 76 75 73 71 70 66 ★★+
Good, typical full-bodied Saint-Émilion; good value.

Ⓡ **Grand-Puy-Ducasse.** Bord. 79 78 76 75 71 70 66 ★★+
Fifth-growth Pauillac, vigorous and sound but lighter than most of that commune; drinkable sooner. Good value.

Ⓡ **Grand-Puy-Lacoste.** Bord. 79 78 76 75 73 71 70 66 61 ★★★
Fifth-growth Pauillac but more classically structured than Ducasse, with more breed and considerable depth; highly regarded (and pricey).

Ⓡ **Grands Échezeaux.** Burg. 79 78 77 76 73 72 71 70 69 66 ★★★★
Among the greatest of red Burgundies, luxuriant fruit, magnificent bouquet, great finesse.

ⓇⓌ **Graves.** Bord. 79 78 77 76 75 71 70 ★★/★★★
District of Bordeaux producing top wines such as Château Haut-Brion and other fine reds; fewer but also excellent dry whites and an abundance of fair to good whites, both sweet and dry.

Ⓦ **Graves Supérieur.** Bord. 79 78 77 ★/★★
Now, by law, the sweet whites of Graves; some improvement in recent years but still rather clumsy and too often oversulfered.

**Graves de Vayre.** Part of Entre-Deux-Mers producing mediocre reds but acceptable whites, especially if young and fresh.

Ⓡ **Griotte-Chambertin.** Burg. 79 78 76 73 72 71 70 69 ★★★+
Worthy younger brother of the great Chambertin, which it adjoins.

(W) **Gros Plant du Pays Nantais.** L.V. ★★
Fresh, dry pleasant white of the Loire near the Atlantic; good, inexpensive choice for seafood but not as full as Muscadet. Drink young. Good value.

(R) **Gruaud-Larose, Ch.** Bord. 79 78 77 76 75 73 71 70 66 62 61 ★★★+
Second-growth Saint-Julien and one of the best: abundant fruit, noble structure and breed.

(RW) **Guiraud, Ch.** Bord. 79 76 75 71 70 67 ★★★
A Sauternes ranked just after Yquem; less concentrated and luscious but quite as elegant. Small quantities of dry white and red also produced. Good value.

(R) **Haut-Bages-Libéral, Ch.** Bord. 79 78 76 75 ★★+
A fifth growth but not up to the best of that level. Pauillac estate recently purchased by Cruse family and appears to be improving; recent wines fairly robust, smooth.

(R) **Haut-Bailly, Ch.** Bord. 79 78 76 75 73 71 70 ★★★
Sturdy, full-flavored Graves; needs time in bottle but exhibits great finesse when mature. Good value.

(R) **Haut-Batailley, Ch.** Bord. 79 78 77 76 75 73 71 70 66 ★★★
Formerly part of Batailley, Pauillac; though smaller it is equally as good with sturdy character and depth.

(R) **Haut-Brion, Ch.** Bord. 79 78 77 76 75 74 73 71 70 67 66 64 62 61 ★★★★
A Graves ranked with Lafite, Latour, Margaux in 1855, the only wine outside the Médoc so honored. Supremely fine still, if not always on a par with the others. Velvet-textured, very long-lived, often good in off-vintages.

**Haut-Médoc.** The best portion of the Médoc embracing its most famous châteaux; also a regional appellation for above-average wines, superior to those labeled simply "Médoc."

(RW) **Hautes-Côtes de Beaune.** Burg. 78 76 73 72 ★★
Vineyards on slopes behind the Côte de Beaune, lighter reds and whites but can be good value.

(W) **Heidsiek, Charles.** One of the top houses of Champagne. Classic, full-bodied style. Luxury CUVÉE: Royal.

(W) **Heidsieck, Dry Monopole.** Champagne firm at Rheims. Luxury CUVÉE: Diamant Bleu.

**Henriot.** Small but top Champagne house now owned by Baron Philippe de Rothschild. Rich, very full-bodied wines.

(R) **Hermitage.** R.V. 78 76 74 72 71 70 69 66 ★★★+
Big generous reds of the northern Rhône that become round and velvety after several years' aging; great ones very long-lived. Good value.

**Hospices de Beaune.** Famous charity hospital in Beaune, scene of annual auction of Burgundy wines each autumn, and owner of portions of several outstanding vineyards on the Côte de Beaune. Wines named for owners include Docteur Peste and Charlotte Dumay.

**Hugel.** A leading firm in Alsace, one of the largest, producing Riesling, Gewürztraminer, Sylvaner.

(R) **d'Issan, Ch.** Bord. 79 78 76 75 73 71 70 ★★★
Historic château at Cantanac, Margaux, recently upgraded wines with the suppleness of Margaux but more robust.

**Jadot, Louis.** Well-respected shipper in Burgundy with several fine vineyards at Corton, Pommard, for example.

(R) **Juliénas.** Burg. 79 78 76 ★★★
One of the sturdier Beaujolais CRUS, not as immediately engaging but balanced and longer-lived.

(R) **Kirwan, Ch.** Bord. 79 78 76 75 71 70 ★★
Good-sized third growth at Cantenac, Margaux, rather lackluster to date but reportedly improving.

(W) **Krug.** One of the smaller Champagne houses; classic, full-bodied wines often considered the connoisseur's Champagne. Luxury CUVÉE: Grande Réserve Blanc de Blancs.

(R) **Lafite-Rothschild, Ch.** Bord. 79 78 77 76 75 71 70 67 66 62 61 ★★★★
Among the world's greatest wines, from Pauillac. The classic claret of elegance and breed, stylish, subtle but astonishing power in great vintages, of this century and the last.

(R) **Lafleur-Pétrus, Ch.** Bord. 79 78 76 75 71 70 66 ★★★
Charming, flavorful wines from one of the smaller Pomerol estates.

(R) **Lafon-Rochet, Ch.** Bord. 79 78 77 75 73 71 70 66 61 ★★+
Fourth-growth Saint-Estèphe now owned by the Tesseron family, who have restored the château and vineyards. Dark, sturdy, typically Saint-Estèphe. Good value.

(R) **La Lagune, Ch.** Bord. 79 78 76 75 73 71 70 66 ★★★
A third growth of the 1855 classification at Ludon (below Margaux). Vineyard replantings and modernization have put this wine in the front ranks; meatier fruit than most Médocs; good balance.

(R) **Lanessan, Ch.** Bord. 79 78 76 75 73 71 70 ★★+
One of the most reputable CRU BOURGEOIS of the Haut-Médoc, firm, full-bodied wines known for long-lived delicacy. Good value.

(R) **Langoa-Barton, Ch.** Bord. 79 78 76 75 73 71 70 67 66 ★★★
Third-growth Saint-Julien and sister château to Léoville-Barton; somewhat lighter than the Léoville but quite good.

(W) **Lanson Père et Fils.** A family-owned Champagne firm in Rheims. Best value: the nonvintage, which is light, dry, and fruity.

(R) **Lascombes, Ch.** Bord. 79 78 76 75 72 71 70 66 64 62 61 ★★★
Second-growth Margaux property restored to excellence largely by former owner Alexis Lichine; fine bouquet and rich, smooth texture. Now belongs to Bass-Charrington.

(R) **La Tache.** Burg. 79 78 77 76 74 73 72 71 70 67 66 62 ★★★★
To some, the noblest of all Bungundies, certainly one of the world's most outstanding (and expensive) wines; deep color, extravagant perfume, lavishly rich yet tremendous noblesse; great vintages live for decades.

(R) **Latour, Ch.** Bord. 79 78 76 75 74 73 71 70 69 67 66 64 62 61 ★★★★
First-growth Pauillac, the most forceful and intense of all, remarkably consistent quality; dark, tannic, and harsh when young but matures into a wine of great nobility and breed with strength for very long life; often superb in off-vintages and excellent value.

**Latour, Louis.** Large, well-known, and highly respected Burgundy shipper, owner of several vineyards such as parts of Corton-Charlemagne.

(R) **Latour-Pomerol, Ch.** Bord. 79 78 77 76 75 74 73 71 70 ★★★
Small Pomerol estate but ample, fruity, beautiful wines made by a member of the Mouiex family of Chateau Pétrus.

(R) **Latricières-Chambertin.** Burg. 79 78 77 76 74 72 71 70 69 66 ★★★+
A GRAND CRU vineyard approaching the strength and nobility of Chambertin but less weighty.

(W) **Laurent-Pérrier.** One of the top shippers in Champagne; luxury CUVÉE, La Grand Siècle, has excellent fruit and finesse.

(R) **Léoville-Barton, Ch.** Bord. 79 78 77 76 75 73 71 70 67 66 64 62 61 ★★★
Excellent second-growth Saint-Julien, full body, fruit, not quite as fine as Léoville-Las Cases, though bigger and occasionally richer.

(R) **Léoville-Las-Cases, Ch.** Bord. 79 78 77 76 75 74 73 71 70 67 66 64 61 ★★★+
Second growth of Saint-Julien and the most outstanding; full, rich fruit, wonderfully perfumed, with great breed, finesse, and long-lasting delicacy at maturity.

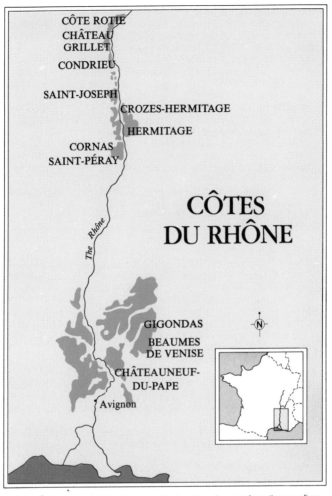

CÔTE ROTIE
CHÂTEAU
GRILLET
CONDRIEU

SAINT-JOSEPH
CROZES-HERMITAGE
HERMITAGE
CORNAS
SAINT-PÉRAY

The Rhône

CÔTES
DU RHÔNE

N

GIGONDAS
BEAUMES
DE VENISE
CHÂTEAUNEUF-
DU-PAPE
Avignon

**THE RHÔNE.** Rhône Valley wines, predominantly red, range from the very fine, full-bodied reds such as Côte Rotie, Hermitage, or Châteauneuf-du-Pape to light regionals labeled simply Côtes du Rhône or Coteaux du Tricastin. Unusual and distinctive whites are made in the region also, such as Condrieu, Château Grillet, Hermitage, and Beaumes-de-Venise, but in far smaller quantities.

ⓡ **Léoville-Poyferré, Ch.** Bord. 79 78 76 75 73 71 70 67 66 61
★★★
Excellent second-growth Saint-Julien, often better than Léoville-Barton with whom it jockeys for position just under Las-Cases; has style and verve.

ⓡ **Loudenne, Ch.** Bord. 79 78 76 75 74 73 71 70 ★★+
Imposing château and well-run CRU BOURGEOIS, of the northern Médoc, owned by Gilbey. Small quantity of dry white Bordeaux Supérieur also produced. Good value.

ⓡ **Lynch-Bages, Ch.** Bord. 79 78 76 75 71 70 66 61 ★★★
Popular fifth-growth Pauillac without the classic breed of the best Pauillac, but robust, rich, and roundly attractive at earlier age.

23

(R) **Lynch-Moussas, Ch.** Bord. 79 78 76 75
Hardly notable fifth-growth Pauillac now under ownership of the family that has Batailley nearby; improvements and expansion underway.

(W) **Macon.** Burg. 79 78 77 76 75 ★★/★★★
Good, dry, full-bodied whites (and small amount of less notable reds) from southern Burgundy seen under appellations Macon-Villages, Macon-Viré, Saint-Veran, and Pouilly-Fuissé. First three appellations very good value. Good value.

(R) **Magdelaine, Ch.** Bord. 79 78 76 75 71 70 ★★★
A great growth of Saint-Émilion near Ausone; full, early maturing.

(RW) **Malartic-Lagravière, Ch.** Bord. 79 78 77 76 75 71 70 ★★+
Good, sound reds and dry, full-bodied whites from classified estate at Léognan, Graves. Good value.

(R) **Malescot-St. Exupéry, Ch.** Bord. 79 78 77 76 75 73 71 70 67 66 61 ★★★
One of the most charming Margaux, with lovely form and structure, beautiful fruit. Good value in its class.

(W) **de Malle, Ch.** Bord. 76 75 73 71 70 67 ★★★
Rich, well-balanced Sauternes from classified growth of the second level. Good value.

(R) **Margaux,** Bord. 79 78 76 75 71 70 ★★/★★★+
Notable commune of the Haut-Médoc, home of Chateau Margaux and several other fine properties. Known for its finely textured, perfumed wines with more delicacy than other Médocs. Appellation also includes communes of Cantenac Soussans and Labarde.

(R) **Margaux, Ch.** Bord. 79 78 77 76 75 71 70 67 66 61 ★★★★
One of the top four first growths of the Médoc, highly esteemed for its delicacy, breed and bouquet, exquisite texture; new owners recently.

(R) **Marquis-de-Terme, Ch.** Bord. 79 78 76 75 71 70 ★★+
A fourth growth of Margaux, rarely great but consistently good, full, and soft.

(RO) **Marsannay.** Burg. 79 78 76 ★★+
Very good rosé from Pinot Noir grape from village in northern Burgundy; dry, full, and fruity. Smaller amount of light red also made. Good value.

**Maufoux, Prosper.** Shipping firm in Burgundy at Santenay offering good Beaujolais, dependable Burgundies mostly from Côte de Beaune.

(R) **Mazis-Chambertin.** Burg. 79 78 76 72 71 70 69 66 ★★★
A GRAND CRU member of the illustrious enclave of Chambertins.

(R) **Mazoyères-Chambertin.** Burg. 79 78 77 76 73 72 71 ★★★
Mostly sold under Charmes-Chambertin label, almost identical.

**Médoc.** Bourdeaux appellation for reds outside the better district of Haut-Médoc; generally good value, never great.

(W) **Mercier.** One of the principal houses of Champagne, now owned by Moët et Chandon.

(R) **Mercurey.** Burg. 79 78 76 72 71 70 69 ★★
Good but not especially distinctive Burgundies from south of the Côte d'Or; fairly good value.

(RW) **Meursault.** Burg. 79 78 76 73 71 70 69 ★★★+
Several superb vineyards produce this dry, full, intriguingly flavored white from the Côte de Beaune. Rich fruit, lingering aftertaste. Best PREMIERS CRUS: Perrières, Charmes, Genevrières. Also smaller quantities of good, sturdy reds, which may be labeled Volnay.

(R) **Meyney, Ch.** Bord. 79 78 76 75 71 ★★
Very good CRU BOURGEOIS at Saint-Estèphe near the Gironde; owned by Cordier, proprietors of Gruaud-Larose and Talbot. Good value.

(R) **Minervois.** Lang. 79 78 77 ★★
Appealing full-bodied reds of VDQS level produced in the hills of the Languedoc; some fresh rosé also made.

®️ **La Mission Haut-Brion, Ch.** Bord. 79 78 77 76 75 73 71 70 66 61 ★★★★
Outstanding Graves, considered on a par with the great Haut-Brion across the road. Rich, broad, round flavors, distinctive bouquet. Small quantity of fine dry white sold as Laville-Haut-Brion.

Ⓦ **Moët et Chandon.** One of the largest and oldest Champagne houses, a part of Moët-Hennessey. Luxury CUVÉE: Dom Pérignon, of worldwide fame.

Ⓦ **Monbazillac.** Bord. 76 75 74 71 ★★+
Sweet, golden dessert wine from Bergerac.

®️ **Monbousquet, Ch.** Bord. 79 78 76 75 ★★
Well-run estate owned by the Querre family of Saint-Émilion; light, attractive wines that mature early.

®️ **Monthélie.** Burg. 79 78 76 72 71 ★★★
Tender, fragrant red Burgundies near Volnay on the Côte de Beaune. Good value.

Ⓦ **Montrachet.** Burg. 79 78 77 76 75 74 73 72 71 69 66 ★★★★
The legendary white of the Côte d'Or—dry, finely balanced, luxuriant fruit; lusciously scented; long, seductive finish. Best is the tiny portion of the vineyard owned by Domaine de la Romanée-Conti.

®️ **Montrose, Ch.** Bord. 79 78 77 76 75 71 70 67 66 64 61 ★★★
Highly respected second growth of Saint Estèphe; formidable, dark, intense wines that mature with great distinction.

®️ **Morey-Saint-Denis.** Burg. 79 78 77 76 73 72 71 70 69 66 ★★★
Notable commune on the Côte de Nuits with several GRANDS CRUS vineyards; and very fine PREMIERS CRUS, often very good value.

®️ **Morgon.** Burg. 79 78 76 ★★★
One of the fullest, sturdiest of the Beaujolais CRUS; needs a good year or two to show its best; also keeps well.

®️ **Moulin à Vent.** Burg. 79 78 76 74 73 ★★★
Biggest, most potent of the nine CRUS of Beaujolais; achieves with age the silkiness of a light Burgundy in superior vintages.

**Moulin des Carruades.** A second-level Pauillac produced at Château Lafite. Soft, fruity, pleasant but lacks the quality of Latour's other label, Les Forts de Latour.

**Mouton-Cadet.** A Bordeaux Supérieur produced by Baron Philippe de Rothschild. Agreeable red of variable quality; fresh dry white is better.

®️ **Mouton-Baronne-Philippe, Ch.** Bord. 79 78 76 75 74 70 66 61 ★★★
Large Pauillac estate owned by Baron Philippe de Rothschild; bold character and bouquet of typical Pauillac, but lighter.

®️ **Mouton-Rothschild, Ch.** Bord. 79 78 77 76 75 73 71 70 67 66 62 61 ★★★★
Won official (and long deserved) rank among the first-growth Pauillacs in 1973; dark, intense, concentrated wines dominated by forceful, penetrating fruit of Cabernet Sauvignon: hard-edged in youth, slow to mature but ultimately rich, with persistent aromas of blackberries and hints of cedar.

Ⓦ **Mumm, G. H. & Cie.** One of the leading houses in Champagne selling Cordon Rouge. Luxury CUVÉE: René Lalou.

Ⓦ **Muscadet.** L.V. 79 78 76 ★★★
Fine, full-bodied dry white of the western Loire near Nantes, labeled SUR LIE. Good acidity makes it superb with shellfish. Sèvre-et-Maine is the inner best district of Muscadet. Good value.

**Muscat.** Fruity, fragrant grape that produces mostly sweet wines.

®️ **Musigny.** Burg. 79 78 77 76 73 72 71 69 67 66 ★★★★
GRAND CRU at Chambolle-Musigny, incomparably fragrant and refined though not as powerful as the biggest GRAND CRUS; has the nobility of Chambertin but more grace. A small quantity of excellent dry white produced also.

Ⓦ **Nairac, Ch.** Bord. 75 73 71 ★★+
Recently restored Sauternes estate; owned by a young American; balanced, well-made wines, steadily improving. Good value.

Ⓡ **Nenin, Ch.** Bord. 79 78 77 76 75 71 70 66 ★★★
One of the larger estates in Pomerol; soft, fruity, engaging wines.

**Nicolas.** Paris's largest wine merchants, who buy wines from many parts of France to ship under their label; several retail stores around France.

Ⓡ **Nuits-St.-Georges.** Burg. 78 77 76 73 72 71 70 69 ★★/★★★
Firm, earthy, full-bodied reds of the southernmost part of the Côte de Nuits just above Beaune. Best vineyards: Les Saint-Georges, Vaucrains, Les Pruliers, Les Cailles, Les Porrets.

Ⓡ Ⓦ **Olivier, Ch.** Bord. 79 78 76 75 71 70 ★★+
Classified property of Graves producing dry whites and reds of sound, rugged character.

Ⓡ **Les Ormes-de-Pez.** Bord. 79 78 77 76 75 73 71 70 ★★+
Mellow and full-bodied Saint-Estèphe CRU BOURGEOIS wine; reliable and consistent. Same owners as Calon-Sègur. Good value.

Ⓡ **Palmer, Ch.** Bord. 79 78 77 76 75 73 71 70 66 61 ★★★+
Third-growth Margaux very near in distinction to the first growths; big, classic, stylish wines of power and elegance.

Ⓡ **Pape-Clement, Ch.** Bord. 79 78 77 76 75 74 72 71 70 66 ★★★
Fine, sturdy Graves from ancient vineyards at Pessac named for thirteenth-century pope. Frequently good value.

Ⓡ **Pauillac.** Bord. 78 76 75 71 70 ★★/★★★★
Famed district and commune of the Haut-Médoc containing three first growths—Lafite, Latour, Mouton—and several other distinguished

# PETITS CHATEAUX

Too numerous to mention individually are many of the better CRUS BOURGEOISES of the Médoc and unclassified chateaux from other Bordeaux regions, often referred to as *petits chateaux*. Generally, they mature earlier and are at their best within 5 years of the vintage. Here are some I particularly recommend, all producing red wines:

Beau-Site, Saint-Estèphe
La Bégorce-Zédé, Margaux
Bel Air Marquis d'Aligre, Margaux
Bellegrave, Pauillac
Bellerose, Pauillac
Capbern, Saint-Estèphe
La Cardonne, Médoc
Chasse-Spleen, Moulis
Cissac, Haut-Médoc
Coufran, Saint-Estèphe
La Couronne, Pauillac
Le Crock, Saint-Estèphe
Croque-Michotte, Saint-Émilion
Dutruch Grand Poujeaux, Moulis
L'Enclos, Pomerol
Fourcas-Hosten, Listrac (Margaux)

Le Gay, Pomerol
Du Glana, Haut-Médoc
Greysac, Médoc
Lafleur, Pomerol
Lagrange, Pomerol
Lanessan, Haut-Médoc
Larose Trintaudon, Haut-Médoc
Laroze, Saint-Émilion
Maucaillou, Moulis
Patache d'Aux, Haut-Médoc
Potensac, Médoc
Reysson, Haut-Médoc
Ripeau, Saint-Émilion
La Tour de By, Médoc
La Tour des Mons, Margaux
Tronquoy-Lalande, Saint-Estèphe

properties. Strongly individualistic wines but typically have great strength and authority, classic structure; are slow to mature but have great staying power.

(R) **Pavie, Ch.** Bord. 79 78 76 75 71 70 66 ★★★
Round, generous and appealing Saint-Émilion from one of the largest of the classed-growth vineyards.

(RW) **Pernand-Vergelesses.** Burg. 79 78 77 76 72 71 70 69 ★★★
Very fine reds and whites from vineyards at Corton and sold mostly under that appellation or Corton-Charlemagne. Its own best: Ile de Vergelesses. Good value.

(W) **Pérrier-Jouet.** One of the top Champagne houses at Épernay. Deluxe CUVÉE: Fleur de Champagne, fruity, elegant, well balanced.

(R) **Pétrus, Ch.** Bord. 79 78 77 76 75 71 70 66 64 62 61 ★★★★
The outstanding Pomerol, ranks with the first growths of the Médoc. Cheval-Blanc and Haut-Brion as the top Bordeaux. Gravelly clay soil gives eloquent expression to Merlot here in full wines of extraordinary finesse and bouquet.

(R) **de Pez, Ch.** Bord. 79 78 77 76 75 71 70 ★★★
A CRU BOURGEOIS of Saint-Estèphe but deserves higher rank for consistently round, soft pleasing wines; excellent value.

(R) **Phélan-Segur, Ch.** Bord. 79 78 77 76 73 71 70
Very good CRU BOURGEOIS of Saint-Estèphe; sound, reliable, aromatic wines.

(R) **Pichon-Longueville-Baron, Ch.** Bord. 79 78 77 76 75 71 70 66 61 ★★★
Elegant, long-lived, aristocratic Pauillac wine but lighter than Pauillacs toward the north.

(R) **Pichon-Longueville-Lalande, Ch.** Bord. 79 78 77 76 75 74 71 70 66 61 ★★★
Across the road from Pichon-Baron, Pauillac wines of similar style but the Baron is weightier, the Lalande delicate, more supple fruit. Often a toss-up as to which is better.

**Pineau des Charentes.** Fortified wine of the Cognac region.

**Pinot Blanc, Pinot Noir.** White and red wine grapes of the Pinot family. Pinot Noir is the red grape for Burgundy and its white juice is used in Champagne.

(W) **Piper-Heidsieck.** Long-established Champagne producer in Reims. Deluxe CUVÉE: Florens Louis Blanc de Blancs.

(R) **la Pointe, Ch.** Bord. 79 78 76 75 71 70 ★★★
Popular Pomerol for good, fleshy wines that ripen quickly.

(W) **Pol Roger.** One of the top Champagne houses at Épernay. Deluxe CUVÉE: Reserve Special.

(R) **Pomerol.** Bord. 79 78 77 76 75 ★★★
Small but very important region of Bordeaux with several excellent properties noted for fine red wines, mainly from the Merlot grape and some Cabernet. Château Pétrus is leading vineyard. Small quantities with regional label, Pomerol, usually quite good.

(R) **Pommard.** Burg. 79 78 76 73 72 71 69 ★★★
One of the largest communes on the southern half of the Côte d'Or, known for firm, very pleasant reds; some, unfortunately, overpriced. Top vineyards: Rugiens, Les Épenots, Chaponnières, Les Arvelets.

(W) **Pommery et Greno.** Large Champagne shipping firm at Reims; classic, full-bodied style Champagne.

(R) **Pontet-Canet, Ch.** Bord. 79 78 77 76 75 73 71 70 67 66 61 ★★★
The top fifth-growth Pauillac and largest of the classified growths, nearly 200 acres, under forward-looking new owners, the Tesseron family. Dark, intense wines often slow to mature, but very appealing when they do. Good value.

(W) **Pouilly-Fuissé.** Burg. 79 78 77 76 75 ★★/★★★
Dry, full-bodied white, the best of the Maconnais but overpriced, lately

pressed by more reasonable Macon-Villages, Saint-Véran. Similar wines of nearby Pouilly-Vinzelles and Pouilly-Loché are also worthwhile.

(W) **Pouilly-Fumé.** L.V. 79 78 ★★/★★★
Fresh, fragrant, fruity dry whites from the Sauvignon Blanc grape, with a distinctly flinty aroma and flavor. (Pouilly-sur-Loire is a different wine of same area made from the lesser Chasselas grape.)

**Premières Côtes de Bordeaux.** District opposite Graves producing average reds, sweet or dry whites and rosés, occasionally good value.

(R) **Prieuré-Lichine, Ch.** Bord. 79 78 77 76 75 71 70 66 ★★★
Lovely Margaux estate at Cantenac restored by present owner Alexis Lichine; soft, delicate, early-maturing, wines with perfumed bouquet. Good value.

**Puisseguin-St.-Émilion.** A part of Saint-Émilion producing robust, full-bodied wines, good but not distinguished.

(W) **Puligny-Montrachet.** Burg. 79 78 76 75 74 73 ★★★
With nearby Chassagne-Montrachet this village produces some of great dry white wines of the world. Various Montrachet vineyards straddle the two districts; other top vineyards include Le Cailleret, Les Combettes, Pucelles, Clavoillon.

(W) **Quarts de Chaume.** L.V. 79 78 76 75 ★★★
Famous sweet golden wine of lush richness, more concentrated with age, made around Angers on the Coteaux du Layon (Anjou).

(W) **Quincy.** L.V. 79 78 ★★
Crisp, dry white similar to Sancerre.

(R) **Rausan-Ségla, Ch.** Bord. 79 78 76 75 71 70 ★★★
Second-growth Margaux but recent vintages patchy; can be full, typical Margaux with appealing bouquet.

(R) **Raussan-Gassies, Ch.** Bord. 79 78 76 75 71 70 ★★
Second-growth Margaux that once included Rausan-Ségla; poor quality in some years has hurt reputation but now under new ownership.

(W) **Rayne-Vigneau, Ch.** Saut. 79 76 75 73 71 70 67 ★★★
One of the best-known Sauternes, rich and full with great depth and power, though occasionally overblown and lacks balance.

(R) **Richebourg.** Burg. 79 78 77 76 75 73 72 71 70 69 66 ★★★★
One of the great GRANDS CRUS of Burgundy at Vosne-Romanée; gloriously rich fruit, plush textures, intense bouquet. Part of the vineyard belongs to the Domaine de la Romanée-Conti; other owners are Louis Gros, Charles Noellat.

(W) **Rieussec, Ch.** Bord. 79 76 75 71 70 67 ★★★+
One of the top first growths of Sauternes, just under Yquem; concentrated, elegant golden sweet wines.

(W) **Roederer, Louis.** One of the leading Champagne shippers in Reims. Luxury CUVÉE: Cristal.

(R) **La Romanée.** Burg. 79 78 77 76 73 72 71 70 66 ★★★★
Tiniest of the GRANDS CRUS, barely 2 acres near Romanée-Conti; wines of great breed, luxuriant fruit, and fragrance.

(R) **La Romanée-Conti.** Burg. 79 78 77 76 73 72 71 70 69 66 ★★★★
4.5-acre plot at Vosne-Romanée yielding the most expensive wine in the world, questionably the best but undeniably great and rare.

(R) **Romanée St. Vivant.** Burg. 79 78 77 76 73 72 71 70 69 66 ★★★★
Another of the noble GRANDS CRUS at Vosne-Romanée, similar to Romanée-Conti but softer, more grace than virility.

(RO) **Rosé d'Anjou.** L.V. ★
Mostly sweetish rosé made in Anjou, occasionally acceptable but Cabernet d'Anjou is better value.

(R) **Ruchottes-Chambertin.** Burg. 79 78 77 76 73 72 71 70 69 66 ★★★
Laudable, durable member of the extended family of Chambertins.

(W) **Ruinart Père et Fils.** One of the oldest Champagne houses in Reims, which is now owned by Moët et Chandon. Delux CUVÉE: Dom Ruinart BLANC DE BLANCS.

SOCIÉTÉ CIVILE DU DOMAINE DE LA ROMANÉE-CONTI
PROPRIÉTAIRE A VOSNE-ROMANÉE (CÔTE-D'OR)

# ÉCHÉZEAUX

APPELLATION ÉCHÉZEAUX CONTROLÉE

*11.234 Bouteilles Récoltées*

N° 04216

L'ASSOCIÉ-GÉRANT

ANNÉE 1971

*H. de Villaine*

*Mise en bouteille au domaine*

ÉCHÉZEAUX. One of Burgundy's greatest wines, Echezeaux is a *Grand Cru* vineyard with an *Appellation Contrôlée* of its own, therefore it can stand alone on the label without the commune name or the words *Grand Cru*. The phrase *mise en bouteille au domaine* means the wine was bottled on the estate where the grapes were grown, the equivalent of chateau-bottled in Bordeaux. These terms do not necessarily carry the guarantee of superior quality they once did. The producer's reputation and track record over recent vintages is an important consideration. The Domaine de Romanée-Conti produces other of the world's greatest wines, including La Tache, Romanée-Conti, and Richebourg.

ⓇⓌ **Rully.** Burg. 79 78 76 75 ★★
Good, dry reds and whites of the Côte Chalonnaise; also known for its sparkling Burgundy.

Ⓡ **Saint-Amour.** Burg. 79 78 ★★★
Soft, fruity GRAND CRU of Beaujolais and the northernmost commune; very tender and appealing wines.

Ⓡ **Saint-Émilion.** Bord. 79 78 76 75 73 71 70 66 ★★/★★★★
Important village and district of Bordeaux producing full, rich wines from slopes overlooking the Dordogne River. Top vineyards: Cheval-Blanc, Ausone. Several surrounding communes may also affix Saint-Émilion to their names; wines often quite good.

Ⓡ **Saint-Estèphe.** Bord. 79 78 77 76 75 73 71 70 ★★/★★★+
Northernmost commune of the Haut-Médoc with several excellent vineyards including Cos d'Estournel, Montrose. Dark, slow-maturing wines with a certain earthy richness of flavor and bouquet.

Ⓡ **Saint-Julien.** Bord. 79 78 77 76 75 71 70 ★★★
Commune in the heart of the Médoc known for fine, classically balanced claret; no first growths but several superb vineyards, including the three Léovilles, Ducru-Beaucaillou, Beychevelle, Gruaud-Larose. Wines with the village name only are among the best regionals in Bordeaux.

Ⓡ **Saint-Pierre-Bontemps-et-Sevaistre.** Bord. 79 78 77 76 75 71 70 ★★+
Light but sound, well-balanced claret, a fourth-growth Pauillac.

Ⓦ **Saint-Véran.** Burg. 79 78 77 ★★★
Dry, stylish, full-bodied white from Macon, good alternative to nearby Pouilly-Fuissé, though not quite as full. Good value.

Ⓦ **Sancerre.** L.V. 79 78 ★★★
Excellent dry white from picturesque hill town on the upper Loire;

BURGUNDY
RED WINE
PRODUCT
OF FRANCE

U.S. REPRESENTATIVES
FREDERICK
**WILDMAN**
AND SONS
NEW YORK CITY

CONTENTS
750 ML
ALCOHOL
13% BY VOLUME

*Fleurie*

APPELLATION CONTROLÉE

*Louis Latour*

MIS EN BOUTEILLE PAR LOUIS LATOUR
NÉGOCIANT A BEAUNE (COTE-D'OR)

**BEAUJOLAIS.** Fleurie is one of the nine *Grands Crus* of Beaujolais in southern Burgundy, all of which are more precisely regulated and produce wines with more definitive character than Beaujolais-Villages or simple Beaujolais. While there are some estate-produced wines, most Beaujolais is bought from local cooperatives or small growers by large shipping firms such as that of Louis Latour, headquartered in Beaune.

crisp, racy fruit, stylishly rendered from Sauvignon Blanc. Region also produces a quite nice rosé from Pinot Noir.

(R) **Santenay.** Burg. 79 78 77 76 72 71 69 ★★★
One of the lighter Burgundies at the southern end of the Côte de Beaune. Some dry whites but the soft, full reds are better. Best vineyards: Les Gravieres, Clos de Tavannes. Good value.

(3) **Saumur.** L.V. 79 78 77 ★★★+
Town on the Loire in Anjou and surrounding district produces pleasant fruity whites from Chenin Blanc, dry or lightly sweet, good sparkling wines, above average Cabernet Franc rosé, and a quite nice red, Champigny, also from Cabernet Franc. All good value.

(W) **Sauternes.** Bord. 79 76 75 73 71 70 67 ★★/★★★★
Region south of the town of Bordeaux (includes Barsac) producing luscious, sweet golden wines, some of the world's finest and perhaps *the* finest—Chateau d'Yquem. Also Climens, Suduiraut, Coutet, La Tour Blanche.

**Sauvignon Blanc.** White grape for fragrant, full-bodied dry wines of Bordeaux and the Loire and, in conjunction with Sémillon, the sweet wines of Sauternes.

(W) **Savennières.** L.V. 79 78 76 75 73 ★★★
Chenin Blanc from Anjou with considerable depth, body, and richness; ages well.

(R) **Savigny-les-Beaune.** Burg. 79 78 77 76 72 71 ★★★
Burgundian town near Beaune producing notable reds with attractively supple fruit; a very small quantity of dry white also made. Top vineyards: Vergelesses, Lavières, Jarrons, Marconnets. Good value.

(RW) **Savoie.** Ju. ★★
Crisp whites, adequate reds similar to those of nearby Switzerland; best known are sparkling Crépy and Seyssel.

Ⓦ **Sigalas-Rabaud, Ch.** Bord. 79 76 75 71 70 67 ★★+
One of the better classed growths of Sauternes, smaller than adjacent Rabaud-Promis, but often more balance and finesse. Good value.

Ⓡⓦ **Smith-Haut-Lafitte, Ch.** Bord. 79 78 77 76 75 71 70 ★★+
Good, sturdy, slow-maturing reds from Graves, bracing dry whites from Sauvignon blanc; often good value.

Ⓦ **Suduiraut, Ch.** Bord. 76 75 71 70 66 ★★★+
Outstanding first growth of Sauternes with rich, creamy texture, splendid balance.

**Sylvaner.** White wine grape, mostly for dry wines of Alsace.

Ⓦ **Taittinger.** Major Champagne shipper at Reims. Deluxe CUVÉE: Comte de Champagnes Blanc de Blancs and Rosé (best of the pink).

Ⓡ **Talbot, Ch.** Bord. 79 78 77 76 75 74 71 70 66 61 ★★★
Consistently good, richly flavored fourth growth at Saint-Julien.

Ⓡⓞ **Tavel.** R.V. ★★★
France's best and most famous rosé; attractive coral bronze color, dry and full-bodied. Drink young.

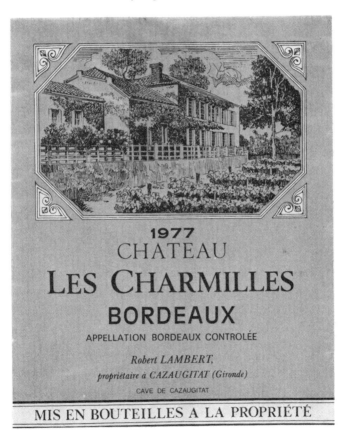

**CHÂTEAU LES CHARMILLES.** The word "château" on a label does not always signify a better wine. The real clue to this wine is in the words that appear beneath the château name, *Appellation* Bordeaux *Contrôlée,* which signify that the wine may legally have come from anywhere in the Bordeaux region. While the wine may indeed have been bottled at the château named (implied by the words *mis en bouteilles á la propriété*) the generalized appellation comes from a region with no appellation of its own. Simple Bordeaux appellations such as this can, however, provide pleasant drinking in good vintages if the price is right.

# French Vintage Chart

Vintage charts should be consulted only as a general guide to the quality of the wines in a given vintage. In every vintage, great or poor, there are exceptions that stand apart from the rest. This chart is, however, more reflective of the better wines of each region than lesser ones. The ratings note the original quality of the vintage—drinkability of the wines today is indicated according to the color code.

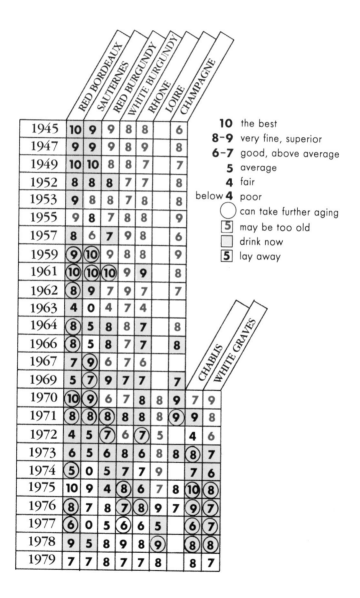

| | RED BORDEAUX | SAUTERNES | RED BURGUNDY | WHITE BURGUNDY | RHONE | LOIRE | CHAMPAGNE | CHABLIS | WHITE GRAVES |
|---|---|---|---|---|---|---|---|---|---|
| 1945 | 10 | 9 | 9 | 8 | 8 | | 6 | | |
| 1947 | 9 | 9 | 9 | 8 | 9 | | 8 | | |
| 1949 | 10 | 10 | 8 | 8 | 7 | | 7 | | |
| 1952 | 8 | 8 | 8 | 7 | 7 | | 8 | | |
| 1953 | 9 | 8 | 8 | 7 | 8 | | 8 | | |
| 1955 | 9 | 8 | 7 | 8 | 8 | | 9 | | |
| 1957 | 8 | 6 | 7 | 9 | 8 | | 6 | | |
| 1959 | (9) | (10) | 9 | 8 | 8 | | 9 | | |
| 1961 | (10) | (10) | (10) | 9 | 9 | | 8 | | |
| 1962 | (8) | 9 | 7 | 9 | 7 | | 7 | | |
| 1963 | 4 | 0 | 4 | 7 | 4 | | | | |
| 1964 | (8) | 5 | 8 | 8 | 7 | | 8 | | |
| 1966 | (8) | 5 | 8 | 7 | 7 | | 8 | | |
| 1967 | 7 | (9) | 6 | 7 | 6 | | | | |
| 1969 | 5 | (7) | 9 | 7 | 7 | | 7 | | |
| 1970 | (10) | (9) | 6 | 7 | 8 | 8 | 9 | 7 | 9 |
| 1971 | (8) | (8) | (8) | 8 | 8 | 8 | (9) | 9 | 8 |
| 1972 | 4 | 5 | (7) | 6 | (7) | 5 | | 4 | 6 |
| 1973 | 6 | 5 | 6 | 8 | 6 | 8 | 8 | (8) | 7 |
| 1974 | (5) | 0 | 5 | 7 | 7 | 9 | | 7 | 6 |
| 1975 | 10 | 9 | 4 | (8) | 6 | 7 | 8 | (10) | (8) |
| 1976 | (8) | 7 | 8 | (7) | (8) | 9 | 7 | (9) | (7) |
| 1977 | (6) | 0 | 5 | (6) | 6 | 5 | | (6) | (7) |
| 1978 | 9 | 5 | 8 | 9 | 8 | (9) | | (8) | (8) |
| 1979 | 7 | 7 | 8 | 7 | 7 | 8 | 8 | | 7 |

**10** the best
**8-9** very fine, superior
**6-7** good, above average
**5** average
**4** fair
below **4** poor
◯ can take further aging
⑤ may be too old
☐ drink now
⑤ lay away

(R) **du Tertre, Ch.** Bord. 79 78 77 76 5 71 70 ★★+
Little-known fifth growth with attractive Margaux-style wines.

**Touraine.** Large region along the Loire, produces copious amounts of sweet and dry white wines, best known being Vouvray; also good reds Chinon and Bourgeuil.

(W) **La Tour-Blanche, Ch.** Bord. 79 76 75 71 70 67 ★★★
First-growth Sauternes that once rivaled Yquem; wines much lighter today and not as concentrated. Estate is government-owned and has a viticultural school.

(R) **La Tour Haut-Brion.** Bord. 79 78 77 76 75 71 70 ★★+
Small, excellent Graves property near the city of Bordeaux popular for stylish, full-bodied reds.

**Trimbach.** Reputable firm in Alsace making very good Riesling, Gewürztraminer, Sylvaner, Pinot Blanc.

(R) **Troplong-Mondot, Ch.** Bord. 79 78 77 76 75 70 ★★+
Among the first growths of Saint-Émilion; round, full-bodied reds, often good value.

(R) **Trotanoy, Ch.** Bord. 79 78 77 76 75 71 70 66 61 ★★★
Rich, flavorsome wines from one of the best Pomerol estates, retain remarkable power in great vintages like 1961.

(R) **Trottevielle, Ch.** Bord. 79 78 77 76 75 71 70 66 ★★★
Eminent first growth of Saint-Émilion; finely tuned wines with abundant fruit and body but well balanced.

(W) **Veuve Clicquot.** One of the top Champagne houses named for the widow Clicquot; rich, full-bodied wines. Special CUVÉE: La Grande Dame.

(R) **Vieux-Chateau-Certan.** Bord. 79 78 77 76 75 71 70 66 61 ★★★+
The leading Pomerol after Pétrus; concentrated fruit, good depth and body, ages with great distinction.

(W) **Vin Jaune.** Ju. ★★
Unusual heavy-ish yellow wines produced at Arbois, a character similar to dry Sherry but lighter and not fortified.

(R) **Volnay.** Burg. 79 78 77 76 72 71 69 ★★★
Delicate, fragrant silky-textured reds of the Côte de Beaune; among the lightest of Burgundies but one of the most engaging. Best vineyards: Caillerets, Clos des Chênes, Clos des Ducs, Champans, Fremiets. Whites from here are labeled Meursault. Volnay-Santenots is red Meursault. Good value.

(R) **Vosne-Romanée.** Burg. 79 78 77 76 72 71 70 66 ★★★/★★★★★
Home of the incomparable GRAND CRUS Romanée-Conti, La Tache, Richebourg, La Romanée, etc., and fine PREMIERS CRUS La Grande Rue, Malconsorts, Les Suchots, Les Beaux-Monts. Simple Vosne-Romanée also quite special.

(W) **Vouvray.** L.V. 79 78 77 ★★/★★★
Full range of whites: dry, semsweet, very sweet, and sparkling. All fruity, fragrant, often delightful; the sweet wines luscious and can age impressively. Excellent value.

(W) **d'Yquem, Ch.** Bord. 78 76 75 71 70 69 68 67 66 62 59 ★★★★
The most celebrated sweet wine in the world from Sauternes; lush, concentrated sweetness with great depth and finesse, glorious aromas of honeyed fruit; ages exceedingly well, often several decades. A full-bodied dry white known as Ygrec is occasionally made.

# THE WINES OF
# ITALY

**I**taly makes more wine than any country in the world. She also exports more and consumes more at home per capita than any other nation, some 30 gallons per person per year.

Vines grow in astonishing variety from one end of the country to the other—from the Tyrol in the extreme northeast to the orange groves of Sicily. Italy's winemaking traditions are centuries old, with wines that evolved largely as accompaniments to local cuisine. Generally, therefore, one will find the better wines in regions where the cuisine is distinctive and varied, such as Tuscany and Piedmont or the Veneto. The grilled meats and game birds so popular in Tuscany, for example, are handsomely set off by fine reds like Chianti Riserva, Vino Nobile, or Brunello di Montalcino. In the northeast around Venice seafood delicacies from the Adriatic are accompanied by fresh dry whites such as Pinot Bianco, Pinot Grigio, and others that are among Italy's best dry white wines.

The Italians' offhand attitude toward wine as a natural adjunct to meals and a part of everyday life has led to a profusion of rather ordinary wines without a great deal to recommend them. Though Italy has always produced excellent wines like Barolo, Barbaresco, Brunello, Chianti Riserva, and others, standards of quality were, for the most part, entirely up to the individual grower. The casual approach to winegrowing and winemaking techniques was prevalent.

All of this began to change in the early 1960s when the government stepped in to set controls for the best wines of each region. In 1963 legislation enacted the *Denominazione di Origine Controllata* (DOC) laws, outlining specific place-names and defining viticultural districts. Grape varieties and minimum alcohol levels were also prescribed. The effect of the DOC laws was a general upgrading of wines at every level, including the best. Improvement continues as more wines are admitted to DOC status.

Recently, a further classification has been proposed for the very finest wines, *Denominazione di Origine Controllata e Guarantita* (DOCG), denomination of origin controlled and guaranteed. Only a few wines are eligible for DOCG status.

# GLOSSARY OF WINE TERMS

**Abboccato.** *Semisweet.*

**Amabile.** *"Amiably" sweet—a little sweeter than* ABBOCCATO.

**Bianco.** *White.*

**Cantina.** *Winery; cantina sociale are local grower cooperatives.*

**Classico.** *Term for superior zone within a* DOC. *Usually the best wine of the region.*

**Colli.** *Literally, "hills."*

**DOC.** *Denominazione di Origine Controllata, wine of controlled name and origin.*

**DOCG.** *Denominazione di Origine Controllata e Garantita, wine of controlled name and origin guaranteed.*

**Dolce.** *Sweet.*

**Frizzante.** *Lightly fizzy.*

**Liquoroso.** *Very sweet and alcoholic dessert wine, sometimes fortified with brandy.*

**Riserva, riserva speciale.** *Reserve wines, aged for a time specified by* DOC *laws, usually in barrel but also in bottle. Minimum, a year or more.*

**Rosato.** *Rosé.*

**Rosso.** *Red.*

**Secco.** *Dry.*

**Spumante.** *Sparkling.*

**Stravecchio.** *Very old.*

**Tenuta.** *Wine estate.*

**Vendemmia.** *Grape harvest, or vintage.*

# PRINCIPAL WINE REGIONS

**Abruzzi** (Abr.)    Mountainous region on the Adriatic, Montepulciano-d'Abruzzi.

**Alto Adige** (A.A.)    Southern portion of Trentino-Alto-Adige. Fertile hills and valleys produce very good varietal wines such as Merlot, Cabernet Franc, Pinot Bianco, Pinot Nero (Noir), and Gewürztraminer. Also Caldaro, Santa Maddalena, Terlano.

**Apulia** (Apu.)    The southeastern heel of Italy's "boot," producing huge quantities of bulk wine, as well as San Severo and Castel del Monte.

**Basilicata** (Bas.)    In the south, known mainly for Aglianico del Vulture.

**Calabria** (Cal.)    Forms the "toe" of Italy's boot shape; noted for Ciro.

**Campania** (Camp.)    South of Naples; volcanic soil on slopes of Mt. Vesuvius produces Lacryma Christi and Vesuvio. Inland there are Taurasi and Greco di Tufo.

**Emilia-Romagna** (E.R.)    Central Italy, gastronomic capital is Bologna. Best known for Lambrusco.

**Friuli-Venezia-Giulia** (F.V.G.)    Hilly, cool climate of the northeast bordering on Yugoslavia; produces several good varietals; Pinot Grigio, Pinot Bianco, Collio Goriziano (around city of Gorizia).

**Latium** (Lat.)    Also known as Lazio. District of Rome, best known are wines from hills south of the city known as Castelli Romani, which include Frascati, Marino, Colli Albani.

**Liguria** (Lig.)    Mountainous Mediterranean coast, capital Genoa. Steep hillside vineyards on rocky coast here produce Cinqueterre, Rossese di Dolceacqua.

**Lombardy** (Lomb.)    Central northern region embracing the Valtellina, known for Grumello, Inferno, Sassella; in the south, Oltrepo' Pavese around the River Po.

**Marches** (Mar.)    Mountainous region on Adriatic, producing Verdicchio, Rosso Conero. Principal wine center is Ancona.

**Piedmont** (Pied.)    Northwestern region bordering France and the Alps. Several of Italy's most famous wines produced: Barolo, Barbaresco, Barbera, Gattinara, Asti Spumante. Turin is the capital: Asti and Alba are principal wine centers.

**Sardinia** (Sard.)    Large island off west coast of Italy. Monica di Cagliari.

**Sicily** (Sic.)    Volcanic island off the southern tip of Italy, largest of Mediterranean. Etna, Corvo, Marsala.

**Trentino** (Tren.)    Northernmost region of Italy bordering on Austria, always linked with Alto-Adige. Principal cities Bolzano and Trento, principal wines same as Alto-Adige, also Teroldego.

**Tuscany** (Tus.)    Italy's leading wine region along with Piedmont, producing Chianti Classico (between Florence and Siena), Brunello di Montalcino, and Vino Nobile di Montepulciano.

**Umbria** (Umb.)    Hilly region in central Italy; best-known wines are Orvieto, Rubesco di Torgiano.

**Veneto** (Ven.)    Large northern region embracing Verona (Soave, Valpolicella, Amarone), Venice (Colli Euganei), Treviso, and Conegliano (Proseco, Venegazzú, Raboso). Tre Venezie refers to areas immediately north and west of Venice.

# WINE GUIDE

Ⓡ **Aglianico del Vulture.** Bas. DOC 78 75 73 71 70 ★★
Made from Aglianico grape and one of southern Italy's better reds. Sturdy, full-bodied; becomes RISERVA after 5 years.

Ⓦ **Albana di Romagna.** E. R. DOC 79 78 ★
Semisweet, often full-bodied white produced in Emilia-Romagna. Best when young.

Ⓦ **Albano.** Lat. 79 78 ★★
One of the dry white village wines from the hills south of Rome; most consumed locally and best when quite young.

Ⓡ **Aleatico.** Red Muscat grape; also the full-bodied sweet wine made from it mostly in Apulia (DOC), Latium, and the island of Elba.

Ⓦ **Alghero.** Sard. 79 78
Fresh, fruity, fragrant dry white from the region around the town of Alghero on Sardinia's northwestern coast.

Ⓡ **Amarone (Recioto Amarone della Valpolicella).** Ven. DOC 78 77 69 67 ★★★
A full-bodied (14–15% alcohol) long-lived type of Valpolicella made from very ripe grapes that are dried after harvest to concentrate sugars. Intense flavors, slightly bitter aftertaste, expensive.

Ⓦ **Asti Spumante.** Pied. DOC 79 78 77 76 ★★★
Sparkling white wine from the Muscat grape made around Asti; fruity and fragrant, usually sweet but some made in dry (brut) style. Good value.

Ⓡ **Barbacarlo.** Lomb. DOC 79 78 76 73 71 70 ★★
Light red, sweet or dry, from around Pavia (Oltrepo' Pavese).

Ⓡ **Barbaresco.** Pied. DOC (G) 79 78 74 71 69 64 62 61 58 ★★★★
One of Italy's best reds from Nebbiolo grape in hills of the Piedmont. Robust, tannic when young, but capable of aging with grace and distinction. Matures sooner than Barolo, to which it is a sort of "younger brother."

THE WINE REGIONS OF **ITALY**

**Barbera.** Grape variety grown in Piedmont producing sturdy, full-bodied reds, very fruity; can be harsh when young but some age well, up to 10 years or more.

Ⓡ **Barbera d'Alba.** Pied. DOC 79 78 74 71 67 ★★★
As above, but produced around Alba. Robust fruit, tannic in youth, ages nicely up to 10 years, sometimes longer. Good value.

Ⓡ **Barbera d'Asti.** Pied. DOC 79 78 74 64 61 ★★★
Somewhat lighter but more refined Barbera than above. Needs minimum 3–4 years aging, best at 5 to 8. Good value.

Ⓡ **Barbera del Monferrato.** Pied. DOC 79 78 74 71 64 ★★
Widely produced in southern Piedmont, varies from light to heavy and full-bodied. Mostly dry, occasionally semisweet and FRIZZANTE.

Ⓡ **Bardolino.** Ven. DOC 77 76 61 ★★
Light red produced near Lake Garda, best when young (and slightly cooled).

Ⓡ **Barolo.** Pied. DOC(G) 79 78 74 71 70 67 65 61 ★★★★
Possibly Italy's best wine, certainly best wine of the Piedmont; dark, ro-

37

bust, powerful, distinctively scented wine, slow to mature but best are very long-lived. Some Barolos spend 5 to 8 years in wood cask. Made from Nebbiolo. Minimum 4 years for RISERVA, 5 for RISERVA SPECIALE.

**Bonarda.** Red wine grape widely grown in Piedmont and Lombardy. Also a light fruity DOC red, Bonarda dell'Oltrepo near Pavia.

®️ **Brachetto d'Acqui.** Pied. DOC 79 78
Cherry red dessert wine, slightly sparkling, with fruity muscat aromas. Best when young and slightly cooled.

**Brolio.** Oldest and most famous Chianti Classico estate founded by the Ricasoli family.

®️ **Brunello di Montalcino.** Tus. DOC(G) 79 77 75 70 67 66 64 61 55 45 ★★★★
Dark, powerful, slow-maturing wine from 100% Sangiovese Grosso. Aged 4 years minimum in wood, 5 for RISERVA. Italy's most expensive wine and one of her most impressive.

®️ **Buttafuoco.** Lomb. DOC 79 78 74 71 ★★
Staunch and fruity red of the Oltrepo' Pavese region in southern Lombardy; name means "spitfire." Best within about 5 years of vintage.

**Cabernet.** The Bordeaux varieties of Cabernet Franc and Cabernet Sauvignon are widely grown in the northeast districts of Trentino-Alto-Adige, Friuli, TreVenezia; some also in Tuscany (see Sassicaia) and Umbria show great future promise.

®️ **Caldaro (Lago di Caldaro).** Tren. DOC 79 78 77 75 69
Full-bodied mellow red with hint of almond aftertaste, from around Bolzano.

®️ **Cannonau.** Sard. DOC 79 77 72 69 64 ★★
Very full-bodied (13–15% alcohol) Sardinian red, both dry and sweet versions; ages well.

Ⓦ **Capri.** Average dry white from island of Capri; no DOC.

®️ **Carema.** Pied. DOC 79 78 74 71 70 ★★
Smooth, medium-bodied red from the Nebbiolo grape, produced near Turin. Good value.

®️ **Carmignano.** Tus. DOC 79 78 77 75 ★★
Warm, fragrant red made from Sangiovese, Cabernet Sauvignon, and other grapes. Similar to Chianti.

**Castel Chiuro.** Good red and white wines of the Valtellina, proprietary labels of a single producer.

**Castel del Monte.** Region in Apulia producing agreeable DOC reds, whites, rosés. Good value.

**Castelli Romani.** Hilly region south of Rome producing several dry whites. See Frascati, Colli Albani, Marino.

®️ **Chianti.** Tus. DOC 79 78 71 70 62 58 ★★
Light, quite pleasant reds from hills surrounding Florence. Includes subdistricts of Rufina, Montalbano, Aretini, Colli Fiorentini, Pisane, Senesi. RISERVA (aged 3 years) often quite good.

®️ **Chianti Classico.** Tus. DOC 79 78 77 75 71 70 ★★★
Superior central district of Chianti between Florence and Siena. Medium to full-bodied red from dozens of fine estates; better vintages capable of aging well, often becoming refined and elegant. RISERVA aged minimum 3 years.

**Chiaretto.** One of Italy's best DOC rosés produced around Lake Garda. Best when young.

Ⓦ **Cinqueterre.** Lig. DOC ★★★
Fragrant whites from the Ligurian coast and La Spezia. Best when young.

®️Ⓦ **Cirò.** Cal. DOC 79 78 77 74 73 69 ★★
Sturdy, full-bodied reds, whites, some rosé; known in the time of the ancient Greeks and consumed at the Olympic games.

Ⓦ **Colli Albani.** Lat. DOC ★★
Gentle dry whites of the Alban hills south of Rome, mostly from Trebbiano grapes, some Malvasia that is slightly sweet. Best when young.

Ⓡ Ⓦ **Colli Euganei.** Ven. DOC ★

Rather light reds and whites produced near Padua, the everyday wines of Venice. Best when young.

Ⓡ Ⓦ **Collio Goriziano.** F.V.G. DOC 79 78 77 ★★+

Eleven wines, mostly white varietals, produced around Gorizia and named for grape varieties (near Yugoslavia); among the best whites are Tocai, Pinot Grigio, Sauvignon, Pinot Bianco. Light reds are Merlot, Cabernet Franc.

Ⓡ Ⓦ **Colli Orientali del Friuli.** F.V.G. DOC ★★

Principal growing region within Friuli-Venezia-Giulia, producing several quite agreeable reds and good whites, such as Pinot Bianco, Pinot Grigio.

Ⓦ **Cortese di Gavi.** Pied. DOC ★★

Mostly fresh, light wine from Cortese grape from southern Piedmont, best from town of Gavi. More full-bodied wines, some aged in small oak, can be extremely good at 2–4 years or longer.

Ⓡ Ⓦ **Corvo.** Sic. DOC 79 78 77 74 71 ★★

Warm, medium-bodied red, flavorful white wines produced near Palermo. Both among southern Italy's best wines, widely exported.

Ⓡ **Dolcetto.** Pied. DOC 79 78 74 ★★

Robust, quick-maturing fruity reds from Dolcetto grape, best of which is Dolcetto d'Alba.

Ⓡ **Donnaz.** Pied. DOC 79 78 74 71 ★★

One of the lightest reds made from Nebbiolo grape in the Val d'Aosta. Agreeable locally, sometimes ages well but not much exported.

Ⓦ **Est! Est! Est!** Lat. DOC ★

Rather ordinary whites, both dry and semisweet, from hilltop town of Montefiascone.

Ⓡ Ⓦ **Etna.** Sic. DOC 79 78 77 75 70 68 ★★

Full, flavorful reds and whites from the volcanic slopes of Mt. Etna. Reds often age extremely well. Good value.

Ⓡ Ⓦ **Falerno.** Camp. 79 78 77 76 ★★

Dry, fairly full reds, some whites made south of Vesuvius. Reds were praised by Romans of antiquity, such as Horace, Pliny, and Ovid, for their longevity. Good but not extraordinary today.

Ⓡ **Fara.** Pied. DOC 79 78 74 71 70 67 ★★

Smooth, fragrant red from Nebbiolo grape, produced near Novarra.

Ⓦ **Fiano.** Camp. DOC 79 78 76 ★★

Dry, pleasant white made from Fiano grape south of Naples.

Ⓡ **Fracia.** Lomb. DOC ★★

Light, fruity red from the Valtellina. Best when young.

Ⓦ **Frascati.** Lat. DOC ★★

Best of the whites from the Colli Albani south of Rome. Soft, fragrant, fruity, very dry. Best when young.

Ⓡ Ⓦ **Frecciarossa.** Lomb. 79 77 76 74 73 ★★

Good reds and whites from Oltrepo' Pavese in southern Lombardy. Whites better known, but red is mellow, balanced.

Ⓡ **Freisa d'Asti.** Pied. DOC 79 78 74 73 70 ★★★

Two styles of red—one dry, fruity, slighty acidic in youth but ages into roundness; the other, sweet, slightly fizzy; most consumed locally.

Ⓡ **Gattinara.** Pied. DOC 79 78 76 74 70 69 68 64 ★★★★

Excellent red from Nebbiolo grape, lighter but more refined than Barolo when young and capable of aging up to 10 years or more. Good value.

**Gavi.** See Cortese di Gavi.

Ⓡ **Ghemme.** Pied. DOC 78 74 73 70 64 ★★★

Another Nebbiolo wine produced near Gattinara. Not quite so fine as Gattinara but sound and appealing. Good value.

**Grappa.** Grape brandy distilled from mass of pulp left after grapes are pressed. Colorless, potent, often fierce spirit. Better ones have fine aromas and complex flavors.

(W) **Greco di Tufo.** Camp. DOC 79 78 77 74 ★★+
  Flavorful, full-bodied dry white, better with a few years of age.

(R) **Grignolino.** Pied. DOC 79 78 74 71 ★★★
  Light pleasant red, very fruity bouquet, produced in Monferrato area of the Piedmont near Asti.

(R) **Grumello.** Lomb. DOC 79 78 75 71 70 69 64 ★★
  From the Nebbiolo grape; one of the best and firmest reds of the Valtellina.

(R) **Inferno.** Lomb. DOC 79 78 75 71 70 69 ★★★
  Similar to Grumello but ages better, developing perfumed bouquet. Best at about five years.

(RW) **Ischia.** Camp. DOC 78 77 75 73 ★★
  Crisp, dry whites from the island off Naples. Some reds produced.

(W) **Lacryma Christi del Vesuvio.** Camp. DOC 79 78 77 74 ★★
  The famous white wine of Naples grown on the slopes of Mt. Vesuvius; name means "tears of Christ." Pleasant but not distinguished. A full-bodied red (Rosso) also produced.

**Lago di Caldaro.** See Caldaro.

(R) **Lagrein.** Tren; A. A. DOC 79 78 77 75 ★★+
  Robust, often meaty red of Bolzano; heartier than Caldaro, not quite as distinguished as Santa Maddalena. Also a dry, full-bodied rosé.

(R) **Lambrusco.** E. R. DOC ★★
  Widely popular light reds in a variety of styles, often frizzy, slightly sweet, and almost rosé. Best when very young and chilled.

**Langhe.** Hills in central Piedmont south of Alba where best Barolo and Barbaresco are produced.

(R) **Lessona.** Pied. DOC 78 74 71 ★★★
  Classically structured, often fruity red of northern Piedmont above Gattinara. Ages well like most Nebbiolo wines but generally lighter in body.

(W) **Lugana.** Lomb. DOC 79 78 76 75 ★★★
  Fragrant, flavorful white (Trebbiano grape) from southern tip of Lake Garda. Fresh, dry, and appealing. Drink young. Good value.

**Malvasia.** White grape producing several sweet wines, the most famous being Malvasia delle Lipari of Sicily and Cagliari of Sardinia.

(W) **Marino.** Lat. DOC ★★
  Fragrant, pale gold white from south of Rome, similar to Frascati, but fuller flavor and body. Best when young.

**Marsala.** Sic. DOC ★★★
  Dark, sweet, and/or dry fortified dessert wine from Sicily. Good by itself and much used in cooking deserts like zabaglione. Good value.

**Merlot.** The red wine grape of Bordeaux, grown mostly in northeastern Italy, producing good, lively reds.

(R) **Monica di Cagliari.** Sard. DOC 79 77 73 72 70 ★★
  Sweet, spicy red from Monica grape, native to Sardinia; a dry red is also made, both up to 13.5% alcohol. Monica di Sardegna is a lighter red with its own DOC.

(R) **Montepulciano d'Abruzzi.** Abr. DOC 79 77 75 74 73 68 ★★★
  Good red from mountainous coast of Abruzzi. Ages well, developing attractive bouquet. Not to be confused with Vino Nobile of Tuscany, though based on same grape.

**Moscato.** Fragrant, fruity grape grown widely throughout Italy. Most famous wine is Asti Spumante.

**Nebbiolo.** One of Italy's best red wine grapes, used for Barolo, Barbaresco, and Gattinara, as well as wines of the Valtellina.

(R) **Nebbiolo d'Alba.** Pied. DOC 79 78 71 ★★
  Attractive red, sometimes declassified Barolo that doesn't meet producer's standards.

(RW) **Oltrepo' Pavese.** Lomb. DOC 79 78 74 ★★
  Hilly region near Pavia that produces several good reds and whites

*Vigneto* **Bricco Asili** *Barbaresco*

*Barbaresco*
1974

VINO A DENOMINAZIONE D'ORIGINE CONTROLLATA

*prodotto ed imbottigliato da*
*Ceretto in Bricco Asili*
*Barbaresco zona d'origine*
*Produzione 7030 b. glie e 950 magnum*
*Bottiglia*

CERETTO
BRICCO ASILI
BARBARESCO - ITALIA

CONT. NETTO LT. 0,720        R.I. 4322 · CN        ALCOOL GR. 13,90

**BARBARESCO.** Most Italian wines are named for the region of origin. Barbaresco is one of the leading red wine districts of the Piedmont in northern Italy. The fact that it is a government-regulated DOC wine is shown by the words *Denominazione d'Origine Controllata* under the vintage date. "Bricco Asili" is the name of a hilltop in the Barbaresco region that yields superior grapes. Ceretto is one of the most reputable producers of Barolo and Barbaresco. 7,030 bottles and 950 magnums of this wine were produced.

from such grapes as Barbera, Bonarda, Moscato, Riesling, to which the suffix dell'Oltrepo' is added in the wine names—Barbera dell'Oltrepo', for example. Good value.

Ⓦ **Orvieto.** Umb. DOC ★★
Fruity, full-bodied whites from region around the hilltop town of Orvieto, near Perugia, mostly dry but some gently sweet, mainly from the Trebbiano grape. Drink young.

**Passito.** Concentrated sweet wines made from sun-dried or partially raisined grapes. Among the best are Tuscany's Vin Santo and Caluso Passito of the Piedmont.

Ⓡ **Piave Rosso.** Tren. DOC 78 77 74 ★
Light to medium-bodied reds made mostly from Merlot and Cabernet.

(W) **Picolit.** F.V.G. DOC ★★★★
Rare and expensive golden dessert wine, sweet or off-dry; made from very ripe, late-harvested grapes in Colli Orientali. Once renowned and favored by popes; most vines now destroyed by disease. Unusual aromas and flavors, probably best sipped alone. Italians call it *vino da meditazione*, a wine for contemplation.

(W) **Pinot Bianco.** Fresh, fragrant, fruity white wines, several of DOC status produced mostly in northeastern districts of Trentino and Friuli. Good value.

(W) **Pinot Grigio.** Firm, dry, fruity white wines from grape of that name, several DOC in regions like Friuli, Trentino, TreVenezie. Excellent value. Best when young.

(R) **Pinot Nero dell'Alto Adige.** Tren. DOC 78 76 75
Light reds of the northeast made from Pinot Noir grape.

(R) **Primitivo.** Red grape widely grown in southern Italy, mostly Apulia, producing warm, fruity, generous wines. Tentatively linked to California's Zinfandel.

(W) **Prosecco di Conegliano.** Ven. DOC 78 75 ★★★
Crisp, dry white produced northwest of Venice from the Prosecco grape, often sparkling and uniquely perfumed, occasionally AMABILE.

(R) **Raboso.** Ven. DOC 79 78 76 75 ★★
Pleasant robust red made near Treviso and the river Piave.

(3) **Ravello.** Red, white, and rosé wines from town of that name along the Amalfi coast; the best are fresh and pleasant.

**Recioto.** Implies extra ripe; term used mostly for full-bodied reds from the Veneto around Verona; wine made from upper portions of grape bunches that get more sun and higher sugars, often sweet. May also be dry and potent, as in Recioto Amarone della Valpolicella.

(R) **Recioto della Valpolicella.** Ven. DOC ★★
Sweet red, occasionally sparkling, or FRIZZANTE, popular in Verona.

(W) **Recioto di Soave.** Ven. DOC ★★
Semisparkling white made from extra-ripe grapes; more full-bodied and strong-flavored than regular Soave. Drink young.

**Riesling.** White grape variety used in northern Italy to make mostly DOC wines in Oltrepo' and Trentino-Alto-Adige.

**Riserva.** See Glossary of Wine Terms.

(RO) **Riviera del Garda Chiaretto.** Ven. DOC ★★
Well-known rosé made near Lake Garda. Strong-flavored, dry, vividly colored. Drink young.

(R) **Riviera del Garda Rosso.** Ven. DOC 79 78 77 76 71 ★
Very full-bodied red version of above, coarser and more robust than other well-known red of the region, Bardolino.

(R) **Rossese di Dolceacqua.** Lig. DOC 79 78 75 71 70 ★★
Warm, full-bodied ruby red wine, faintly bitter in aftertaste; popular along Italian Riviera. Superiore bigger, longer-lived.

(R) **Rosso Conero.** Mar. DOC 78 77 75 74 ★★
Robust, fruity red based on Montepulciano grape of Tuscany, produced around Ancona on Adriatic coast. Good value.

(R) **Rosso delle Colline Lucchesi.** Tus. DOC 79 78 77 75 ★★
Medium-bodied red that is produced around Lucca, similar in style to Chianti.

(R) **Rubesco di Torgiano.** Umb. DOC 78 77 75 74 71 ★★★
Excellent red produced near Perugia. Robust, full-flavored, and capable of aging extremely well. Excellent value.

**Rufina.** One of the subregions of Chianti.

**Sangiovese.** Principal red wine grape used for Chianti and other reds of Tuscany. Sangiovese Grosso is used for big reds like Brunello, Vino Nobile di Montepulciano, and Tignanello.

(R) **Sangiovese di Romagna.** E. R. DOC 78 75 71 ★+
Widely produced everyday red north of Bologna; in good vintages improves with age.

**Castello di Uzzano**

CHIANTI CLASSICO

DENOMINAZIONE DI ORIGINE CONTROLLATA

**1974**
RISERVA

*Conti Castelbarco Albani*
*Masetti*

GREVE in Chianti Classico (Firenze)

680/FI

MESSO IN BOTTIGLIA AL CASTELLO

PRODUCE OF ITALY

ALCOHOL 12.5% BY VOLUME    ®    NET CONTENTS 3/4 QUART

IMPORTED
BY    A L M A D É N    SAN JOSE    ✠    I M P O R T S    CALIFORNIA    Sole Agents
for the
United States
of America

**CASTELLO DI UZZANO.** There are numerous fine estates in the Chianti Classico region of Tuscany, a specifically defined area between Florence and Siena with its own DOC separate from other Chianti regions such as Rufina or Fiorentina. As a *Riserva*, the wine by law must be aged a minimum of 3 years before release. "Greve" is one of the principal wine towns of the Classico region and "Castello di Uzzano" one of its best estates. *Messo in bottiglia al castello* means estate-bottled.

Ⓡ **Sangue di Giuda.** Lomb. DOC 79 77 ★★
    Hearty, tannic red from southern Lombardy (Oltrepo' Pavese). Name means "blood of Judas."

③ **San Severo.** Apu. DOC 79 78 77 ★★
    Dry, sturdy white and red wines, some rosé, produced near town of Foggia; quality has improved in recent years, especially for red.

Ⓡ **Santa Maddalena.** Tren. DOC 79 78 76 75 74 ★★
    One of the best reds of northeastern Italy near Bolzano, made from Schiava, full-bodied, flavorful, generally well-balanced. Good value.

Ⓡ **Sassella.** Lomb. DOC 79 78 75 71 ★★
    Good, medium-bodied red from the Valtellina made from Nebbiolo. Ages well in good vintages. Good value.

Ⓡ **Sassicaia.** Tus. DOC 79 78 77 75 ★★★★
    Relatively new and superior red made from 100% Cabernet Sauvignon produced on coastal heights near Livorno. Big and tannic in youth, ages well; very small production. Interesting, expensive wine.

**Sauvignon Blanc.** White grape variety used in northeast, principally Friuli, to produce dry, fragrant, fruity white wines labeled Sauvignon. Very good value.

Ⓡ **Savuto.** Cal. DOC ★★
Big, sturdy red of southern Italy.

**Schiava.** Red wine grape used in northern Italy for superior reds such as Santa Maddalena and Lago di Caldaro.

Ⓡ **Sfursat.** Lomb. DOC 79 75 71 ★★
Full-bodied concentrated red of Valtellina made of partially dried grapes. Ages well but limited production. Also known as Sforzato.

Ⓡ **Sizzano.** Pied. DOC 79 78 74 71 ★★
Agreeable red made from Nebbiolo grape, produced around Novara.

Ⓦ **Soave.** Ven. DOC ★★★
Italy's best-known white wine produced near Verona in ancient walled town of Soave. Fresh, light, fruity, very pleasant wine, though popularity and expanded production have resulted in some unevenness. Best when young; often good value.

Ⓡ **Spanna.** Pied. 78 76 74 71 68 64 61 ★★+
Sturdy, full-bodied red made from Nebbiolo. *Spanna* is local name for Nebbiolo grape from lower slopes around Gattinara region. Capable of long aging, often requires it. Good value.

Ⓡ **Taurasi.** Camp. DOC 79 77 75 71 68 58 ★★★
Full-bodied, complex red; tannic and harsh in youth but ages impressively into harmonious wine of some finesse. Expensive.

Ⓦ **Terlano.** Tren. DOC ★★
Several dry agreeable whites produced around Bolzano. Drink young.

Ⓡ **Teroldego.** Tren. DOC 79 78 76 71 ★★
Leading red wine of Trentino. Berryish fruit, well-balanced wine of medium body. Good value locally.

Ⓡ **Tignanello.** Tus. 78 75 71 ★★★★
Proprietary label from Antinori estate in Chianti region of Tuscany. Fine, well-structured wine made from Sangiovese and Cabernet Sauvignon. Made in Bordeaux style, becomes elegant with age, though quite good at 5 to 7 years.

Ⓦ **Tocai.** Tren.; F.V.G. DOC 79 78 77 ★★★
One of the better whites of the northeast. Aromatic, with a dry, crisp, slight almond aroma. Good value.

Ⓦ **Torre di Giano.** Umb. DOC ★★★
Fragrant, full-bodied, flavorful white from the Longarotti estate near Torgiano. Drink young. Good value. Also lesser wines labeled simply Torgiano.

Ⓦ **Traminer.** Tren. DOC ★★
Delicate fragrant white of the Italian Tyrol, mostly northeast. Traminer Aromatico is name for Gewürztraminer, spicy dry white. Drink young. Good value.

**Trebbiano.** Leading white grape of central Italy, mainly Tuscany and Umbria, producing several DOC whites such as Trebbiano di Toscano (also known as Bianco di Toscano) and Orvieto. Generally fruity, flavorful though some lesser local versions quite ordinary. Known in France as Uqni Blanc.

**Trentino-Alto-Adige.** Extreme northeastern province of Italy. Mountainous cool climate producing several DOC wines mostly named for grape varieties.

ⓇⓌ **Valdage.** Broad DOC category of reds and whites, mostly named for grape variety and made around Trento.

Ⓡ **Valgella.** Lomb. DOC 79 78 71 70 69 ★★
Sturdy red wine of the Valtellina, slow to mature. After 4 years aging becomes RISERVA. Good value.

Ⓡ **Valpantena.** Ven. DOC 78 77 ★★
Light red produced east of Verona, similar to Valpolicella but of lesser quality.

(R) **Valpolicella.** Ven. DOC 79 78 77 74 ★★★

One of Italy's best light reds produced northwest of Verona. Smooth, round, fruity wines generally best within five years of vintage, though some last longer. Often best when slightly cooled.

**Valtellina.** Principal wine-producing region of Lombardy, a mountainous region east of Lake Como known for sturdy, generous reds such as Grumello, Sassella, Inferno, and Valgella.

(RW) **Velletri.** Lat. DOC 79 78 ★★

Agreeable whites and rather better reds from town of Velletri in the hills south of Rome.

(R) **Venegazzú.** F.V.G. 78 77 74 ★★★

Very fine red wine from little town of that name above Treviso. Made from Cabernet Sauvignon, Malbec, and Merlot, very full-bodied (over 13% alcohol) and aged in small oak. At 4 years becomes Riserva di Casa, developing fine bouquet, complexity, and finesse. Expensive. Some white wine produced under the name as well.

**Verdiso.** A white grape producing light fresh whites around the town of Conegliano in Friuli and the sparkling wines of Prosecco.

(W) **Verduzzo.** F.V.G. DOC ★★

Dry, fragrant whites from grape of that name produced near Piave above Venice. Some sweet sparkling wines also produced.

(W) **Vermentino.** Lig. ★★

Popular dry white wine along Italian Riviera, very good with seafood. Drink young. Good value.

(W) **Vermentino di Gallura.** Sard. DOC ★★

Full-bodied dry white wine produced in northern Sardinia from Vermentino grape.

**Vernaccia.** Old and honored white grape variety producing dry and sweet pale golden wines.

(W) **Vernaccia di San Gimignano.** Tus. DOC (G) 78 77 75 ★★★

Best-known whites made from Vernaccia grape. Mostly dry and somewhat austere in youth, softens with a couple of years in bottle. Some sweet wines also made. Other Vernaccias are Vernaccia di Oristano of Sardinia and Vernaccia di Serrapetrona from the Marches.

(R) **Vino Nobile di Montepulciano.** Tus. DOC 78 77 75 70 68 67 ★★★★

Excellent noble red wine from Montepulciano near Siena. Made mostly from Sangiovese grosso. Deeply colored, rich flavors and aromas, ages extremely well. Good value.

**Vin santo.** Rich, usually sweet, white wines made from dried grapes. Not well known outside Italy, but many of the leading estates produce their own. Tuscany's are the most famous.

(W) **Zagarolo.** Lat. DOC ★★

Agreeable whites from hill town of Zagarolo south of Rome. Similar to Frascati, but smaller production and less well known.

# Italian Vintage Chart

Vintage charts serve primarily as general guides to the quality of wines in each vintage; in both good and bad years there are exceptions to the general rating. Some regional wines, such as Barolo or Chianti, have numerous producers, and one can expect to find on occasion considerable variation of style among them.

This vintage chart covers only red wines. For white wines, generally the younger and fresher they are, the better. There are two Italian whites, however, that improve with a few years of bottle age: Greco di Tufo and Vernaccia di San Gimignano.

| | AMARONE | BARBARESCO | BARBERA | BARDOLINO | BAROLO | BRUNELLO DI MONTALCINO | CABERNET TRENTINO | CAREMA | CHIANTI | CHIANTI CLASSICO (RISERVA) | CIRO ROSSO | CORVO ROSSO | GATTINARA | GHEMME |
|---|---|---|---|---|---|---|---|---|---|---|---|---|---|---|
| 1961 | 8 | 9 | 8 | 6 | (10) | 6 | 6 | | 5 | 6 | 7 | | 8 | 6 |
| 1962 | 8 | 8 | 8 | 9 | 8 | | 4 | | 7 | 9 | 5 | | 5 | 8 |
| 1963 | 7 | 2 | 4 | 6 | 4 | | 6 | | 4 | 4 | 7 | | 2 | 4 |
| 1964 | 10 | 10 | 9 | 8 | 10 | (10) | 10 | | 6 | 9 | 5 | | 10 | 9 |
| 1965 | 6 | 6 | 6 | 6 | 7 | 6 | 2 | | 5 | 5 | 5 | | 5 | 6 |
| 1966 | 8 | 2 | 2 | 6 | 5 | (7) | 6 | | 5 | 5 | | | 5 | 5 |
| 1967 | 8 | (8) | 7 | 7 | 8 | (8) | 6 | | 5 | 8 | 5 | | 5 | 5 |
| 1968 | (8) | 6 | 6 | 7 | 7 | (6) | 4 | | 7 | 8 | 10 | | 8 | 7 |
| 1969 | (9) | (7) | 7 | 9 | (7) | (7) | 10 | | 7 | 8 | 2 | | (8) | 7 |
| 1970 | (7) | (8) | 8 | 7 | (7) | (10) | (10) | 8 | (7) | (9) | 5 | | (8) | 8 |
| 1971 | (8) | (10) | (10) | 8 | 10 | (9) | 7 | 8 | (7) | (9) | 5 | 8 | 5 | 5 |
| 1972 | (7) | 2 | 2 | 5 | 4 | 5 | 4 | 5 | 5 | 5 | 5 | 8 | 3 | 4 |
| 1973 | 8 | 6 | 5 | 7 | 5 | 6 | 4 | 5 | 5 | 5 | (7) | 8 | 5 | 5 |
| 1974 | (9) | 9 | (8) | 7 | (8) | (6) | 4 | 8 | 7 | (7) | (7) | (8) | (9) | (8) |
| 1975 | | (5) | (5) | 8 | (6) | (9) | 6 | (5) | (8) | 9 | (5) | (7) | (6) | (5) |
| 1976 | 6 | (5) | (5) | 8 | (6) | (5) | (6) | 5 | 5 | 5 | 2 | (5) | (8) | (7) |
| 1977 | 8 | 5 | 2 | 8 | 6 | (7) | (6) | 2 | (8) | (8) | (7) | (6) | 5 | (5) |
| 1978 | 8 | 9 | 7 | 6 | 7 | (8) | 8 | 7 | 7 | 7 | 6 | 6 | 7 | 6 |
| 1979 | | 8 | 8 | 8 | 9 | | 7 | 8 | 9 | 8 | 8 | 8 | 8 | 8 |

| | | |
|---|---|---|
| **10** | the best | ○ can take further aging |
| **8-9** | very fine, superior | 5̄ may be too old |
| **6-7** | good, above average | ▦ drink now |
| **5** | average | 5̄ lay away |
| **4** | fair | |
| below **4** | poor | |

| GRIGNOLINO | GRUMELLO | INFERNO | LAMBRUSCO DI SORBÁRA | MERLOT TRENTINO | MONTEPULCIANO D'ABRUZZO | NEBBIOLO D'ALBA | SASSELLA | SFURSAT | TAURASI | TORGIANO | VALPOLICELLA | VINO NOBILE DI MONTEPULCIANO | |
|---|---|---|---|---|---|---|---|---|---|---|---|---|---|
| 8 | 8 | 8 | 10 | 8 | 6 | 10 | 8 | 8 | 10 | | 7 | 6 | 1961 |
| 5 | 5 | 5 | 4 | 6 | 6 | 8 | 5 | 5 | 4 | | 8 | 8 | 1962 |
| 4 | 5 | 5 | 6 | 4 | 7 | 4 | 5 | 5 | 4 | | 7 | 4 | 1963 |
| 5 | 10 | 10 | 4 | 8 | 4 | 8 | 10 | (10) | 8 | | 9 | 8 | 1964 |
| 5 | 4 | 4 | 5 | 4 | 7 | 6 | 4 | 4 | 6 | | 6 | 4 | 1965 |
| 5 | 5 | 5 | 4 | 6 | 6 | 4 | 5 | 5 | 8 | | 7 | 6 | 1966 |
| 5 | 5 | 5 | 6 | 5 | 6 | 8 | 5 | 6 | 8 | | 8 | (10) | 1967 |
| 5 | 5 | 5 | 6 | 5 | 9 | 5 | 5 | 5 | 10 | | 7 | (8) | 1968 |
| 5 | 7 | 7 | 6 | 9 | 4 | 5 | 7 | 8 | 6 | | 8 | 8 | 1969 |
| 5 | (8) | (8) | 7 | 6 | 5 | 5 | (8) | (8) | 8 | | 7 | (10) | 1970 |
| 7 | (8) | (8) | 8 | 8 | 5 | (10) | (8) | (8) | 8 | (9) | 8 | 5 | 1971 |
| 2 | 6 | 6 | 5 | 4 | 5 | 2 | 6 | 5 | 6 | 8 | 8 | 5 | 1972 |
| 5 | 6 | 6 | 6 | 4 | 7 | 5 | 6 | 6 | (8) | 8 | 7 | (8) | 1973 |
| 8 | 6 | 6 | 6 | 6 | 7 | 5 | 6 | 5 | (6) | (7) | 7 | 6 | 1974 |
| 2 | 6 | 6 | 7 | 5 | 8 | 5 | 6 | (6) | (8) | (7) | (8) | (10) | 1975 |
| 5 | (5) | (5) | 6 | (6) | 5 | (5) | (6) | 4 | (6) | (5) | 6 | 4 | 1976 |
| 4 | (5) | (5) | 6 | (5) | (8) | (5) | (5) | (5) | 10 | (6) | (8) | 8 | 1977 |
| (6) | 5 | 5 | 6 | (7) | 6 | (6) | 5 | 5 | 8 | 7 | 7 | 8 | 1978 |
| 7 | 8 | 8 | 8 | 8 | 8 | 7 | 8 | 8 | 8 | 9 | 9 | 9 | 1979 |

THE WINES OF

# GERMANY

ermany's two million acres of vineyards produce some of the world's most delightful wine. Along her famous wine rivers (where Rhine wines come in brown bottles and Mosel wines in green bottles) the views are spectacularly scenic, with steep vine-covered hills rising dramatically from the river banks, and villages of quaint and picturesque charm clustered below. The overall quality of German wines—mostly white, though a little red is produced—is very high. Wines at the middle level, Qualitätswein, are light, fragrant, fruity, and very easy to drink. The best, and Germany's best represents extraordinary distinction at highest levels, are her naturally sweet wines made from the Riesling grape, considered by some the supreme white wines of the world.

Although German nomenclature seems forbiddingly complicated, especially when it appears in forceful gothic, it is worth trying to understand the terminology, for the sublime experience that certain wines afford. The label information for Germany is the most precise in the wine world, and very often what is *not* on the label tells you as much as what is there.

The key words indicate ripeness of the grapes at harvest or pinpoint geographic origin. The geographic breakdown is this: There are 11 regions designated for quality wines (the 9 most important are discussed in Principal Wine Regions). Within each region there are subdistricts known as *Bereichs*. Bereich Bernkastel, for instance, covers most of the Mittel-Mosel. Within each Bereich, several of the better vineyards may constitute a further subgroup known as *Grosslage*, such as Bernkastler Badstube. These wines are of higher grade than Bereich wines. Better wines still come from the most precise geographic site of all, the individual vineyard, or *Einzellage*, as in Bernkasteler Doktor. The suffix "er" is usually added to wines using a village name. Thus, a wine from the town of Winkel becomes Winkeler, one from Graach, Graacher. This works similarly for certain outstanding vineyards where the vineyard name appears by itself (Steinberger, Scharzhofberger). The inclusion of a vineyard name following a village name is a good indication of superior quality.

The other quality indicators are based on ripeness of the grapes, or "must-weight," at harvest. The simplest quality category is *Tafelwein*, ordinary table wine that conforms to minimum quality standards. It is inexpensive, undistinguished, though often agreeable. The next step up is *Qualitätswein bestimmte Anbaugebiete* (QbA)—wine of specified region. Tafelwein and QbAs may legally add sugar before fermentation to make up for insufficient ripeness—a usual occurrence since Germany's vineyards are the north-

# GLOSSARY OF WINE TERMS

**Edelfaule.** *Noble rot, the beneficial mold* Botrytis cinerea *that penetrates grape skins, releasing moisture but concentrating sugars and flavors.*

**Eiswein.** *Literally, "ice wine." Rare, sweet wine made in the unusual instance when a drop in temperature freezes grapes that are still on the vine. The grapes are pressed while still frozen. Usually of the Auslese level of sweetness, and expensive. Can occur as late as January or February after harvest.*

**Erzeugerabfüllung.** *Estate-bottled, wine from a single vineyard.*

**Halb-Trocken.** *Half-dry.*

**Keller.** *Cellar.*

**Perlwein.** *Semisparkling.*

**QbA.** Qualitätswein bestimmte Anbaugebiete. *Quality wine of designated regions. The middle level of German wines to which sugar may be added (before fermentation) when grapes do not fully ripen. Subject to approval before the government quality control board.*

**QmP.** Qualitätswein mit Prädikat. *Quality wine with special attributes. The top 5 levels of German wines, made only in years when the grapes ripen fully and no sugar is added. In ascending order of quality and natural sweetness they are:*

**Kabinett.** *Driest of the QmP wines.*

**Spätlese.** *Late-picked, from grapes left on the vine to ripen further and develop higher sugars. Wines are generally lightly sweet and good acidity makes them suitable with food, even such richly flavored dishes as game in Germany.*

**Auslese.** *Late-picked, selected bunches of grapes, affected by* Botrytis cinerea *(see Edelfäule). Naturally sweet but not heavy, can be excellent summer apéritif or just by itself. Auslese and the two following QmPs are only made in superior vintages.*

**Beerenauslese.** (BA). *Late-ripened selected berries. Only those attacked by* Botrytis *are used, resulting in small quanties of luscious sweet wines among the finest in the world.*

**Trockenbeerenauslese.** (TBA). *Selected dried berries—ultra-ripe grapes left to dry until the sugars concentrate. Incredibly rich, honeyish wine with remarkable balance, depth, and longevity. The ultimate in German wine; a single bottle may cost several hundred dollars.*

**Tafelwein.** *Table wine; lowest classification of wines. It is ranked below QbA.*

**Trocken.** *Dry. By itself on a label, generally means safe for diabetics.*

**Weingut.** *Wine estate.*

**Weinkellerei.** *Winery.*

---

ernmost in Europe, on the same latitude as Newfoundland. More years than not, the grapes cannot develop adequate sugar on their own, and without added sugar, the wines would be hard, acidic, and unpleasant. At the QbA level, most of the sugar is converted to alcohol, leaving wines that are basically dry.

The next level takes a quantum leap—*Qualitätswein mit Prädikat* (QmP), quality wines with special attributes, those that have graduated "with honors," so to speak. They are made with naturally ripened grapes that develop higher sugars and thus can be made only in good years when weather permits. The great vintage years in Germany are those that result in the greatest number of QmP wines. There are five levels within this category. In ascending order of sweetness, they are *Kabinett*; *Spätlese*; *Auslese*; *Beerenauslese* (BA); and *Trockenbeerenauslese* (TBA). (See Glossary of Wine Terms.)

The latter three represent the pinnacle of German wines. Their exquisite balance of sweetness and acidity, never cloying, is the Riesling's response to unique combinations of soil and climate. They are wines of remarkable subtlety, elegance, and profound depth and are incomparably perfumed with the rich scent of honeyed fruit or hints of herbs, wildflowers, or exotic spices.

Some people find German wines too sweet to go with food. But do not be too quick to embrace that idea. In Germany, as well as among connoisseurs throughout the world, wines of Kabinett or Spätlese status are often superb choices with richly flavored dishes, particularly game. Many QbAs and Kabinetts are quite dry; Spätleses are usually lightly sweet or off-dry. There is a renewed trend in Germany toward drier wines, often labeled *Trocken* (dry) or *Halb-Trocken* (half-dry). The wines of Franconia (Franken) wines, those that are sold in a *Bocksbeutel* (squatty green flagon), are also dry, for the most part.

As for the superior levels of naturally sweet wines, Auslese and above, they are most appropriate with dessert or just by themselves. They are wines for special moments.

# PRINCIPAL WINE REGIONS

**Ahr.** A tributary of the Rhine north of Koblenz, known mostly for red wines, rarely exported.

**Baden** (Bad.) Southern Germany's wine region, bordered by Switzerland and Alsace and embracing the Black Forest. Districts such as Ortenau, Kaiserstuhl-Tuniberg, and Bodensee produce good, fresh wines and occasionally some that are more distinguished. Also a few red wines from the Spätburgunder grape.

**Franken, or Franconia** (FrK.) Located in the upper Main valley either side of Würzburg. Mostly, agreeable wines made from Müller-Thurgau and Sylvaner, that come in a flagon-type bottle known as a Bocksbeutel.

**Lagename** Vineyard name.

**Mittelrhein** The "middle Rhine" from Bonn to Bingen, a lesser region of some 2,000 acres producing light wines that are mostly consumed by tourists in the region. Leading Bereich: Bacharach.

**Mosel-Saar-Ruwer** (M-S-R.) The Mosel, leading tributary of the Rhine, produces some of Germany's most exquisite wines—paler, more acid than those of the Rhine regions but also more flowery and spicy—as well as huge quantities of very ordinary wines from large Bereichs like Bernkastel and Zell. The Riesling grape is grown almost exclusively. The best wines come from specific vineyards in the leading wine towns of Bernkastel, Piesport, Wehlen, Ürzig, Brauneberg, and Zeltingen, which make up the Mittel-Mosel. The Saar and Ruwer rivers, tributaries of the Mosel at Trier, also produce some wines with the distinctive floral aromas and spiciness of flavor that mark wines of the Mosel.

**Nahe** (Na.) A tributary of the Rhine near Bingen producing very good wines from Riesling, Sylvaner, and Ruländer. Principal wine towns are Kreuznach and Schloss Böckelheim.

**Rheingau** (Rhg.) Acknowledged as Germany's premier wine region with vineyards facing south on the north bank of the Rhine between Hochheim and Rüdesheim. Excellent QbAs and some of the world's finest sweet wines from famed vineyards such as Schloss Vollrads, Steinberg, and Schloss Johannisberg, the best very long-lived.

**Rheinhessen** (Rhh.) Large growing region on the south bank of the Rhine opposite the Rheingau and turning southward up the Rhine at Mainz. The best wines from vineyards in Nierstein, Nackenheim, and

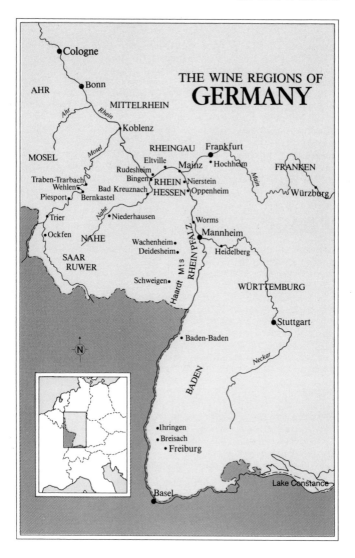

THE WINE REGIONS OF
# GERMANY

Oppenheim are made from Riesling and some Sylvaner. Müller-Thurgau predominates in the Hessen, however, and a great deal of Liebfraumilch, Germany's best-known blend, is made here. The greatest wines compare with those of the Rheingau, though tend to be somewhat softer and not as classically structured.

**Rheinpfalz** (RpF.)  Germany's largest wine region, over 50,000 acres of vineyards below the Rheinhessen on the upper Rhine's western banks. The vineyards are back from the river here, the best on low, east-facing slopes of the Haardt Mountains around the towns of Deidesheim, Forst, Ruppertsberg, Wachenheim, and Bad Dürkheim. Lesser wines have more earthiness and body than most German wines, but QmP wines such as AUSLESE, BA, and TBA show great noblesse and breed. Leading producers of the Pfalz, known locally as the "three Bs," are Bassermann-Jordan, Bürklin-Wolf, and von Bühl.

# FURTHER REGIONAL DESIGNATIONS

**Anbaugebiete** (Gebiet) Wine region. There are 11 designated by German law, 9 of which are shown on the map on page 51, the two lesser ones are Hessiche Bergstrasse and Württemberg.

**Bereich** Subregion of a Gebiet, such as Bereich Niersteiner of the Rheinhessen; a Bereich may include several villages and vineyard sites (Grosslages) but no vineyard name appears on the label since wines may come from any part of the region.

**Einzellage** Individual vineyard site, the smallest geographic designation to appear on a German wine label, usually producing the best wines.

**Grosslage** "Composite" site. A grouping of several vineyards within a Bereich. There are 11 Grosslages in Bereich Nierstein, the most famous of which is Niersteiner Gutes Domtal.

# VINTAGES

Because German wines taste so fresh and appealing within a few months of bottling, the refinements they acquire with maturity—nuance, harmony, elegance—are not always readily appreciated or explored. The fact is, however, that Germany's finest wines improve considerably with bottle age, and often require it to be at their best. An example is the 1976 vintage, which exhibits much more grace, balance and depth at present than it did earlier on. Vintages that yield wines of exceptional quality and ripeness, those of KABINETT status and above, invariably improve in bottle, particularly if acidity is in good proportion. The wines can then be extremely long-lived, up to ten years and beyond.

The following list of vintages indicates which vintages are best for keeping.

**1979.** Greatly reduced by frost in some regions, notably Mosel-Saar-Ruwer, the Nahe, Franconia, and Rheinhessen. Bigger crops in the Rheingau (very good); Rheinpfalz; and Baden. Generally 70% QbA, 25 to 30% QmP wines, mostly KABINETT and SPÄTLESE, a few AUSLESE in the Rheinhessen and Mosel, which should prove good keepers.

**1978.** A late warm harvest, also reduced by frosts the previous spring. Generally good; warmer on the Rhine that produced mostly KABINETT, SPÄTLESE. 80% was QbA for drinking soon.

**1977.** Big, useful vintage, mostly QbAs of appealing freshness for drinking now; some KABINETTS, best in the Rheinpfalz.

**1976.** Excellent quality but reduced quantity. High percentage of QmP wines with very high sugars, some extraordinary wines. Best from Rhine regions, rich though perhaps not as balanced as 1975. Twenty percent KABINETT, 30% AUSLESE, some BAS, TBAS. Needs time to develop, best will be very long-lived.

**1975.** Excellent year for Rieslings, mostly KABINETT and SPÄTLESE of fine, austere balance on the Rhine, superb AUSLESEN on the Mosel, also the Rheinpfalz. Will improve further with time.

**1974.** Variable quality, most no higher than KABINETT level; not suitable for keeping.

**1973.** Large harvest, mostly attractive wines but low acidity, particularly among Mosels; most should be drunk now.

**1972.** Large harvest, average quality, now over the hill.

**1971.** Superlative. Perfectly balanced QmP wines that will continue to develop, though showing beautifully now.

Earlier great vintages whose wines are still fine: **1967, 1966** (Mosel), **1964, 1959, 1953, 1949, 1945.**

# WINE GUIDE

(R) **Ahr.** Ahr. 79 78 76 75 ★/★★
Major region for red wines from Spätburgunder grape, from towns along the Ahr River such as Ahrweiler, Bad Neuenahr, Walporzheim. Pale, some very agreeable but not distinguished.

(R) **Assmannshausen.** Rhg. 79 78 76 75 ★★
Town along the Rhine famous for its red wine from the Spätburgunder grape.

**Auslese.** See Glossary of Wine Terms.

(W) **Avelsbach.** M-S-R 79 78 76 75 73 71 ★★★
One of the better wine villages near Trier, falls within the Grosslage Trierer Römerlay, but best vineyards are Hammerstein, Altenberg, Herrenberg.

(W) **Ayl.** M-S-R. 79 78 76 75 73 71 ★★★
Leading village along the Saar in the Grosslage Scharzberg. Outstanding vineyards: Ayler Kupp, Herrenberg.

**Bad Dürkheim.** See Dürkheim.

**Badische Bergstrasse/Kraichgau.** A leading Bereich in northern Baden, supplies much local wine to Heidelberg.

**Bad Kreuznach.** See Kreuznach.

**Bassermann-Jordan.** Excellent producer along the Rheinpfalz at Deidesheim, with vineyards also in Forst, (Forster Jesuitengarten) and Ruppertsberg. Highly regarded wines, especially of AUSLESE level or higher.

**Beerenauslese.** See Glossary of Wine Terms.

**Bereich.** See Further Regional Designations.

(W) **Bernkastel.** M-S-R. 79 78 76 75 73 71 ★★/★★★★
The principal wine town of the Mosel, finest wines are among Germany's best from the famous Bernkasterler Doktor vineyard; others are Lay, Graben, Bratenhofchen, Matheisbildchen. Best Grosslage: Badstube; the other, Kurfurstlay, also produces good wine.

(W) **Bernkastel, Bereich.** M-S-R. 79 78 76 ★★
One of Germany's largest Bereichs, includes wines from several towns along the Mosel between Zell and the Ruwer (Mittel-Mosel). Often ordinary. Very pleasant in ripe vintages but best when young and fresh.

(W) **Bingen.** Rhh. 79 78 76 73 71 ★★/★★★
A leading wine town on the Rhine near its juncture with the Nahe. Best vineyards: Scharlachberg, Kirchberg, Rosengarten. Also a Bereich for the west Rheinhessen.

**Blauburgunder.** A clone of Pinot Noir, grown mainly in the Ahr.

(W) **Blue Nun.** Largest selling Liebfraumilch from the firm of Sichel. Semisweet but generally fresh and well-balanced.

**Bocksbeutel.** Flagon-shaped bottle with flat sides used for Franken wines.

(W) **Bockstein.** M-S-R. 79 78 76 75 73 71 ★★★
One of the best vineyards in Ockfen on the Saar, known as Ockfener Bockstein.

(W) **Bodenheim.** Rhh. 79 78 76 75 ★★
Wine town in the Rheinhessen. Good wines for the most part, from Sylvaner grape unless otherwise labeled (some Riesling).

**Bodensee.** Minor district of Baden near Lake Constance.

Ⓦ **Brauneberg.** M-S-R. 79 78 76 75 73 71 ★★/★★★
Major wine town along the Mosel. Excellent, often rich sweet wines of top class from vineyards such as Juffer, Juffer-Sonnenuhr, and Klostergarten. Grosslage: Kurfurstlay. Good value.

Ⓦ **Breisach.** Bad. 79 78 76 75 ★★+
Town in Bereich Kaiserstuhl-Tuniberg. Best-known vineyard, Vulkanfelsen, produces good Gewürztraminer.

**Breisgau.** Bereich, minor district in southern Baden near Kaiserstuhl.

**Buhl, von.** One of the three principal growers in the Rheinpfalz, extensive holdings in top vineyards of Deidesheim, Forst, Ruppertsberg; very fine wines, especially of KABINETT level and above.

**Bürklin-Wolf.** Another of the top three producers (with Bassermann-Jordan and von Bühl) in the Rheinpfalz, with excellent vineyards such as Hohenmorgen in Deidesheim, Gerumpel in Wachenheim, and Ungeheuer in Forst.

Ⓦ **Crown of Crowns.** Langenbach's widely-sold Liebfraumilch.

Ⓦ **Deidesheim.** Rpf. 79 78 76 75 73 71 ★★/★★★★
Quaint, charming town in the Rheinpfalz. Rich, aromatic, full-bodied wines. Several top vineyards: Hohenmorgen, Paradiesgarten, Nonnenstück, Herrgottsacker, Leinhöhle, Langenmorgen, Maushöhle, and others known for outstanding QmP wines.

**Deinhard.** Large firm headquartered in Koblenz, with several quality vineyards in the Mosel (including part of Bernkasteler Doktor) and the Rheinpfalz.

Ⓦ **Dhron.** M-S-R. 79 78 76 75 73 71 ★★/★★★
Wine town on the Mosel, falling within Grosslage Michalsberg (Piesporter), some wines sold as Neumagen-Dhron. Best wines from Hofberg vineyard.

**Diabetiker Wein.** Dry wines with minute residual sugar, safe for diabetics, and becoming something of a trend among medium-quality wines.

Ⓦ **Dienheim.** Rhh. 79 78 76 75 73 71 ★★
Wine village south of Oppenheim producing moderately good wines in the Grosslage Krötenbrunnen or vineyards such as Falkenberg, Herrenberg, and Kreuz.

**Dom.** "Cathedral," word seen on wine labels of certain church-owned properties.

**Domtal.** See Niersteiner.

**Dunneg, Otto.** Well-known grower of the upper Mosel.

Ⓦ **Durbach.** Bad. 79 78 76 75 ★★+
Wine village in central Baden, producing mostly light, drinkable wines; the best are Rieslings, Ruländers okay. Best vineyards: Wolf-Metternich and Staufenberg.

ⓇⓌ **Dürkheim, Bad.** Rpf. 79 78 76 75 73 71 ★★/★★★
Largest wine-producing town of the Rheinpfalz; considerable quantities of moderate reds; whites, especially Riesling, are best from such vineyards as Herrenmorgen, Hochbenn, and Spielberg. Grosslage: Feuerberg.

**Egon Müller.** Top producer of the Mosel, with important holdings such as Scharzhofberger in Wiltingen.

**Eiswein.** See Glossary of Wine Terms.

Ⓦ **Eitelsbach.** M-S-R. 79 78 76 75 73 71 ★★★
Town on the Ruwer producing quite fine, fragrant whites from leading vineyards of Karthauserhofberg and Marienholz; others included in Grosslage Trier Römerslay.

Ⓦ **Eltville.** Rhg. 79 78 76 75 73 71 ★★★/★★★★
Top wine-producing town of the Rheingau, producing classic, extremely fine, elegant wines from such estates as Schloss Eltz, von Simmern, and the Staatsweingüter (state-owned domain). Important vineyards: Sonnenberg, Langenstück, Taubenberg, Sandgrub.

# VINEYARD NAMES

Vineyards in Germany often have amusing and colorful names that have special significance in the region. Among the more interesting ones are these:

**Apotheke**: apothecary
**Drachenstein**: the dragon's stone
**Engelsberg**: mountain of the angel
**Feuerberg**: fire mountain
**Gerumpel**: clutter
**Hasensprung**: hare's leap
**Hergottsacker**: God's acre
**Himmelreich**: heavenly domaine
**Honigberg**: honey mountain
**Hohenmorgen**: high noon
**Kirchenpfad**: church path
**Klostergarten**: cloister garden
**Königsfels**: the king's rock

**Kupfergrube**: copper pit
**Liebfraumilch**: dear lady's milk
**Maushöhle**: mousehole
**Nacktarsch**: naked bottom
**Nonnenstück**: the nun's plot
**Paradiesgarten**: paradise garden
**Pfaffenberg**: mountain of the friar
**Sandgrube**: sand pit
**Sonnenberg**: sun mountain
**Sonnenuhr**: sun dial
**Taubenberg**: mountain of the dove
**Ungeheuer**: monster
**Vulkanfelsen**: volcano rock

**Eltz, Schloss.** A leading wine-estate in the Rheingau, with vineyards in Eltville, Kiedrich, Rauenthal, Rudesheim. The Schloss or castle and cellars are in Eltville. Generally superb wines.

(w) **Enkirch.** M·S·R. 79 78 76 75 ★★+
Small town on the middle Mosel producing fresh, very agreeable light wines. Grosslage: Ürziger Schwarzlay.

(w) **Erbach.** Rhg. 79 78 76 75 73 71 ★★★/★★★★
Wines of great distinction, powerful, long-lived, intensely fragrant. Best estate: Marcobrunn, but also Steinmorgen, Honigberg, Siegelsberg, Schlossberg, Michelmark.

(w) **Erden.** M·S·R. 79 78 76 75 73 71 ★★/★★★
Small village along middle Mosel; strong-flavored, very good wines from Treppchen, Busslay, Pralat, Herrenberg vineyards. Grosslage: Ürziger Schwarzlay.

**Erzeugerabfüllung.** See Glossary of Wine Terms.

(w) **Escherndorf.** Frk. 79 78 76 75 ★★/★★★
Wine-producing town in Franconia, second to Würzberg in quality. Top vineyards: Lump, Berg. Grosslage: Kirchberg.

**Feine, feinste, hochfeinste.** Quality terms formerly used to denote a producer's best wine. No longer legal.

(w) **Forst.** Rpf. 79 78 76 75 73 71 ★★/★★★★
One of best wine-producing towns of the Rheinpfalz, excellent wines that are intensely fragrant and complex of KABINETT level or above. Top vineyards are Kirchenstück, Jesuitengarten, Ungeheuer, and Pechstein. Wines of the Grosslage Mariengarten, such as Bürklin-Wolf's, are reliable. Good value.

**Franken.** See Principal Wine Regions.

(w) **Geisenheim.** Rhg. 79 78 76 75 73 71 ★★/★★★
Famous for its wine school on the Rhine; includes also good Rieslings from Rothenberg, Fuchsberg, Klauserweg, and other vineyards.

**Gewürztraminer.** The spicy traminer grape of Alsace, planted to small extent in Germany, mostly Baden and Rheinpfalz.

**Goldener October.** Proprietary names of St. Ursula Liebfraumilch and Moselblümchen.

(w) **Graach.** M·S·R. 79 78 76 75 73 71 ★★/★★★+
One of the Mosel's leading wine towns; fragrant, quite fine wines from

such estates as Himmelreich, Josephshofer, Abstberg. Some of best properties belong to von Kesselstatt family.

**Grosslage.** See Principal Wine Regions.

**Gutedel.** Lesser grape variety known elsewhere as Chasselas, grown mostly in southern Baden.

ⓦ **Hallgarten.** Rhg. 79 78 76 75 73 71 ★★/★★★★
Excellent wines, among the most forceful of the Rheingau from vineyards upland, well above the Rhine, specifically Jungfer, Hendelberg, Schönhell, and Würzgarten. Hallgarten is also the name of a well-known wine firm in London.

ⓦ **Hattenheim.** Rhg. 79 78 76 75 73 71 ★★/★★★★
Consistently good to outstanding wines, including top vineyards Marcobrunn and Steinberg, whose names appear alone on label. Others: Nussbrunnen, Pfaffenberg, Wisselbrunnen, Mannberg. Also the Grosslage Hattenheimer Deutelsberg.

**Hessiche Bergstrasse.** Lesser wine region near Frankfurt, and Germany's smallest. Mostly average wines, little exported.

ⓦ **Hochheim.** Rhg. 79 78 76 75 73 71 ★★/★★★
Major wine town on the eastern edge of the Rheingau; elegant wines but rather softer than rest of Rheingau. Best vineyards are Domdechaney, Kirchenstück, Hölle. Also a Grosslage: Hochheimer Daubhaus.

**Hock.** Old English term for Rhine wine, anglicized from Hochheimer.

**Huxelrebe.** One of the newer, early-ripening, frost-resistant grape varieties grown in Germany, mainly the Rheinpfalz.

ⓡⓦ **Ihringen.** Bad. 79 78 76 ★
Mostly average wines from one of best-known wine towns in Baden.

**Iphofen.** One of Franconia's best wine-producing villages, particularly wines from the Julius Echter-Berg vineyard.

**Jesuitengarten.** Forster Jesuitengarten in the Rheinpfalz is one of Germany's top vineyards, world-famous.

ⓦ **Johannisberg.** Rhg. 79 78 76 75 73 71 ★★/★★★★
Perhaps the Rheingau's top wine-producing vineyards dominated by the famous castle and vineyard, Schloss Johannisberg overlooking the Rhine. Graceful wines, the best have exquisite breed and bouquet; can be very long-lived. Other top estates: Holle, Klaus, Schwartzenstein. Johannisberg Erntebringer is the Grosslage; the Bereich is simply Johannisberg and includes the entire Rheingau.

**Josephshofer.** Important vineyard in Graach owned by von Kesselstatt.

**Kabinett.** See Glossary of Wine Terms.

**Kaiserstuhl-Tuniberg.** Leading Bereich of Baden; the name comes from the steep volcanic hills.

ⓦ **Kallstadt.** Rpf. 79 78 76 75 73 71 ★★/★★★
Good to excellent wines with rich, sometimes earthy flavor. Best vineyard: Annaberg, also Horn, Kronenberg.

ⓦ **Kanzem.** M-S-R. 79 78 76 75 73 71 ★★/★★★+
Important wine village near Wiltingen on the Saar with excellent vineyards: Sonnenberg, Altenberg, Schlossberg, Horecker; wines rank with those of Wiltingen or Ockfen but often more full-bodied.

ⓦ **Kasel.** M-S-R. 79 78 76 75 ★★
Leading wine village of the Ruwer, producing good but light fragrant wines. Good value. Grosslage: Trierer Römerlay.

**Kerner.** One of the newer grape varieties developed for earlier ripening and resistance to frost.

**Kesselstatt, von.** A leading wine-growing family of the Mosel owning some of the best vineyards in Graach, Piesport, Kasel, and Wiltingen.

ⓦ **Kiedrich.** Rhg. 79 78 76 75 73 71 ★★/★★★★
Small wine town set above the Rhine near Rauenthal, with wine often as good, especially from such vineyards as Grafenberg, Sandgrub, and Wasserros.

**Kloster Eberbach.** Famous 12th century monastery, once a center of German viticulture, now site of the German Wine Academy that holds seminars and tastings and conducts tours to German wine regions.

(W) **Königsbach.** Rpf. 79 78 76 75 ★★+
Small village near Diedesheim, with good wines from such vineyards as Idig, Jesuitengarten, Ölberg, and Reiterpfad.

(W) **Kreuznach, Bad.** Na. 79 78 76 75 ★★+
Principal town on the Nahe, also known as a spa for its mineral waters; several good vineyards include Hinkelstein, Brückes, Kahlenberg, Kauzenberg. Kreuznach is also the Bereich name for a large quantity of regional wines.

**Krov.** Town on the Mosel, most famous for its regional wine of the Grosslage Krover Nacktarsch, which is quite ordinary wine.

**Liebfrauenberg.** Grosslage of the Rheinpfalz.

(W) **Liebfraumilch.** A semisweet QbA blended from Riesling, Sylvaner, or Müller-Thurgau grapes grown in various Rhine regions such as the Rheinhessen, Rheinpfalz, Nahe, and Rheingau. Touted as the wine that "goes with everything"—but that only if you like rather sweet wines with food. Can be balanced and pleasant on its own.

(W) **Lieser.** M-S-R. 79 78 77 76 75 ★★
Small village near Bernkastel producing good but somewhat heavy-ish wines for the Mittel-Mosel. Grosslagen: Beerenlay, Kurfürstlay. Good value.

(RW) **Lorch.** Rhg. 79 78 77 76 75 ★/★★
Town on the Rhine at the northern end of the Rheingau, though wines not as typical of Rheingau and many based on Sylvaner, Kerner, some red Spätburgunder. Best vineyards: Pfaffenwies, Bodental, Steinberger.

(W) **Marcobrun.** Rhg. 79 78 77 76 75 73 71 ★★★★
Outstanding vineyard at Erbach (part of it lies also in Hattenheim) producing Rieslings of fine bouquet and elegance.

**Markgräflerland, Bereich.** A lesser district in Baden. The Gutedel, or Chasselas, grape is widely grown for wines best consumed young; little exported.

**Matuschka-Greiffenklau, Graf.** Owners of the outstanding Rheingau vineyard, Schloss Vollrads near Winkel.

(W) **Maximin Grünhaus.** M-S-R. 79 78 77 76 75 73 71 ★★★/★★★★
Acclaimed estate on the Ruwer at Mertesdorf producing QmP wines of great delicacy and distinction. Three superb vineyards: Herrenberg, Bruderberg, Abstberg.

**Mittelrhein.** See Principal Wine Regions.

**Mittel-Haardt.** Best section of the Rheinpfalz, including towns of Diedesheim, Forst, Rüppertsberg, Wachenheim, and Dürkheim.

**Morio Muskat.** One of the newer, early-ripening grape varieties, a crossing between Sylvaner and Pinot Blanc. Yields wines with flowery, muscat bouquet, hence its name. Most vineyards in the Rheinhessen and Rheinpfalz.

(W) **Moselblümchen.** Literally, "little flower of the Mosel," the Mosel's Liebfraumilch, a blended TAFELWEIN that may come from anywhere in the region. Generally sweet, some better than others, but rarely of very good value.

**Mosel-Saar-Ruwer.** See Principal Wine Regions.

**Moselle.** The name of the Mosel in France, where it originates. Commonly used as alternate (though not strictly correct) name for wines from the Mosel-Saar-Ruwer.

**Müller-Thurgau.** Productive grape variety yielding fruity, low-acid wines, often attractive and agreeable, now more widely planted than Riesling, especially in Rheinhessen and Rheinpfalz.

(W) **Münster.** Actually two towns on the Nahe, Bad Münster and Münster-Sarmshein, producing average to very good wines.

(W) **Nackenheim.** Rhh. 79 78 77 76 75 71 ★/★★★
Prominent wine village adjoining Nierstein that is noted for some of best wines from the Rheinhessen. Leading vineyards: Rothenberg, Engelsberg, Schmitts-Kappelle. Grosslagen: Gutes Domtal, Spiegelberg.

**Nahe.** See Principal Wine Regions.

**Neumagen-Dhron.** See Dhron.

Ⓦ **Niederhausen.** Na. 79 78 77 76 75 73 71 ★★/★★★+
One of the Nahe's best wine towns with superb wines from vineyards such as Hermannsberg, Hermannshöhle, Pfingstweide, Steinberg. Good value.

Ⓦ **Nierstein.** Rhh. 79 78 77 76 75 73 71 ★/★★★+
Principal wine town of the Rheinhessen and very large vineyard areas. Produces superb wines from vineyards such as Hipping, Kranzberg, Glöck, Bildstock, Pettenthal, Ölberg, Heiligenbaum, Hölle. Without vineyard name the wine may be ordinary, as from Bereich Nierstein and Grosslage Niersteiner Gutes Domtal, both of which produce large quantities. Wines labeled Riesling are best.

Ⓦ **Norheim.** Na. 79 78 77 76 75 73 71 ★★/★★★
A leading wine village on the Nahe; best wines from Kafels, Kirschheck, Klosterberg, good wines from Grosslage Burgweg.

Ⓦ **Oberemmel.** M-S-R. 79 78 77 76 75 73 71 ★★★
Wine town on the Saar near Wiltingen; good Rieslings of QmP level, flowery but subtle. Best vineyards: Rosenberg, Hutte, Karlsberg, and Altenburg Scharzberg. Grosslage: Wiltinger Scharzberg.

Ⓦ **Ockfen.** M-S-R. 79 78 77 76 75 71 ★★/★★★★
Outstanding wine village on the Saar. Steep vineyards of Riesling producing some of Germany's most distinguished and highly perfumed wines—particularly AUSLESEN, BA, TBA. Vineyards: Bockstein, Herrenberg, Geisberg, and Heppenstein. In lesser years (1977, 1973) can be too acid. Grosslage: Scharzberg.

Ⓦ **Oestrich.** Rhg. 79 78 77 76 75 ★★
Large village in Rheingau producing good but generally not outstanding wines. Best vineyards are Doosberg, Lenchen, Klosterberg.

Ⓦ **Oppenheim.** Rhh. 79 78 77 76 75 73 71 ★★/★★★
Wine town below Nierstein known for good to superior wines, softer than Niersteiners but generally more reliable in quality. Best vineyards: Kreuz, Sackträger, Daubhaus, Herrenberg, and others. Grosslages: Guldenmorgen and Krötenbrunnen.

Ⓦ **Ortenau.** Bad. 79 78 77 76 ★★+
One of the best Bereichs in Baden, producing soft pleasing wines. Good value.

**Palatinate.** Alternative name for the Rheinpfalz (English).

Ⓦ **Piesport.** M-S-R. 79 78 77 76 75 71 ★★/★★★★
Important town on the Mittel-Mosel famous for very fragrant, fruity wines, the best of which carry vineyard name such as Goldtröpfchen, Gunterslay, Falkenberg, or Schubertslay. Wines labeled Piesporter Michelsberg (Grosslage) dependable. Good value.

**Prumm, J.J.** Owner of fine vineyards along the Mosel at Wehlen, Graach, and Bernkastel.

Ⓦ **Randersacker.** Frk. 79 78 77 76 75 ★★+
One of the best wine-producing towns in Franconia, most of it dry.

Ⓦ **Rauenthal.** Rhg. 79 78 77 76 75 73 71 ★★★
Village on the Rheingau behind Eltville; excellent wines known for spicy bouquet and fruit, generally outstanding in top vintages. Grosslage: Rauenthaler Steinmacher. Best vineyards: Baiken, Langenstück, Gehrn, Wulfen. Good value.

**Rheingau, Rheinhessen, Rheinpfalz.** See Principal Wine Regions.

**Riesling.** Germany's best grape, giving wines of excellent fruit, bouquet, and breed.

Ⓦ **Rüdesheim.** Rhg. 79 78 77 76 75 73 71 ★★/★★★+
Popular town in the Rheingau noted for excellent wines from better vineyards like Bischofsberg, Drachenstein, Kirchenpfad; also those west of town with Berg attached to vineyard name: Berg Rottland, Berg Roseneck, Berg Schlossberg. Grosslage: Burgweg. Not to be confused with Rüdesheim on the Nahe that produces lesser wines.

**Ruländer.** The Pinot Gris grape in Germany; produces fresh, attractive wines in Baden, but rather dull ones elsewhere.

CARDINAL CUSANUS STIFTSWEIN

MOSEL·SAAR·RUWER          GEGR. 3. XII. 1458

**Brauneberger Juffer**
Auslese
Qualitätswein mit Prädikat
Amtliche Prüfungsnummer 2 576238 . 76
ERZEUGERABFÜLLUNG ST. NIKOLAUS·HOSPITAL·BERNKASTEL/MOSEL

MITGLIED DER
PRÄDIKATSWEIN-
VERSTEIGERER DER
MITTELMOSEL E.V.
BERNKASTEL-KUES

Bastian, Neumagen                                        1596

**BRAUNEBERGER JUFFER.** Brauneberg is one of the leading wine towns along the Mosel River ("er" is commonly suffixed to village names on wine labels). Juffer is the name of its best vineyard. Vineyard names on German labels generally signify superior wines. *Qualitätswein mit Prädikat* is the term for the highest quality level in German wines, and the word *Auslese* indicates that the wine is naturally sweet, made from late-harvested, very ripe grapes. *Erzeugerabfüllung* means estate-bottled. *Amtliche Prüfungsnummer* is the wine's identity number registered with the government testing bureau.

Ⓦ **Ruppertsberg.** Rpf. 79 78 77 76 75 73 72 71 ★★/★★★+
One of the four leading wine towns along the Rheinpfalz; good wines from better vineyards owned by Bassermann-Jordan, Bürklin-Wolf and von Bühl. Good value.

**Ruwer.** See Principal Wine Regions.

**Saar.** See Principal Wine Regions.

**Scharzberg.** Grosslage lying partly in Wiltingen, partly in Oberemmel on the Saar River. Not as good as formerly.

Ⓦ **Scharzhofberg.** M-S-R. 79 78 77 76 75 73 71 ★★★/★★★★
Distinguished vineyard in Wiltingen, largely owned by family of Egon Müller, others. Known for supremely fragrant, full-flavored but elegant wines; those from great vintages very longlived.

**Scheurebe.** New variety developed by crossing Sylvaner and Riesling, producing full-bodied, aromatic wines; planted mainly in Rheinhessen, Rheinpfalz, and Franconia.

Ⓦ **Schloss Böckelheim.** Na. 79 78 77 76 75 ★★/★★★
The town with the best vineyards on the Nahe, such as Königsfels, Kupfergrube, Felsenberg, Heimberg, Mühlberg. Also now a Bereich that includes several villages producing only average wines.

**Schloss Johannisberg.** See Johannisberg.

Ⓦ **Schloss Reinhartshausen.** Rhg. 79 78 77 76 75 73 71 ★★★+
Important estate in the Rheingau between Erbach and Hattenheim, including portions of vineyards in both towns.

Ⓦ **Schloss Vollrads.** Rhg. 79 78 77 76 74 73 71 ★★★/★★★★
Perhaps the most famous of all German estates (at Winkel) and one of the largest, producing dependably good to incomparable QmP wines in top vintages.

**Schmitt Söhne.** Large firm with vineyards in many regions; average to good wines, several in the TROCKEN style.

**Schoppenwein.** Wine served in restaurants by the glass or in pitchers.

**Schwarzwald.** The Black Forest, in Baden.

**Sichel Söhne.** Large producer of quality German wines, including Blue Nun Liebfraumilch.

59

1975

# Bereich Johannisberg Riesling

QUALITÄTSWEIN · RHEINGAU

A. P. Nr. 1 234 567 8 78

Alc. 10% by Vol.                    1 PT. 7.5 FL. Oz.

Abgefüllt für:

FREDERICK WILDMAN and SONS, GmbH
Bingen · Germany

70 cl e

**BEREICH JOHANNISBERGER.** *Bereich* is the regional term covering a broad area and numerous vineyards within a given wine district, in this case the whole of the Rheingau. Johannisberg is a principal town of the region, and the wine is made from the Riesling grape. *Qualitätswein* is the middle level of quality in German wines. Bereich Johannisberger wines are generally above average and represent good value.

**Simmern, von.** Owners of fine vineyards in Hattenheim, Eltville, Rauenthal.

**Sonnenuhr.** "Sun-dial." Several vineyards so-named, the best and most famous at Wehlen on the Mosel.

**Spätburgunder.** Name for the Pinot Noir grape in Germany.

**Spätlese.** See Glossary of Wine Terms.

**Staatsweingut.** State wine domain. There are state-owned vineyards in several leading wine regions, including the Rheingau (Steinberg vineyard), Rheinhessen, Mosel, and Nahe.

Ⓦ **Steinberg.** Rhg. 79 78 77 76 75 73 71 ★★★/★★★★
Celebrated state-owned vineyard and estate at Hattenheim in the Rheingau. Wines range from good QbA to QmP wines of unsurpassed quality, fine and powerful, impressive depth.

**Steinwein.** Commonly used term for Bocksbeutel wines that are from Franconia.

**Südliche Weinstrasse.** Bereich name for southern Rheinpfalz.

**Sylvaner.** Grape variety of lesser distinction than Riesling but producing fresh, clean, often softer wine; leading grape for Franconia.

**Tafelwein.** See Glossary of Wine Terms.

**Thanisch, Dr.** Prominent vineyard owners in Bernkastel, including a portion of the famous Doktor vineyard.

Ⓦ **Traben-Trarbach.** M-S-R. 79 78 77 76 75 ★★
Two towns on the Mosel across the river from one another that share good vineyards such as Schlossberg, Hühnerberg, Ungsberg. Grosslage: Schwarzlay. Good value.

Ⓦ **Trier.** M-S-R. 79 78 77 76 75 71 ★★★
Famous town on the Mosel near its confluence with Ruwer. Several important wine firms headquartered here; appellation also includes vineyards of Avelsbach and Eitelsbach.

Ⓦ **Trittenheim.** M-S-R. 79 78 77 76 75 ★★+
Light, appealing wines, best when quite young and fresh except in great vintages. Best vineyards: Apotheke, Altarchen, and Felsenkopf. Grosslage: Michelsberg. Good value.

**Trocken.** See Glossary of Wine Terms.

**TbA.** See Glossary of Wine Terms.

(W) **Ürzig.** M-S-R. 79 78 77 76 75 71 ★★/★★★
Little village on the Mittel-Mosel known for spicy, intensely fruity wines. Best vineyard is Würzgarten. Grosslage: Ürziger Schwarzlay, average quality. Good value.

(W) **Wachenheim.** Rpf. 79 78 77 76 75 71 ★★★/★★★★
One of the four top wine towns along the Rheinpfalz known for exceptional Rieslings in superior vintages. Vineyards Gerümpel, Böhlig, Rechbächel, Goldbächel, and Altenburg produce lovely wines, similar to but lighter than Deidesheimer or Forster. Grosslagen: Mariengarten, Schenkenböhl, Schnepfenflug. Good value.

(W) **Waldrach.** M-S-R. 79 78 77 76 75 ★★+
Wine village on the Ruwer producing light, attractive wines. Vineyards: Krone, Ehrenberg. Grosslage: Trierer Römerlay.

(W) **Walluf.** Rhg. 79 77 76 75 73 ★★/★★★★
Previously Nieder-Walluf and Ober-Walluf, two villages now combined. Good Rieslings, generally less fine than best Rheingau.

(W) **Wehlen.** M-S-R. 79 78 77 76 75 71 ★★★/★★★★
Wine village on the Mittel-Mosel near Bernkastel with equally fine vineyards, many owned by J. J. Prüm family. Sonnenuhr is best, followed by Klosterberg, Nonnenberg. Grosslage: Münzlay.

(W) **Wiltingen.** M-S-R. 79 78 77 76 75 71 ★★/★★★★
Best wine village on the Saar (and one of Germany's best altogether) from some of the steepest and best vineyards in Germany, including Scharzhofberger. Austere, complex, exceptional wines in good vintages, steely-edged in poor ones. Other good vineyards: Braune Kupp, Braunfels, Klosterberg. Grosslage: Scharzberg. Fair to good.

(W) **Winkel.** Rhg. 79 78 77 76 75 73 71 ★★★/★★★★
Home of Schloss Vollrads, Rheingau's most famous estate, but also generally superior wines. Top vineyards include Hasensprung, Jesuitengarten, Gutenberg, Schlossberg, and Bienengarten.

(W) **Wintrich.** M-S-R. 79 78 77 76 75 ★★+
Lesser village along the Mosel producing light, fragrant attractive wines, the best from Riesling. Grosslage: Kurfürstlay.

**Winzergenossenschaft.** Wine growers' cooperative. Also known as *Winzerverein.*

(W) **Worms.** Rhh. 79 78 77 76 75 ★★
Lesser town in the Rheinhessen, site of Liebfrauenstift vineyard, thought to be origin of name Liebfraumilch, of which a great deal is produced in the Hessen.

(W) **Württemburg.** Dry wines of average to good quality produced along the Neckar River around Stuttgart.

(W) **Würzburg.** Frk. 79 78 77 76 75 ★★★/★★★
Famous for beer as well as wine in traditional Bocksbeutel, called "Würzberger Stein." Good, flavorful wines from Riesling and Sylvaner mostly; among Germany's driest and good with food. Top vineyards: Stein, also Innere Leiste, Abtsleite, and Pfaffenberg.

(W) **Zell.** M-S-R. ★/★★
Village on the Mosel best known for its wine, Zeller Schwarze Katz, the "Black Cat of Zell." More famous than good, but often agreeable, usually inexpensive. Also the name for the Grosslage. Zell is the Bereich.

(W) **Zeltingen.** M-S-R. 79 78 77 76 75 71 ★★/★★★★
One of the Mosel's most reputable wine villages (includes also village of Rachtig) and the largest on the Mittel-Mosel. Best wines comparable to nearby Wehlen; top vineyards: Sonnenuhr, Schlossberg, Himmelreich, Deutschherrenberg. Grosslage: Münzlay, also good, but simple regional Zeltingers are rather ordinary.

# THE WINES OF SPAIN & PORTUGAL

**T**he best wines of Spain and Portugal are the famous fortified wines—Sherry, Port, and Madeira—and these are treated in the chapter on "Fortified Wines." Spain and Portugal produce large quantities of red, white, and rosé table wines. Spain is, after Italy and France, the largest producer of wine in the world. Until recently, old-fashioned and often primitive techniques in some cases produced wines of mostly indifferent quality, particularly among white wines. But there have always been exceptions, however, notably among the reds, such as the Riojas of Spain.

The Rioja of northern Spain is an area of over 100,000 acres that in 1979 produced more than two million cases of wine, predominantly red produced in the style of traditional red Bordeaux. This is more than just coincidence, for when the vine pest phylloxera wiped out vineyards in Bordeaux in the 1880s, many Bordeaux vintners came to Rioja to start again. Though not all of them stayed, their influence on viticulture, winemaking techniques, and aging in wood remained and the region still has strong connection with Bordeaux today. Most Rioja white wines were usually heavy in character and often spent so long in wood that they lacked freshness. The use of new stainless steel fermenters and other modern equipment is bringing about improvements. Rioja wines are excellent value for the wine drinker, the best are labeled Reserva.

Other good wines are produced in Catalonia, particularly in the Panadés region near Barcelona. Torres is the leading producer in this region.

Portugal's fresh and lively rosés are widest known, but she also produces sound and agreeable red and white wines, particularly the sturdy Dão among reds and the very young whites known as *vinho verde*. Portuguese wines are becoming more popluar because the better ones are such bargains in the current wine market of escalating prices.

## PRINCIPAL WINE REGIONS OF SPAIN

**Andalusia** (And.)    Southwestern coastal province of Spain best known for the fortified wines from Jerez de la Frontera—Sherry. Another fortified wine, Malaga, is produced in the coastal city of that name.

**Catalonia** (Cat.)    Northern Mediterranean region near Barcelona. Some very good reds produced around Tarragona and Panadés; producers of Spain's best sparkling wines also located in this region.

**La Mancha** (L.M.)    Large region in central Spain (land of Don Quixote) producing mostly bulk table wines of ordinary quality and some popular fruity and agreeable reds and whites from the Valdepeñas district.

**Rioja** (Rio.)    Spain's most important region for table wines, named for the Rio Oja, a tributary of the Rio Ebro that runs practically the entire length of the region. It is divided into three distinct sections: Rioja Alta, or upper Rioja, whose capital is Haro; Rioja Alavesa (also known as Ala-va), which produces 65 percent of total production and are considered the best; and Rioja Baja, or lower Rioja, to the east of the other two, which produces coarser, more alcoholic wines.

# PRINCIPAL WINE REGIONS OF PORTUGAL

**Alto Douro** (A.D.)    The upper Douro Valley in northern Portugal where steep, terraced vineyards supply the grapes for Port. (See chapter on "Fortified Wines.") The city of Porto gave Port its name and its suburb, Vila Nova de Gaia, is where most of the shipping firms have their warehouses, or lodges.

**Madeira** (Mad.)    Island in the Atlantic nearly 400 miles off the coast of Morocco, producing fortified Madeira wines (see chapter on "Fortified Wines") such as Bual, Servial, and Malmsey.

Other wine-growing regions are scattered through Portugal from the north to the Algarve (Alg.), producing mostly everyday table wines of agreeable quality. The best wines are often named for the region where they are grown—Vinho Verde (V.V.); Dão; Colares (Col.); Ribatejo (Rib.); and Bucelas (Buc.); for example—and will be treated in the Wine Guide: Portugal.

THE WINE REGIONS OF
**SPAIN &
PORTUGAL**

# WINE GUIDE: SPAIN

(RW) **Age Bodegas.** Rio. ★★★
Producer of good, light- to medium-bodied red wines under the well-known label Siglo; the bottles wrapped in burlap bags. Good value.

(W) **Alella.** Cat. ★★
White wine from the village of Alella near Barcelona, rather sweet though one of the most popular Catalonian whites.

(R) **Alicante.** City on the Costa Blanca south of Valencia and the name for locally produced wines, mostly sweet red, some full-bodied and dry.

(RW) **Berberana.** Rio. ★★★
Firm in Logroño; label names to look for include Carta de Plata, Carta de Oro, and Gran Reservas. Good value.

(RW) **Bodegas Bilbainas.** Rio. ★★★
A leading Rioja producer, Viña Pomal red, Brillante rosé, and white wines, Cepa de Oro (dry). Good value.

(3) **Campo Burgo.** Rio. ★★★
Principal brand names for the red, white, and rosé wines of leading Rioja producer in Logroño, de la Torre y Lapuerta. Good value.

(3) **Campo Viejo de Savin.** Rio. ★★★
Producer in Logroño whose principal wines are exported under the Campo Viejo label; very good RESERVAS.

**Clarete.** Term used for light red wine; also brand name for a light Rioja by Cune.

(W) **Codorniu.** Cat. ★★★
Producer of good sparkling wine by the traditional French *méthode champenoise* in Catalonia at San Sadurnyi de Noya; largest such facility in the world. Blanc de Blancs is one of their best.

(RW) **Companhia Vinícola del Norte de Espana (CVNE).** Rio. ★★★
A leading producer of the Rioja Alta with several good brands, Cune Clarete and Vina Real Resrevas, among the reds, and the dry white Monopole. Good value.

(R) **Coronas.** Cat. ★★/★★★
Light but firm dry red from the Torres firm in Catalonia. Gran Coronas Reserva, made with a percentage of Cabernet Sauvignon and aged in oak cask, is more substantial and ages well. Good value.

(R) **Domecq Domain.** Rio. ★★
Rioja produced by Pedro Domecq, the famous Sherry and Brandy house in Jerez.

**Don Jacobo.** Brand name for the Rioja wines of Bodegas Corral, which is located in Logroño.

(RW) **Faustino Martinez.** Rio. ★★
Producer known mainly for reds labeled Faustino I, Faustino V, VII. Good value, particularly among jug wines.

(3) **Federico Paternina.** Rio. ★★★
Leading producer of the upper Rioja. Banda Azul is a popular light red, Banda Dorada a white, but the most impressive are Gran Reserva and Vina Vial, which are aged longer in wood and can be quite firm and full-bodied. Good value.

**Franco-Españolas.** Rioja producer; recommended labels are the red Sin Rival and white Diamante.

(W) **Freixenet.** Cat. ★★
Large producer of sparkling wines made by the traditional *méthode champenoise,* under such labels as Carta Nevada Brut or Semi-Secco, Cordon Negro Brut and Brut Nature.

(RW) **Jean Leon.** Cat. ★★★
Proprietor of excellent vineyards in the Panadés region of Catalonia (as well as owner of La Scala restaurant in Los Angeles). Pioneer producer of Chardonnay and Cabernet Sauvignon in Spain; the Cabernet is especially interesting.

SPAIN
# GLOSSARY OF WINE TERMS

**Año.** *Year. 4°, 6° indicates the age of the wine when bottled.*
**Blanco.** *White.*
**Bodega.** *Storage warehouse or above-ground "cellar"; in Rioja refers to the entire wine-producing facility; elsewhere in Spain, the name for a little shop.*
**Cosecha.** *Vintage, or harvest.*
**Criado y embotellado por....** *Phrase meaning "grown and bottled by...."*
**Dulce.** *Sweet.*
**Embotellado de origen.** *Estate-bottled. Wine bottled on the property where the grapes were grown.*
**Espumoso.** *Sparkling.*
**Medio-seco.** *Semidry.*
**Reserva.** *Term for best wines, set aside for longer aging. In Rioja, Reservas must spend two years in wood at minimum.*
**Rosdao.** *Rosé.*
**Seco.** *Dry.*
**Tinto.** *Red.*
**Vendimia.** *Vintage, harvest.*
**Viña.** *Vineyard.*
**Viño de mesa.** *Table wine.*

---

**(RW) La Rioja Alta.** Rio. ★★★
Producer of very good Riojas such as Viña Arana and several well-aged RESERVAS.

**(RW) López de Heredia.** Rio. ★★★
One of the oldest and most reputable of Rioja producers in Haro, whose Viña Tondonia reds and whites are widely known and very popular. Good value.

**(3) Lan, Bodegas.** Rio. ★★/★★★
New, large producer in the Rioja Alta making good reds, fresh whites, and rosés.

**Málaga.** See chapter on "Fortified Wines."

**Mallorca.** This Mediterranean island produces a few interesting reds.

**(RW) Marqués de Cáceres.** Rio. ★★★
One of the newer producers in Rioja Alta using modern techniques and generally less aging in wood. Very good RESERVA. A line of inexpensive wines is marketed under the Rivarey label. Good value.

**(RW) Marqués de Murrieta.** Rio. ★★★
One of the oldest and best Rioja producers. Distinctive reds, particularly the Reserva and Castillo Ygay. Murrieta whites have unique, intriguing flavor as well.

**(RW) Marqués de Riscal.** Rio. ★★★
Another of Rioja's most reputable producers, known for its deep, earthy reds aged long periods in oak, becoming rather elegant with time, like a well-aged Bordeaux.

**(W) Montilla-Moriles.** And. ★★★
Superb, unusually full-bodied wine from two villages in Andalusia, south of Cordoba. Often reaches 14 to 17% alcohol, although it is not fortified; not to be confused with Sherry, fortified wines, and Amontillado. Some of the locally produced wine is, however, sent to Jerez for blending into Sherry.

CONTENTS 730 ml.
ALCOHOL 13%
BY VOLUME
CONTENTS 24,7 Fl. Oz.

FREDERICK
WILDMAN
AND SONS
NEW YORK CITY

RED RIOJA
TABLE WINE
PRODUCE OF SPAIN

**IMPERIAL**
1970
*Compañía Vinícola*
*del Norte de España*
HARO, RIOJA
EMBOTELLADO EN BODEGA

CUNE IMPERIAL RESERVA. A red wine from one of the leading Rioja producers. As a *Reserva* (though not noted on the label), it is one of the best wines from this firm and has received longer aging in oak casks than regular Riojan reds that normally spend 2 or 3 years in oak. This wine is dry, smooth and shows considerable complexity that will continue to evolve in bottle over the next few years.

**Muga.** Red wine from producer of that name in the Rioja Alava; the RESERVA is known as Prado Enea.

**Olarras.** Rio. ★★+
Now, forward-looking BODEGA in Logroño, styling its wines after Bordeaux. Most successful wines are the Cerro Anon (Iron Knoll), Tinto Riserva, and Olarra Reservas. The whites and rosés are dry and fresh. Good value.

**Palacio.** Large producer in the Rioja Alavesa. Best values are the reds Nobella, and Glorioso.

**Panadés** (also Penedés). Specified region near Barcelona producing good red wines, including some made from Cabernet Sauvignon. Leading town is Vilafranca del Panadés.

**Penafiel.** L.M. ★★
Robust red wine from Valdepeñas, made near Valladolid southwest of Rioja, on the River Duero.

**Priorato.** Cat. ★/★★+
Sturdy, dark red wine from Tarragona, one of Barcelona's better table wines, also a sweet, darkly white fortified wine.

**Rioja Santiago.** Rio. ★/★★
Best known for Yago Santgria, but also a good Rioja Reserva known as Yago Condal.

Ⓦ **Rueda.** White wines of high alcohol (up to 17%) that develop Sherry-like aromas from a special yeast (flor) that forms as the wine ferments; produced near Valladolid in Old Castile.

Ⓡ **Sangre de Toro.** Cat. ★★
Literally, "blood of the bulls." Sturdy reds from the town of Toro in Catalonia, and the brand name for pleasant, everyday reds from the firm of Torres.

**Sangria.** Red wine punch (white wine occasionally used) made by adding citrus fruits, sugar, and brandy to the wine; serve chilled.

Ⓡ **Sarria, Seniorio de.** Navarra ★★+
Reputable producer near Pamplona of balanced, fruity, occasionally elegant reds. Similar in style to Riojas.

**Torres.** Family-owned firm in Panadés making reds and whites, especially Gran Coronas Reservas, Gran Sangre de Toro, and Viña Sol.

Ⓡ **Vega Sicilia.** Old Castile ★★★
Excellent, long-lived, and very rare Spanish red wine produced near Valladolid; worth seeking out when in the area.

ⓇⓌ **Viña del Oja.** Rio. ★★
Leading brand name for Rioja Producer in Rioja Alavesa, Vizcaina Rojas. RESERVAS appear under the Sommelier label.

Ⓦ **Viña Sol.** Cat. ★★+
Fresh, dry white made by the Torres firm of Tarrgona. Gran Viña Sol has more body and fullness.

# WINE GUIDE: PORTUGAL

**Algarve.** Southern coast of Portugal producing mostly ordinary table wines, often unbottled and referred to as *vinhos de consumo.*

**Aveleda.** Estate in northern Portugal producing one of the best-known VINHOS VERDES.

**Avelar.** Brand name for average to good red, white, and rosé wines of Caves Velhas.

**Bual.** See chapter on "Fortified Wines."

Ⓦ **Bucelas.** Buc. ★★★
Light, fragarant, dry white wines from a delimited area 25 kilometers north of Lisbon, often only 11% alcohol, very pleasant drinking.

Ⓦ **Carcavelos.** Carcavelos ★★★
Rich and generous sweet white wine, often reaching between 18 and 20% alcohol. Chilled, it makes a fine apértif wine.

Ⓡ **Cartaxo.** Rib. ★★★
Popular red table wine from the Ribatejo region northeast of Lisbon, often the carafe wine in the city's restaurants.

Ⓢ **Caves Aliança.** One of Portugal's largest wine companies, producing range of wines from many of the better regions, including Dão, Vinho Verde (Casal Mendes), rosé.

Ⓦ **Casal Mendes.** V.V. ★★+
The VINHO VERDE produced by Caves Aliança; fresh, dry, and one of the best of the "green wines."

Ⓦ **Casal Garcia.** One of the most popular and largest selling VINHOS VERDES from Sogrape, Portugal's largest producer.

Ⓢ **Casaleiro.** Brand name for the wines produced by Caves Dom Teodosio, such as rosés, Dão, and VINHO VERDE.

(RW) **Cepa Velha.** Proprietary name for the wines of one of Portugal's quality producers, Vinhos de Monção, among them the very good VINHO VERDE Alvarinho.

(R) **Colares.** Col. ★★

Mountainous region near Sintra to the west of Lisbon; formerly produced Portugal's most esteemed red wine, full-bodied and long-lived. Most is made much lighter today but occasionally older, impressive wines can be found; they are worth looking for.

(R) **Dão.** Dão ★★/★★★

Portugal's best-known red wine, produced in north-central region. Robust, round, occasionally harsh when young but generally ages well. Good value. Full-bodied whites are also produced to lesser extent.

---

PORTUGAL
# GLOSSARY OF WINE TERMS:

**Adega.** *Winery, or storage cellars.*
**Branco.** *White.*
**Colheita.** *Vintage.*
**Doce.** *Sweet.*
**Espumante.** *Sparkling.*
**Garrafeira.** *Producer's "private stock," or best wines.*
**Madura.** *Mature, used to distinguish regular table wines from the young "green wines,"* vinhos verdes.
**Quinta.** *Farm or estate.*
**Rosado, rosario.** *Rosé.*
**Seco.** *Dry.*
**Selo de guarantita.** *Seal of guaranteed origin for wines from demarcated regions.*
**Tinto.** *Red.*
**Vinho verde.** *"Green," or young wine.*

---

(R) **Douro.** A.D. ★★

The river region of the north famous for Port but also the name for local table wines of ordinary to good quality.

(RO) **Faisca.** A best-selling sweetish sparking rosé from the large producer J. M. de Fonseca.

(R) **Grao Vasco.** Dão ★★+

Widely known brand name for the very good Dão of Sogrape. Good value.

**Green wine (vinho verde).** Portugal's famous and unique young wines, mostly white, from grapes picked at earliest ripeness when acidity is high. Refershing, giving a slight prickle on the tongue, and fragile; often delightful and should be consumed as young as possible. The whites are superior to red or rosé. All should be well-chilled.

**Lagosta.** Brand name for line of wines produced by Real Companhia Vinícola do Norte de Portugal. Widely known, generally good.

(RO) **Lancers.** One of Portugal's most popular carbonated rosés. This wine is sold worldwide.

**Malmsey.** See chapter on "Fortified Wines."

(WRO) **Mateus.** Brand name for Sogrape's carbonated rosé and white wines. Mateus Rosé is currently the largest-selling wine in the United States.

(W) **Moscatel de Setúbal.** Setúbal ★★/★★★

Very good sweet muscat wines made at Setúbal, southeast of Lisbon. Two versions are made: a 6-year-old that is lightly sweet, fresh and well-balanced, and a 25-year old wine that is much darker and more concentrated; both reach 18% alcohol.

Ⓡ **Perequita.** Rib. ★★★
Robust red from the Perequita grape made by the firm of J. M. Fonseca. A very agreeable red. Good value.

**Ribatejo.** Growing region along the Tagus River in central Portugal producing better than average red wines and some whites.

**Ribeiro & Irmao.** A leading producer of table wines, including Ribeiros, a sweet white VINHO VERDE.

**Sercial.** See chapter on "Fortified Wines."

**Serra & Sons.** Producer of quality table wines under the brand names of Justina and Serra.

Ⓡ **Serradayres.** Rib. ★★
A good, solid drinkable red from the Ribatejo region in central Portugal. Good value.

**Sogrape.** Sociedad Comercial dos Vinhos de Mesa de Portugal, Portugal's largest wine company owned by the Guedes family. Some of its best include the VINHO VERDES Casal Garcia, Aveleda, Mateus, and Dão.

Ⓡ **Terras Altas.** Dão ★★+
Sound and reliable Dão from the firm of J. M. Fonseca. Good value.

ⓇⓇ **Villa Real.** A village north of the Douro and the wines from surrounding area, mostly light reds and a good quantity of rosé.

Ⓦ **Vinhos Verdes.** The delimited region between the Minho and upper Douro rivers; the region where Portugal's famous "green wine" (VINHO VERDE) is made.

# THE WINES OF
# AUSTRIA

ustria's wine industry has recently geared up for much wider export, and more of her pleasant, gentle, German-style white wines (a few reds of lesser quantity and quality are produced) are appearing in international markets. They range from dry and lively to quite sweet and luscious, using German-quality designations that indicate degree of natural sweetness in the wines: Kabinett; Spätlese; Auslese; Beerenauslese (BA); and Trockenbeerenauslese (TBA). See Glossary of Wine Terms in "The Wines of Germany."

The better wines for export come from the eastern provinces of Lower Austria (Wachau, Krems, and Langenlois) and Burgenland. Most wine labels bear the name of the grape variety, such as Gruner Veltliner, Rheinriesling, and Blaufrankisch, and usually names derived from the village of origin, such as Kremser, Ruster, and Gumpoldskirchener ("er" is always added to the town name).

Austria is also known for very fresh, young wines called *heurigen*, which are sold only in cafes and taverns in Vienna and its suburbs.

## WINE GUIDE

Ⓦ **Apetlon.** Burgenland ★★
   One of the better wine villages on the shores of the Neusiedlersee in Seewinkel; agreeable dry whites, some very good sweet wines of Spätlese and Auslese level. Good value.

   **Ausbruch.** An Austrian term for very sweet, rich wines that fall between the BA and TBA levels; the best are from Rust.

Ⓦ **Baden.** Vienna ★/★★★
   Town and surrounding region below Vienna producing spicy, fresh whites, some quite pleasant, especially those of Gumpoldskirchen.

   **Blauburgunder.** Pinot Noir grape; also called Spätburgunder.

   **Blaufrankisch.** Austria's name for a Gamay-like red grape, giving dry, fruity wines.

   **Bouvier.** Native white grape variety producing soft, fragrant white wines.

   **Burgenland.** One of the principal wine-producing regions in eastern Austria near Hungary with vineyards surrounding the large, shallow

70

Lake Neusiedl (Neusiedlersee); produces some of Austria's greatest wines, including sweet noble Auslese, Ausbruch, and TBA. Most famous wine center: Rust.

(W) **Durnstein.** Wachau ★★/★★★
A leading village of the Wachau district west of Vienna along the Danube, known for fresh and charming white wines from mostly Gruner Veltliner and Rheinriesling. Good value.

(RW) **Eisenstadt.** Burgenland ★★/★★★
Important wine village in foothills above Neusiedlersee; site of the famed Esterhazy firm.

**Esterhazy.** Old Austrian family with excellent estates in Burgenland producing some of Austria's finest wines; headquartered in Eisenstadt.

(W) **Grinzing.** Vienna ★★+
Vienna's suburb, famous for its lively young heurigen wines sold in restaurant wine gardens.

**Grüner Veltliner.** White wine grape used for Austria's most typical wines—young, fresh, fruity, often with a spicy zest and stylish appeal. Best when young, quite young.

(W) **Gumpoldskirchen.** Vienna ★★/★★★
One of Austria's most charming wine villages near Vienna, producing delightful whites from mostly Rotgipfler and Spätrot grapes. Good value.

**Heurigen.** Young wines sold in taverns (also called heurigen ) following the vintage. See page 72.

(RW) **Kloch.** Steiermark ★★
Best-known wine village of the southernmost province, producing some good Traminer.

(RW) **Klosterneuburg.** Vienna ★★+
Famous monastery and town above Vienna that is now a viticultural school and still produces wines, such as Klostergarten, a soft, dry red. Good value.

(W) **Krems.** Wachau ★/★★★
Leading wine town of the Wachau district along the Danube west of Vienna, with wines mostly from Grüner Veltliner, Rheinriesling. Good value.

**Langenlois.** Town west of Vienna giving its name to surrounding area, producing some good whites from Grüner Veltliner and some unassuming reds.

**Lenz Moser.** Austria's largest private proprietor and a strong influence on the upgrading of Austrian wines. Good wines from several regions, including Krems, Apetlon; also brands such as Schluck, Malteser, Blue Danube.

(RW) **Mörbisch.** Burgenland ★/★★★
One of the leading wine towns of Burgenland; good, sweet wines, light but ordinary reds.

**Müller-Thurgau.** White wine grape yielding mild but fragrant wines.

**Muscat Ottonel.** A muscat variety common to eastern Europe; mostly sweet wines.

**Neuberger.** White grape variety used in some wines from Krems, Langenlois, Gumpoldskirchen, and sections of Burgenland.

**Neusiedlersee.** Large lake in Burgenland affecting the climate of surrounding vineyards; mists off the lake during harvest foster growth of the noble mold *Botrytis cinerea* for splendid sweet wines.

(W) **Nussdorf.** Vienna ★★
One of Vienna's suburbs popular for the young heurigen wines.

(RW) **Oggau.** Burgenland ★★/★★★
Wine village near Rust on the Neusiedlersee producing outstanding Ausbruch and other sweet wines. Good value.

**Pinot Blanc.** Also known as Weissburgunder in Austria, a white variety producing dry, crisp, rather full-bodied wines, occasionally made sweet as impressive Ausbruch, Beeren, and TBA.

(W) **Podersdorf.** Burgenland ★/★★★

Wine village east of Lake Neusiedl in Burgenland that produces average dry whites but fine, sweet BAs and TBAs. Good value.

**Portugieser (Blau Portugieser).** A red wine grape producing dark, medium-bodied, rather bland wines.

(R) **Pottlesdorf.** Burgenland ★★

One of the few communities known in Austria for its red wines, light, drinkable quality.

**Qualitätswein.** Wine that has passed official examination for meeting specified standards of quality, noted on a seal that is affixed to the neck of the bottle.

**Retz.** One of the growing regions of Lower Austria just north of Krems and Langenlois, important for its white wines, mostly light, dry Gruner Veltliner or Müller-Thurgau.

**Rheinriesling.** The true German Riesling grape, not widely grown; the name Riesling by itself on a label usually refers to a quite different strain of the variety developed in Italy, sometimes called Welschriesling.

# HEURIGEN WINES

One of the most delightful aspects of Viennese life is the tradition of drinking Heurigen, or the new wines from the previous vintage. During spring and summer—sometimes drifting well into autumn—the wine taverns (also called *Heurigen*) of Vienna and suburbs such as Grinzing resound with the lilting music of zithers and violins. The gardens of each tavern are strung with lanterns and filled each evening by the local citizenry who come to enjoy wholesome food and quaff the fresh, fruity, slightly green and spritzy white wines—by the steinful or the pitcherful. Many of these young wines are too light and fragile to withstand travel, you must travel to Vienna to experience their special charm.

**Rotgipfler.** White wine grape used mainly in the wines of Gumpoldskirchen to give zestful, full-flavored fruity wines; often combined with another white grape such as Spätrot or Zierfandler.

**Ruländer.** White grape, also known as Pinot Gris, used in making soft whites, mostly in Styria.

(W) **Rust.** Burgenland ★/★★★

One of Austria's leading wine towns on Lake Neusiedl, producing some of her most outstanding sweet white wines, especially Ausbruch, a Rust specialty; fine Auslese also. Good value.

**St. Laurent.** Richly colored red wine grape with pronounced flowery fruity aroma.

(W) **Schloss Grafenegg.** Krems ★★/★★★

Wines from this well-known estate owned by the Metternich family are sound, reputable-quality dry whites, with some quite fine Auslese, mainly from Gruner Veltliner and Rheinriesling.

(W) **Schluck.** Wachau ★★

Fresh, dry white produced in quantity in the Wachau from the Welschriesling grape, best when quite young. Good value.

**Seewinkel.** Dry, sandy region east of Lake Neusiedl making mostly mild whites; name means "sea corner."

**Spätrot.** White grape variety often used in conjunction with Rotgipler to make the popular Gumpoldskirchener.

**Spitzenwein.** Term used to refer to the better table wines, higher level than Tischwein.

**Steiermark.** Southernmost growing region in Austria, known also as Styria. Mostly mild, pleasant wines, some good flavorful Traminer. Leading wine town is Kloch.

(w) **Thallern.** Vienna ★★+

Small wine village near Gumpoldskirchen making similar wine; also famed for its old church and monastery, Heiligenstift. Good value.

**Tischwein.** Everyday table wine, below the level of Spitzenwein.

(RW) **Traiskirchen.** Vienna ★★

Another of the wine villages near Gumpoldskirchen that produces lively, spicy wines, mostly white and best when young.

**Veltliner.** See Gruner Veltliner.

**Vienna.** Austria's capital and an important wine center, with vines surrounding and within the city and its suburbs; famous for young wines of the most recent vintage sold by glass or pitcher in the popular and numerous heurigen, or wine taverns.

(RW) **Vöslau, Bad.** Baden ★★

Resort town south of Vienna and below the town of Baden producing dark, soft, agreeable reds, some quite full-bodied, made from Portuguesier and Blaufränkisch, and a lesser amount of whites.

**Wachau.** One of Austria's most famous wine districts along the Danube west of Vienna, producing good whites from Gruner Veltliner and Rheinriesling, among Austria's best. Leading wine towns: Durnstein, Loiben, Stein, Weissenkirchen, and Krems on its eastern edge.

**Weinviertal.** "Wine quarter," a large growing region north of Vienna toward the Czech border, including towns of Retz, Falkenstein, Mailberg, Eggenburg, and others; known mostly for whites.

**Weissburgunder.** Pinot Blanc grape.

**Welschriesling.** A lesser strain of Riesling developed in Italy yielding light white wines without the finesse of true German Riesling.

**Wien.** Vienna.

**Zierfändler.** Zestful white grape (also known as Spätrot) used in Gumpoldskirchener; native to Austria.

# THE WINES OF
# SWITZERLAND

witzerland produces mostly dry white wines and some light to medium-bodied reds. The best of both have a briskness about them that is often as bracing as the alpine air of the surrounding countryside. The Swiss drink a lot of wine and import far more than they produce (about 28 million gallons) with only limited quantities available for export.

The principal wine-producing cantons, or districts, are the Valais along the Rhône River Valley in the south, the Vaud above Lake Geneva, and the slopes above Lake Neuchatel. Whites are made mostly from the lesser Chasselas grape that here gives crisp, dry wines known as Fendant, Dorin, or Neuchatel. Reds are made from Pinot Noir or Gamay, often a blend of the two; Ticino, the section bordering Italy to the southeast, produces Merlot. Wines are also made in the northern and eastern parts of Switzerland bordering Germany and Austria but are rarely seen outside the region.

## WINE GUIDE

Ⓦ **Aigle.** Vaud ★★
   Town in the Chablais region east of Lake Geneva producing good dry whites known as Dorin.

   **Amigne.** Old white grape of the Valais making pleasantly scented but rather heavy, dry white wines.

   **Arvine.** Another old-time white of the Valais but produces dry wines rather livelier than Amigne.

   **Chablais.** Region between the Vaud and Valais cantons south of Lake Geneva. Best wines are Dorin from villages of Aigle, Bex, Yvorne.

   **Chasselas.** Leading white grape of Switzerland known by different names such as Dorin (the Vaud); Fendant (the Valais); and Neuchatel.

Ⓡ **Cortaillod.** Neuchatel ★★
   Light red from the village of Cortaillod made from Pinot Noir; also a pale rosé made here called Oeil de Perdrix.

Ⓦ **Dezaley.** Vaud ★★★
   Good full-fruited Dorin from the slopes of Lavaux between Lausanne and Montreux, one of Switzerland's best whites.

74

(R) **Dole.** Valais ★★+

Usually considered Switzerland's best red, produced from Pinot Noir with some Gamay blended in; medium but sometimes full-bodied and then powerful with rich fruit and fragrance.

(W) **Dorin.** Vaud ★/★★★

The name by which white wines from the Chasselas are known in the canton of Vaud; full, dry, fruity but generally lighter than the Fendant of the Valais.

(W) **Ermitage.** Valais ★★

Sturdy, flavorful white wine that is made from the minor grape variety Marsanne.

(W) **Fendant.** Valais ★/★★★

Dry whites from the Chasselas grape from the Rhône River Valley. Fendant de Sion (wine center of the Valais) or Mont d'Or are often Switzerland's most potent, flavorful white wines.

(W) **Johannisberg.** Fragrant, soft white from Sylvaner or Müller-Thurgau in the Valais.

**Malvoisie.** Sweet, perfumed dessert wine from the Valais made from ripe Pinot Gris.

**Merlot.** Red grape of Bordeaux fame used to make reds in Ticino, the Italian-speaking section of Switzerland. The best is labeled Viti.

(3) **Neuchatel.** Neuchatel ★/★★★

Reds and rosés from Pinot Noir; dry whites from the Chasselas, some sparkling or semisparkling. They are referred to as "the star wines of Switzerland."

**Nostrano.** Red vin ordinaire of Ticino.

(RO) **Oeil de Perdrix.** Neuchatel ★★

The light rosé from Pinot Noir from around Lake Neuchatel; name means "eye of the partridge" and refers to the wine's color.

**Perlan.** Another name for the Chasselas grape for the dry white wines of the Mandement district west of Geneva.

(W) **St.-Saphorin.** Vaud ★★

Crisp dry white from the Lavaux area.

(R) **Salvagnin.** Vaud ★★

Dry reds from the slopes overlooking Lake Geneva, made from Pinot Noir and/or Gamay; lighter than Dole of the Valais.

**Spätburgunder.** Name for the Pinot Noir red grape in Germany and Switzerland; Blauburgunder is occasionally used also.

**Ticino.** Southeastern section of Switzerland bordering Italy, known mostly for reds: Merlot, Viti, Nostrano.

**Valais.** One of Switzerland's most important wine regions along the Rhône River Valley between the cities of Brig and Martigny. Known mostly for dry white Fendant and red Dole, both among the country's best wines.

**Vaud.** Largest wine region in Switzerland bordering northern shores of Lake Geneva with vineyards on steep slopes above Lausanne and Vevey. The dry white Dorin is its best wine; some dry reds (Salvagnin) also made.

(R) **Viti.** Ticino ★★+

Name for the best quality Merlot of the Italian-speaking Ticino region.

(W) **Yvorne.** Vaud ★★★

Firm, full-bodied white wines from the village of Yvorne in the Chablais region east of Lake Geneva.

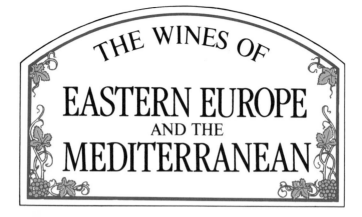

# THE WINES OF EASTERN EUROPE AND THE MEDITERRANEAN

he wines of eastern Europe that we are most likely to see come from Hungary, Romania, Bulgaria, and Yugoslavia, all of whom produce tremendous quantities of wine, and have done so for centuries. Relatively few wines are exported to the West. But those that are in many cases represent each country's best. Because of expanded plantings of Cabernet Sauvignon and some Pinot Noir, red wines seem to be the most interesting. The labels, with some exceptions as noted, generally show place name and grape variety.

The wide variety of wines produced around the Mediterranean don't really have much in common other than the fact that their growing regions are, for the most part, hot and dry, a climate shared by Sicily and other parts of southern Italy. Only Greece, Cyprus, and Israel export to any great, or identifiable, extent. The wines of Algeria, Tunisia, Morocco, and other countries of the Middle East are mostly sold locally or exported in bulk for blending.

## Hungary

Hungary's most famous wine, the gloriously sweet Tokaji Eszencia (Tokay), was well known in Europe during the Crusades. Made in the northeast part of the country near the USSR-Czech border, its intense, concentrated sweetness, comparable to the finest Sauternes and Trockenbeerenauslesen (TBAs), was prized for centuries by European royalty. Legend has it that Catherine the Great deployed a special troop of Cossacks to guard her supply of it. Today it is extremely rare.

Hungary's red and white table wines come largely from the western half of the country on the Great Plain of the Danube, Somlo near the Austrian border and around the shores of Lake Balaton. Another important region is north of Budapest around the town of Eger. On wine labels place-names end in "i," thus Debrö becomes Debröi, Eger becomes Egri. Native grapes such as Furmint (Tokay), the red Kadarka, and white Leányka are the main varieties, though Olasz Riesling is also widely grown. Cabernet Sauvignon and Pinot Noir are becoming increasingly important.

# WINE GUIDE: HUNGARY

**Aszu.** The German equivalent of Auslese, signifying overripe grapes that make the sweetest, best Tokaji. Grapes often affected by noble rot (*Botrytis*).

Ⓦ **Badacsony.** Balaton ★★/★★★
Some of Hungary's best white wines, both dry and sweet, come from this volcanic hill on the north shore of Lake Balaton from Welschriesling, Szürkebarat, and Kéknyelu grapes. Good value.

ⓇⓌ **Balaton.** Balaton ★★+
Lake Balaton is known as "the Hungarian sea," and is Europe's biggest lake. Vines grow all around it, some of the best from Badacsony. Softer but still pleasing whites from Welschriesling, Furmint, and Sylvaner are made in other districts around the lake and Cabernet Sauvignon in some parts shows promise. Good value.

**Bársonyos Császár.** Northern hill country between Lake Balaton and the city of Budapest, best known for the dry whites of Mór.

Ⓦ **Debrö.** Mátraaljai ★★+
Town in the foothills of the Matra Mountains to the north, famous for its fragrant, semisweet wine Debröi Hárslevelü.

ⓇⓌ **Eger.** Mátraaljai ★★+
Important wine town best known for its famous red Egri Bikavér, but also white Leányka and the thick fruity Médoc Noir (Merlot).

Ⓡ **Egri Bikavér.** Mátraaljai ★★+
Hungary's best-known dry red made from the Kadarka grape; "bikaver" means bull's blood and the wine was once stronger and darker than today; now mostly round, mellow, medium-bodied; ages fairly well. Good value.

**Eszencia.** The sweetest Tokaji, a concentrated elixir made practically drop by drop from raisined Furmint grapes to make the rarest of Tokaji wines; reputed to have miraculous healing powers but almost never seen now.

Ⓦ **Ezerjó.** Mór ★★★
Móri Ezerjó, one of Hungary's finest dry white wines, comes from sandy hill vineyards of Mór; distinctive full aromas and flavor.

**Furmint.** The great white grape that makes Tokaji as well as some very good whites in Balaton.

**Hárslevelü.** White wine grape whose name translates as "lime-leaved," referring to the shape of the leaves. Most famous wine comes from Debrö, usually lightly sweet.

**Kadarka.** Hungary's most widely grown red grape, making mostly fullish dry, mellow reds, Egri Bikavér being the best known.

Ⓦ **Kéknelyü.** Balaton ★★★
Interesting green-gold white wine made from the grape of the same name in the Badacsony district; heady, spicy aromas, bracing flavors.

Ⓦ **Leányka.** Eger ★★
Delicate semidry white wine from a grape whose name means "young girl."

**Mátraaljai.** District in northern Hungary in the foothills of the Matra Mountains; best-known wine towns are Debrö and Eger.

**Mecsek.** Hilly region in southern Hungary known for its reds from Pinot Noir and Kadarka from Vilány and Székszard districts. Good Cabernet now coming from Hajós.

**Monimpex.** State-controlled export syndicate with headquarters located in Budapest.

**Mór.** Wine town in northern Hungary well-known for its dry white Móri Ezerjó.

**Nagyburgundi.** Hungarian name for Pinot Noir grape, which makes particularly good reds in the Vilány-Siklós district in southern Hungary (Mecsek).

**Olasz Riesling.** Italian or Welschriesling that makes moderate to good white wines.

(W) **Pecs.** Mecsek ★★+

Growing region in southern Mecsek region near Vilány that produces good, balanced whites from Furmint, Welschriesling, and Pinot Blanc.

**Puttonyos.** Term appearing on Tokaji Aszu labels that signifies the amount of sweet raisined grapes that were used to make the wine; one *putt*, or basket, added to the wine makes it lightly sweet; five *puttonyos*, the maximum, makes it intensely sweet.

(W) **Somló.** Mt. Somló ★★★

White wine from an extinct volcano in northern Hungary; concentrated dry and sweet wines, highly regarded by Hungarians.

(R) **Sopron.** Burgenland ★★

An extension of Austria's Burgenland into a small corner of Hungary, best known for its light reds made from Gamay.

**Szamorodni.** The driest of the wines from Tokaj made from normally ripened grapes; term means "as it comes."

(R) **Szekszárdi Vörös.** Mecsek ★★

Dark red from the Kadarka grape in one of Hungary's growing regions in the south; robust wines that need aging to be palatable.

(W) **Szürkebarát.** Balaton ★★

Hungarian name meaning "grey friar" given to Pinot Gris grape; makes rather heavy, rich dessert wine in the Badacsony district.

(W) **Tokaji.** Tokaj ★★/★★★★

Hungary's splendid and famous white wine, especially Aszu, the sweetest (except for Eszencia, which is almost unobtainable today); produced in northeastern Hungary in foothills of the Carpathian mountains from the Furmint grape. Szamorodni is the drier version, Aszu the sweet, and the number of puttonyos indicates degree of sweetness.

(R) **Vilány.** Mecsek ★★/★★★

Good reds from Pinot Noir known as Vilanyi Burgundi are quite good from this southern district, which makes reds from Kadarka also, though rather less impressive. Good value.

# Yugoslavia

Slovenian whites and Dalmatian reds jump first to mind among Yugoslavian wines because they were among the earliest and most widely seen outside the country. But Croatia and Serbia make the largest quantities of Yugoslavian wines, including well-balanced dry whites from Sauvignon Blanc and Traminer. Ljutomer whites from Slovenia near the Austro-Hungarian border are widely exported, made mostly from Rheinriesling, Sylvaner, and Pinot Blanc grapes. Numerous wines are made from native grapes such as Grk, Plavać Mali, Posip, and Prokupac, among others. Yugoslavia's up and coming wines, however, are varietals based on Cabernet; Merlot, Gamay, Sauvignon Blanc, Traminer and Riesling, and Pinot Blanc.

## WINE GUIDE: YUGOSLAVIA

**Amselfelder.** Spätburgunder. Serbian red from the Pinot Noir grape, popular export to Germany where it gets its name.

**Bijelo.** Term for white wine.

**Cabernet Sauvignon.** Increasingly grown in various regions of Yugoslavia; average to good dry reds, the best from Istria.

**Crno.** Literally, "black," the term for red wine.

**Ĉviĉek.** Light red or rosé from native variety grown in Slovenia.

**Dalmatia.** The coastal province on the Adriatic between Rijeka and Dubrovnik, known for numerous reds, both sweet and dry, some quite potent.

**Dingaĉ.** Heavy-bodied sweet reds from the Plavać Mali grape made along the Dalmatian coast.

**Grk.** Native Yugoslavian grape making mostly sweet, strong-flavored, full-bodied wines on the Dalmatian coast.

**Istria.** Peninsula jutting out from northern Yugoslavia above Dalmatia, producing some good Cabernet and Merlot.

**Kosovo.** Newly modernized wineries and vineyards in this region between Serbia and Macedonia may soon produce some of Yugoslavia's better wines; currently best known is Amselfelder.

**Laski Rizling.** Slavic name for the Italian Riesling.

**Ljutomer.** Source of Yugoslavia's best whites from Slovenia, mostly flavorful Riesling.

**Merlot.** The Bordeaux red grape now grown with some success in Istria and western Slovenia.

**Navip.** Large growers' co-operative in Belgrade producing a range of table wines including medium reds from Merlot, Prokupac.

**Plavać Mali.** The native grape resonsible for reds of Slovenia and Dalmatia such as Dingaĉ, Postup, and others.

**Posip.** Dry, full-bodied white made along the Dalmatian coast and islands just off it.

**Postup.** Popular sweet, strong-bodied red wine of the Dalmatian coast.

**Prokupac.** Another native red grape grown in Serbia and Macedonia to produce dark, robust reds and richly colored rosé.

**Prosek.** Potent dessert wine made from very ripe red grapes resulting in concentrated sweetness and high alcohol. A Dalmatian favorite.

**Ruzica.** A dark rosé made from Prokupac, Yugoslavia's best.

**Serbia.** Yugoslavia's largest grape-growing region producing the greatest quantity of table reds and whites.

**Sipon.** Actually Hungary's Furmint grape, small amounts grown in Slovenia, making good sweet wines.

**Slavonia.** District bordering Slovenia to the east, and northern part of Croatia, producing mostly white wines of middling interest.

**Slovenia.** Northern region whose capital is Ljubljana and whose Ljutomer whites are Yugoslavia's best.

**Tigrovo Mljeko.** "Tiger's Milk," a brand of sweet, white dessert wine, a local specialty of eastern Slovenia.

**Žilavka.** Flavorful, dry, aromatic white wine of Bosnia-Hercegovina in central Yugoslavia, around the town of Mostar.

# Greece

Birthplace of Dionysus, the god of wine, who according to legend passed on his precious knowledge of how to make it to the peoples of ancient Greece. Best-known survivor from antiquity is Retsina, the pungent resinated wine made around Athens in Attica. It is best served very cold. The greatest quantity of wine comes from the Peloponnese but wines are also produced in Macedonia, Thessaly, Hellas, Thrace, and most of the islands, notably Crete.

# WINE GUIDE: GREECE

**Achaia Clauss.** One of the two leading Greek producers headquartered in Patras on the Peloponnese peninsula. Best wines: Castel Daniels, Santa Helena.

**Attika.** The region around Athens that produces most of the country's Retsina.

**Cambas.** The other leading producer in Greece and largest exporter headquartered in Athens.

**Castel Danielis.** Vintage-dated dry red produced by Achaia Clauss. Varying quality but sometimes quite good.

**Crete.** Largest island of the Mediterranean that makes a considerable quantity of wine, the best being red Mavro Romeiko.

**Demestica.** Brand name for light, dry reds and whites of Achaia Clauss; moderately good and dependable.

**Hymettus.** Dry white wine made around Mt. Hymettus near Athens; also Cambas's line of dry red and dry white wines.

**Kokkineli.** Resinated rosé, sometimes called red Retsina, but generally more pink in color. Also best very cold.

**Lindos.** Agreeable white wine from the island of Rhodes.

**Malvasia.** Sweet wines from the ancient variety Monemvasia that appears to have originated in the southern Peloponnese; probably the forerunner of Madeira's Malmsey.

**Mavro.** Greek word for black, signifying darker reds.

**Mavrodaphne.** Luscious sweet red wine from Patras whose name means "black laurel." A dessert wine taken at room temperature.

**Mavro Romeiko.** One of the best red wines, from the island of Crete; dry, dark, and robust.

**Mavroudi.** Sturdy, dark red produced in Attica around Delphi.

**Naoussa.** Good dry red from the town of Naoussa in Macedonia.

**Peloponnese.** Large peninsula almost separated from the rest of Greece by the Corinthian gulf; the country's largest wine region.

**Pendeli.** Dry, full-bodied Attican red produced by the firm of Cambas.

**Retsina.** The famous resinated wine of Greece, mostly white, and best when very cold, a favorite with Greek food. Fully half the country's wine is resinated; the pink version is Kokkineli.

**Rhodes.** Famous island near the Turkish mainland producing dry white Lindos and Malvasia.

**Samos.** Luscious sweet Muscat from the island of Samos in the Aegean; widely exported.

**Santa Helena.** Pleasant, fresh, dry white of the northern Peloponnese.

**Santorin.** Island above Crete producing pleasant dry white and a potent sweet Vino Santo from sun-dried grapes.

# Cyprus

Winemaking traditions on Cyprus are among the oldest in the world, but the island has lately boosted exports of dry, full-bodied table wines that are finding ready acceptance in the world market. While not particularly distinguished, they are sound, well made, and inexpensive. Commandaria, a dessert wine of 14 to 15% alcohol, was legendary as far back as the Crusades for its intense, concentrated but uncloying richness. Though obviously lighter today than centuries ago, it can be a pleasant and lighter alternative to fortified wines, brandy, or liqueur.

Cyprus also produces the full range of sherries, long popular in Europe, the best of which are aged in outdoor soleras, as in Spain. Most of the Cypriot wine names have historic associations.

# WINE GUIDE: CYPRUS

**Afames.** Dry red table wine made by the co-operative in Limassol, Sodap.

**Amathus.** Full-bodied dry white made with some Muscat from the smallest of the four leading producers, Loel.

**Ambrosia.** Average dry table red produced by Etko, known in Cyprus as Olympus.

**Aphrodite.** Dry, full-bodied white wine from the Keo firm, named after the goddess said to have been born out of the sea off the southern coast.

**Arsinöe.** Sodap's crisp, dry white wine with a slightly bitter aftertaste.

**Bellapais.** Slightly *pétillant*, or semidry, white named for the historic abbey at Kyrenia.

**Coeur de Lion.** Sturdy, dry coral-colored rosé, the island's best.

**Commanderia.** Cyprus's famous dessert wine named for the command headquarters (Grande Commanderie) of the Knights Templars in the time of the Crusades; dark, burnished amber wine of rich, balanced sweetness made from red and white grapes dried in the sun in the Troodos Mountains.

**Domaine d'Ahera.** Wood-aged dry red from the firm of Keo; lighter than Othello.

**Etko.** One of the four leading producers of Cyprus, owned by Haggipavlu of Limassol. Olympus Red, Muscat, dry and cream sherries.

**Hermes.** Light, dry red from the firm of Loel.

**Keo.** A leading producer in Limassol with a full range of wines, especially Othello, Aphrodite, and Commanderia.

**Limassol.** Cyprus' largest coastal city and the center of the wine industry.

**Loel.** Smallest of the four top producers producing Hermes, Amathus, and Negro, a dry red blended from recently imported varieties such as Grenache and Carignane. Chateau de Lusignan Commanderia.

**Mavron.** The dark red grape native to Cyprus.

**Nefeli.** Fresh, dry white named after a sister of Bacchus, from Etko.

**Olympus.** The tallest mountain in the Troodos range in central Cyprus; also a brand name of table wines and sherries from Etko.

**Othello.** One of the island's best reds, dry, full-bodied, well balanced; made by Keo.

**Paphos.** Historic and picturesque port on the southwest coast; also a wine-growing region in the low hills surrounding it.

**St. Panteleimon.** Assertive semisweet wine named after a charitable saint.

**Sherry.** Cyprus's full range of fortified wines in the sherry style, from dry fino to sweet cream, some quite good, such as Keo's Fino and some of the sweeter ones; others quite bland and characterless.

**Sodap.** The growers' co-operative at Limassol and largest of the island's producers. Arsinöe, Afames, St. Barnabus Commanderia.

**Troodos.** Mountains in the central part of Cyprus west of Nicosia; cool climate and annual rainfall make it the best for growing wine grapes, especially Commanderia and certain white wines.

**Xynisteri.** The white grape native to Cyprus.

# Romania and Bulgaria

These iron curtain countries ship very few wines to the West as yet, but those they do export are quite good. Romania, lying on the same latitude as France, has modernized her ancient traditions of winemaking over the last two decades. The best wines come mainly from the foothills of the Carpathian Mountains and the southern plains of the Danube bordering Bulgaria and the Black Sea. Cabernet Sauvignon and Pinot Noir are the most successful red varieties—they are dry, mellow, and easy to drink. Italian Riesling is the leading white, along with Chardonnay and Aligoté. Native varieties such as Feteasca, Perla, and Cotnari are also quite popular in Romania.

Bulgaria is more modern still. Its now-thriving wine industry was not created until halfway through the twentieth century, following World War II. The wines of Bulgaria come from broad flat plains in the north and central parts of the country (mostly reds) and east toward the Black Sea (mostly white varieties) with scattered vineyard regions in the south and west. Most of Bulgaria's sizable production (sixth in world production) is exported to Russia, some to Germany and England. Presumably we soon will get more in the West since Bulgaria's robust, vigorous Cabernet has been so well received. The Chardonnay is also good, with surprising varietal character and body in a wine so inexpensive.

The wines of both countries represent good value for everyday table wines.

# Israel

Israel's flourishing vineyards were started in the 1800s by Baron Edmond de Rothschild, who sent a staff of experts and vine cuttings from his own vineyards in Bordeaux to get production underway. Today there are over 15,000 acres under cultivation in four principal areas: the slopes of Mount Carmel, some of which are at elevations of nearly 3,000 feet; the Judean hills from Hebron to Jerusalem; upper Galilee near the Jordan River; and along the Mediterranean from Haifa to Natanya.

More than 800 growers belong to the principal co-operative that markets wines under the brand name Carmel. Kosher wines, mostly sweet reds and whites, were major exports until recently, but expanded plantings of European varietals such as Cabernet Sauvignon, Sauvignon Blanc, Chenin Blanc, Grenache, and French Colombard show promise of better wines to come. These are the wines to look for from Israel. Other leading producers are Askalon, Benyaminah, Eliaz, Israeli Distillers, and Richon-le-Zion.

# Algeria

This North African country once supplied France with enormous quantities of red wines for blending. Algeria is one of the few countries in the world where vineyards have actually decreased in the last decade. Most of her dark, sturdy red wine is now exported to the USSR and Germany, as well as other African nations. Typical hot country wines, they are, for the most part, low in acidity and high in alcohol. Sound, more balanced wines come from the hill vineyards of Medea, the Haut-Dahra, Mascara, and Zaccar, all west of Algiers.

# Morocco

Morocco produces the smallest quantity of the North African countries and its wine industry is the youngest, begun only in the last 50 years. The grapes are largely the same as in Tunisia, with sturdy red varieties such as Alicante Bouschet, Carignane and the Cabernets predominating. Reds and rosés from Cabernet Franc are often agreeable, especially with the country's spicy cuisine. They are most likely to be encountered only while traveling there, however, as most of the wine for export is shipped in bulk to European markets where it is used for blending.

# Tunisia

In ancient Carthage, viticulture and winemaking were well established centuries before Christ. The leading grape varieties today are Alicante Bouschet, Cabernet, Carignane, Pinot Noir, Grenache, and Muscat. Some of the reds, such as Coteaux de Carthage, are considered reasonably good examples of sturdy, hot-country reds. New efforts at quality control have been undertaken recently, and Tunisia is increasing its exports to European countries such as Switzerland, West Germany, and Great Britain.

# THE WINES OF
# THE
# UNITED STATES

**A**merica's wine regions are concentrated mainly in coastal areas just inland from the Atlantic and Pacific oceans. The earliest immigrants to both places attempted to grow wine grapes from vines they brought with them from their homelands in France, Spain, Italy, Germany, and other parts of Europe. Severe winters and native diseases defeated these efforts in New England, Virginia, and elsewhere along the east coast, so the settlers developed native varieties such as Concord, Niagara, Delaware. California, however, was more accommodating to the European vine, *Vitis vinifera,* especially varieties like Cabernet Sauvignon and Riesling. By the second decade of the twentieth century, the California wine industry was flourishing, but it virtually halted in 1919 because of Prohibition.

Over the last two decades, a dramatic revolution has taken place in America's wine industry. Consumption increased from half a gallon per capita annually in 1960 to some two gallons per capita today (still tiny in comparison to France or Italy, where 25 gallons is more like it). Vineyards have expanded east, west, and in between. California is by far the most important region with over 70% of production, and increasing quantities of wine are exported to England, France, and Germany. New York State and the Pacific Northwest regions follow in terms of size, but several other states are making serious attempts at winegrowing so that one day America's *vins du pays* may be quite widespread.

# California

California's dynamic wine industry is at an exciting stage of growth, change, and expansion. It is an extremely young industry, having started virtually from scratch in the years after Prohibition, a 14-year hiatus that brought winemaking (except for sacramental wines) to a standstill. Progress in the 1940s and 1950s was sluggish, with dessert and other sweet, fortified wines dominating production. It accelerated dramatically in the mid-1960s, however, with the infusion of a group of new winemakers who created much excitement with wines of intense varietal character and complexity, particularly those from Cabernet Sauvignon, the leading red grape variety, and Chardonnay, the leading white grape. California's unique red grape, Zinfandel, also moved to premium status during this time.

The key to quality in California is varietal labeling—wines named for grape variety, such as the three named above, Pinot Noir, Chenin Blanc, and so on—and the reputation of the winery. A listing of California Grape Varieties appears on page 90, followed by a listing of individual wineries (Wine Guide: California).

The industry is in such a period of flux that quality ratings in many cases can be only tentative. Not only do new wineries constantly appear, seemingly overnight, but there are sometimes tremendous changes within the wineries themselves—winemakers come and go, ownership changes hands, certain types of wines may be added or dropped from a winery's product line, particularly those that purchase grapes instead of (or, in addition to) growing their own. Even the style of a given wine may change from year to year, being rather sweet in one vintage but totally dry the next, or vice versa. New growing regions are emerging as well, all of which leads to some confusion for the consumer. In the end, it means that the only way to keep up is to taste the wines frequently. Fortunately, California wines are generally so good—and improving—that such a task is not only useful but a very pleasurable pastime indeed.

The wineries included in the Wine Guide are those with a reasonable chance of national distribution and a few whose reputations have stretched well beyond the boundaries of California, even if the wines have not. Wines named in each entry are those for which the winery is particularly known. Those in **bold** type are especially recommended.

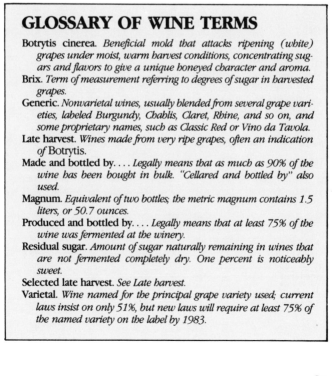

# GLOSSARY OF WINE TERMS

**Botrytis cinerea.** *Beneficial mold that attacks ripening (white) grapes under moist, warm harvest conditions, concentrating sugars and flavors to give a unique honeyed character and aroma.*

**Brix.** *Term of measurement referring to degrees of sugar in harvested grapes.*

**Generic.** *Nonvarietal wines, usually blended from several grape varieties, labeled Burgundy, Chablis, Claret, Rhine, and so on, and some proprietary names, such as Classic Red or Vino da Tavola.*

**Late harvest.** *Wines made from very ripe grapes, often an indication of* Botrytis.

**Made and bottled by. . . .** *Legally means that as much as 90% of the wine has been bought in bulk. "Cellared and bottled by" also used.*

**Magnum.** *Equivalent of two bottles; the metric magnum contains 1.5 liters, or 50.7 ounces.*

**Produced and bottled by. . . .** *Legally means that at least 75% of the wine was fermented at the winery.*

**Residual sugar.** *Amount of sugar naturally remaining in wines that are not fermented completely dry. One percent is noticeably sweet.*

**Selected late harvest.** *See Late harvest.*

**Varietal.** *Wine named for the principal grape variety used; current laws insist on only 51%, but new laws will require at least 75% of the named variety on the label by 1983.*

# PRINCIPAL WINE REGIONS OF CALIFORNIA

Geographic appellations are becoming increasingly important in California as knowledgeable consumers become familiar with regional distinctions. As yet, however, changing styles of winemaking and new and expanded plantings make it difficult in many cases to pin down specific regional character. Some areas, to be sure, have established enough of a track record for consumers to know what they can expect from the wines. We know that classic Cabernet Sauvignon of a certain style is produced in central Napa around Oakville and Rutherford; the fiercest Zinfandels seem to originate in Amador, and other areas with strong geographic identity are beginning to appear. In this decade regional characteristics will become much more defined, as young vineyards mature and winemakers extract the maximum from soil and climate factors.

Stating on the label where the grapes were grown is now common practice instead of merely a trend as it was a few years ago. For grape origin to appear on a vintage-dated VARIETAL, the law requires that 95% of the grapes come from the area named and 75% for nonvintage wines. Following is a discussion of the principal growing regions.

## Central Coast

**Santa Clara**    South of San Francisco Bay, this large area was one of California's earliest wine regions. Almadén planted vineyards in the 1850s, as did Paul Masson and Mirassou a bit later—all today among the largest of California's premium wineries. There are only pockets of vineyards left in most of Santa Clara Valley, as urban sprawl overtook most of the prime vineyard land in the 1950s and 1960s. Mirassou still has an important vineyard in San Jose. To the west, the hillside vineyards of Mount Eden, Martin Ray, David Bruce, and Ridge produce some of the state's most intense and interesting wines. In the south around Gilroy there are a number of wineries growing mostly Zinfandel and Cabernet and a bit of Pinot Noir.

**Alameda County (Livermore Valley)** (Alameda)    The Livermore Valley southeast of San Francisco is known mostly for white grapes like Chardonnay, Sauvignon Blanc, and Riesling, which do well in gravelly soil that gets very little rain. Wente Bros. and Concannon were pioneers here, both of whom tout it as a good region for reds too, especially Petite Sirah.

**Santa Cruz Mountains** (S.C.M.)    North of the town of Santa Cruz, this lush, green mountainous region once boasted 40 wineries that dwindled to almost none. New, small operations have cropped up recently and the cool climate and soil composition have lured those in quest of Pinot Noir, some of which is formidable; also good Chardonnay and Riesling.

**San Benito** (S.Ben.)    As vineyard acreage in Santa Clara decreased, wineries had to search elsewhere for it. Of the 4,500 acres in San Benito County, 95% belong to Almadén at Paicines and Cienega near Hollister. All types of varieties are planted, but Cabernet and Chardonnay predominate.

**Monterey** (Mon.)    Almadén went to San Benito; Paul Masson, Mirassou, and Wente expanded into Monterey County; the broad Salinas Valley, once the "salad bowl" of the nation, was ripped up and replanted with wine grapes in the 1960s and 1970s. Monterey has a long, cool growing season, with good drainage and morning mist that often foster development of BOTRYTIS CINEREA (the beatific mold that concentrates grape-

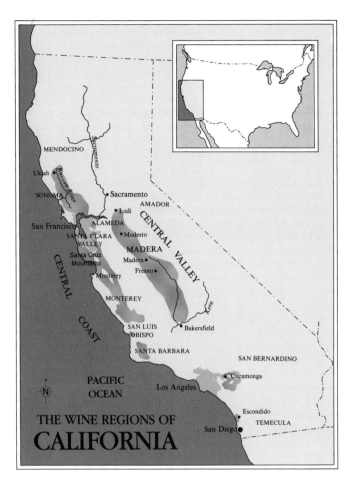

THE WINE REGIONS OF
# CALIFORNIA

sugars and flavors to result in delectable, naturally sweet wines), which produces interesting sweet Riesling and Sauvignon Blanc. A curious vegetal quality has affected Monterey wines at times, particularly the reds, possibly due to the intense VARIETAL character of grapes growing on their own rootstocks (instead of grafted onto phylloxera-resistant roots like most of the world's wine grapes), as well as the region's climatic factors. Certain vineyard practices seem to reduce this flavor. Some experts feel that as the vines mature it will become less noticeable. Main vineyard areas run from Gonzales down to Greenfield and King City. High up on the Gavilan benchlands overlooking the valley are Paul Masson's Pinnacles Vineyard and tiny Chalone Vineyard.

**San Luis Obispo** (S.L.O.)  One of California's newer and very promising wine regions with vineyards around Paso Robles and Santa Maria; appears good for all varieties, especially Zinfandel, Cabernet, Merlot, Chardonnay, Chenin Blanc, and unusual Pinot Noir.

**Santa Barbara County** (S.Barb.)  The cool plateaus of the Santa Ynez Valley produce good reds and whites with distinctive regional character; early-ripening varieties like Pinot Noir, Merlot, Riesling, and Chardonnay are especially good. A region to watch.

87

**Amador** (Ama.)    In the foothills of the Sierras east of Sacramento Amador can hardly be considered coastal, yet its climate and wines are more nearly like those of the coastal counties. Hilly country and high plateaus make rich, full-bodied wines: hefty Zinfandel, Cabernet, even Sauvignon Blanc; small lots of Barbera and Nebbiolo, too. Place-names like Fiddletown, Sutter Creek, and Shenandoah Valley guarantee very concentrated wines.

# Cucamonga-San Bernardino (Cuc.-S.B.)

**This region** east of Los Angeles was the earliest wine-growing region, planted with mission grapes brought by the Spanish friars in the late eighteenth century. The region was best known for dessert varieties, including some astonishing Angelica. The tentacles of urban Los Angeles have enveloped most of the vineyards, though a few stands of Zinfandel, Grenache, Mission, and Palomino survive in patches.

# North Coast Counties

**Mendocino** (Men.)    Mountainous region famous for pears and apples, north of Napa and Sonoma. Fairly warm, though cool at night in places, and planted mostly in red varieties to date, though Chardonnay, Riesling, and Gewürztraminer from Anderson Valley, west of Ukiah, are promising. Chenin Blanc and French Colombard also do well. Largest producers here are Fetzer and Parducci. Grapes are also grown next door in Lake County, mostly in the southern region around Clear Lake.

**Napa Valley** (Napa)    California's most famous wine region, mostly because of the concentration of old, well-established names like Beaulieu, Beringer, Christian Brothers, Inglenook, and Martini and a growing number of newer ones that continue to add luster to the name. Small and compact, the narrow valley curves northward between two mountain ranges for about 35 miles, only 7.5 miles at its widest. Over 25,000 acres of vineyards cover the valley floor and pockets of hillside or mountaintop. Most plantings are of noble varieties, such as Cabernet Sauvignon, Chardonnay, Riesling, Pinot Noir, Zinfandel, and Chenin Blanc.

The central part of the valley around Oakville and Rutherford yields outstanding Cabernet Sauvignon found in the Reserves of Beaulieu, Inglenook, Robert Mondavi, Heitz Martha's Vineyard, and Freemark Abbey Bosché. East of the Silverado Trail above the town of Napa is another good region for Cabernet, the Stag's Leap area.

The cool Carneros region in southern Napa—fog-bound hills overlooking San Pablo Bay with a climate similar to that of Burgundy—yields excellent Pinot Noir and Chardonnay. The northern end of the valley, bounded by the town of Calistoga, is the warmest, planted mostly in Zinfandel, Chenin Blanc, some Pinot Noir, Merlot, and Chardonnay. Mountain vineyards in the ranges bordering the valley produce some of Napa's most intense wines, mainly Cabernet and Chardonnay. To the east of the valley proper are Pope Valley and Chiles Valley.

**Sonoma** (Son.)    Separated from Napa Valley by the Mayacamas Mountains, its grape-growing industry is older than Napa's, but the lay of the land is very different—a broad, sprawling terrain of plains, valleys, and rolling hills that accommodates cattle ranches and fruit orchards as well as vineyards. The first grapes were planted in the south around the town of Sonoma that Jack London made famous as the "valley of the moon." Sebastiani and Buena Vista are here. In northern Sonoma, Alexander Valley is becoming known for its Cabernet, Zinfandel, Gewürztraminer, and Chardonnay, as is nearby Dry Creek. The cool, foggy reaches of the Russian River Valley, often attended by morning fog, yield fine Riesling, Chardonnay, and Pinot Noir. Kenwood, between Santa Rosa and Sonoma, is another important region, and Bennett Valley is just starting to emerge, south of Santa Rosa.

# San Joaquin Valley (S.J.V.)

**This inland** central valley stretches from Lodi to Bakersfield, a hot wide plain between the ridges of the coastal range and the Sierras—nearly 300 miles of over half a million acres of grapes. The giants are located here: Gallo, United Vintners, Guild, Franzia, and others. Table grapes are grown, but the region supplies 80% of California's wine grapes, including hybridized varieties developed to suit the climate—Ruby Cabernet, Emerald Riesling, Carnelian. Grapes for dessert wines also come from here.

# Temecula (Tem.)

**California's** southernmost district, a microclimate east of San Diego, cooled by Pacific breezes and sheltered from desert heat by Palm Springs mountains. Callaway is the best-known vineyard here. The most successful varieties appear to be whites: Riesling, Sauvignon Blanc, and Chenin Blanc. Very intense Zinfandel and Petite Sirah.

# VINTAGES: CALIFORNIA

Contrary to what you may hear, vintages in California are quite different from one another. While the region rarely suffers dismal or catastrophic years, as happens in the northern regions of Europe, complications can occur. Rain during the harvest is always unfortuante; if excessive, it tends to dilute the quality and flavor of the grapes. Too much heat can also be a problem, causing grape sugars to soar too fast while simultaneously reducing the acidity that gives vitality and balance to a wine. Following is a discussion of recent California vintages in the coastal counties.

1979. Biggest crop in history but problems in some areas due to rain. Napa and Sonoma particularly hard-hit by storms following heat spells, throwing the grapes into a state of arrested development. Some Cabernet in the north coast counties never ripened sufficiently. Early-ripening varieties, such as Pinot Noir, Chardonnay, Riesling, and Merlot, did quite well in all regions, benefiting from warm, dry weather in August and early September. Overall, this year appears better for whites than reds, except in Amador, where Zinfandel should be good.

1978. Until 1979, the biggest crop to date. Superb white wines, especially Chardonnay and Sauvignon Blanc. Vines seemed to recover quickly and healthily from previous two years of drought. High sugars for reds make the vintage somewhat similar to 1974; most regions report superb wines.

1977. Second year of drought. Somewhat variable but extremely good in many instances, mostly reds. Reduced quantity, down as much as 50% from drought conditions and some frost in spring. Uneven ripening required successive pickings in some areas with different parts of the vineyard reaching desired sugar levels at different times. Chardonnays not as rich as 1978, nor as balanced as 1976, but many Cabernets, Zinfandels, and Pinot Noirs are excellent, especially along the central coast from the Santa Cruz Mountains to Santa Barbara County.

1976. First year of drought, quantity reduced by half but some Cabernets of great intensity from small berries loaded with flavor and extract, particularly Napa and Sonoma; also full, balanced Chardonnay, the best holding nicely.

1975.  A cool year, with some uneven ripening, overshadowed by big, powerful 1974s. Reds were dark and tannic but lower in alcohol and generally more austere, but capable of achieving great elegance in time; Zinfandel richer in fruit than Cabernet. Good Chardonnay in Napa Sonoma.

1974.  Considered by some the best vintage to date; big, powerful wines, especially among reds (Cabernet, Zinfandel), which are very high in alcohol. Very concentrated reserve wines whose value is now realized and they are correspondingly expensive; some will be very long-lived. Best whites holding but should be consumed now.

1973.  Cool growing season, rainy during harvest. Somewhat thinner wines but some elegant Cabernets drinking extremely well now.

1972.  Cool, rainy, generally quite poor, though a few pleasant reds from warmer regions.

1971.  Average to good, some Cabernets from central Napa still impressive. Warm-region reds (like Barbera, Zinfandel) did better.

1970.  A great year for reds, particularly Cabernet, which is still growing in bottle and showing very well; will last several more years.

1969, 1968.  Both great years for Cabernet, some Zinfandel, Pinot Noir, burgundy.

# GRAPE VARIETIES: CALIFORNIA

**Alicante Bouschet.** Deeply colored red grape grown mostly in the central valley for blending with paler reds; Papagni Vineyards makes a sturdy VARIETAL of it.

**Barbera.** Red wine grape from the Italian Piedmont. Widest plantings in San Joaquin Valley yield soft, mild wines, but tart, somewhat astringent fruit in young wines from the cooler coastal counties that develop rich warmth and roundness with age.

**Cabernet Sauvignon.** California's best red grape and the single most widely produced VARIETAL; styles range from mellow fruitiness to classic elegance to darkly tannic with intense, concentrated fruit; ages extremely well.

**Carignane.** Prolific and widely grown in warmer regions for its dark, paunchy fruit; used mostly for blending but occasionally made as an interesting VARIETAL.

**Charbono.** Red grape similar to Barbera, making dark, thick, densely fruity wines that age nicely. Limited plantings in Napa, mostly at Inglenook; also by Papagni in Madera.

**Chardonnay.** California's noblest white grape, yielding dry wines ranging from crisp, apple-like freshness to more pronounced VARIETAL character and complexity, often with added dimension from aging in small oak barrels; the best are comparable to fine white Burgundy.

**Chenin Blanc.** Productive, widely-grown white wine grape. Usually off-dry or lightly sweet, but increasingly popular drier versions are full-flavored, racy, stylish.

**Emerald Riesling.** Hybrid white grape developed in California with rather faint Riesling character but good acidity, fruity, and occasionally rather tart; popular with seafood.

**Flora.** Cross between Sémillon and Gewürztraminer; flowery, delicate white with a touch of spice and light sweetness; not widely known (or grown) as yet.

**Folle Blanche.** Clean, crisp, rather acidic white, produced as a VARIETAL only by Louis Martini; elsewhere used for blending.

VINTAGE 1973    BOTTLED JUNE, 1977

Bottle № **5779** of a total of 27,950 bottles

**Heitz Cellar**

NAPA VALLEY
**CABERNET SAUVIGNON**

ALCOHOL 13% BY VOLUME
PRODUCED AND BOTTLED IN OUR CELLAR BY
**HEITZ WINE CELLARS**
ST. HELENA, CALIFORNIA

MARTHA'S VINEYARD

HEITZ CELLARS. The better California wines are varietals, made predominately of a single grape variety, such as the Cabernet Sauvignon above. Varietal wines currently must contain 51% of the grape variety named (75% as of 1983), but for top producers such as Heitz the amount is always considerably more—in this case 100%. Martha's Vineyard in Napa Valley is the specific plot of land where the grapes were grown. Such vineyard designation calls attention to wines with a consistently distinct regional character.

**French Colombard.** Very productive white, widely grown for GENERIC blends but newly popular as a VARIETAL; bracing acidity usually modified by a touch of sweetness; often fresh and appealing.

**Fumé Blanc.** Another name for Sauvignon Blanc.

**Gamay.** Also known as Gamay Noir or Napa Gamay. The French Beaujolais grape, but tends to be heavier and more "serious" in California. Whole berry fermentation (carbonic maceration) often used for lighter, fruitier wines.

**Gamay Beaujolais.** Misnamed, actually a clone of Pinot Noir but most is made in a light, fruity style. More widely grown than Gamay Noir.

**Gewürztraminer.** Good, spicy white grape; very fragrant, usually lightly sweet; most drier styles often excellent with more intense VARIETAL character and aroma.

**Green Hungarian.** Minor white grape for ordinary but occasionally zesty wines; popular mostly for its romantic name, but not Hungarian in origin.

**Grenache.** Widest grown red grape for rosé, most rather sweet; occasionally also a red VARIETAL of no particular note.

**Grey Riesling.** Not a true Riesling but a lesser white variety yielding agreeably fruity wines; best when very young and fresh.

**Johannisberg Riesling.** Also known as White Riesling and the true Riesling of Germany. One of California's best, widely grown; ranges in style from fresh and off-dry to richly sweet and complex LATE-HARVEST styles, comparable to Germany's fine Auslese and TBA (see "The Wines of Germany").

**Merlot.** Excellent red grape, often used for blending with Cabernet but increasingly a VARIETAL on its own, making sound, solid reds of suppleness and grace.

**Muscat (Moscato).** The grape for light, sweet, fragrant, and often delectable white wines named for various muscat varieties, such as Canelli, Frontignan, Alexandria; some wines also labeled Moscato Amabile.

**Petite Sirah.** Dark, purple red grape, not the true Syrah of great Rhône reds but a minor variety known as Duriff. In warmer regions, yields soft, fruity wines of mild character but dense, tannic, more complex ones from cooler regions near the coast, also Livermore Valley.

**Pineau de la Loire.** Another name for Chenin Blanc.

**Pinot Blanc.** Yields full-bodied dry whites, more austere than Chardonnay and much less known, though recently more popular.

**Pinot Noir.** The great red grape of Burgundy seems to have lost something in translation (or transplantation), yielding rather pretty, light wines in California but lacking richness and depth; a few achieve it, so the quest, fortunately, continues.

**Pinot St. George.** Sturdy variety, grown mostly for use as rootstock, but Christian Brothers and Almadén make agreeable reds of rather distinctive flavor.

**Ruby Cabernet.** A cross between Carignane and Cabernet bred for the warm central valley where it is very successful, with reasonable hints of Cabernet character. More intense versions occasionally made in cooler, mountainous regions.

**Sauvignon Blanc.** White grape, excellent for dry, fruity white wines either in the style of the Loire (Fumé Blanc) or fuller bodied dry Graves.

**Sémillon.** Mostly seen as Dry Sémillon making a mild, rather stony white, crisp and fresh, at best. A few efforts at sweet wines (affected by BOTRYTIS) are interesting, with several experiments in the works, particularly in Monterey.

**Sylvaner.** Sharper, and similar to, Riesling though of secondary rank and used frequently for blending. Can be quite good and fresh.

**Syrah.** The true Syrah of the Rhône, first made by Joseph Phelps in Napa Valley. Dark, sturdy, attractive.

**Zinfandel.** California's most popular red VARIETAL with a wide range of styles from light and fruity to heavy, LATE-HARVEST types. In between are medium styles of ripe, berryish, or spicy aromas and more concentrated fruit, as well as more classic, complex claret styles that age well.

# WINE GUIDE: CALIFORNIA

Ⓡⓦ **Ahern.** Los Angeles ★★
  Small operation in San Fernando Valley that buys grapes up north, including Zinfandel and Sauvignon Blanc; available mostly in Los Angeles.

Ⓡⓦ **Ahlgren.** S.C.M. ★★/★★★
  Small, new winery near Boulder Creek making good, chewy **Cabernet**, Chardonnay, and big Zinfandel.

(RW) **Alexander Valley Vineyards.** Son. ★★/★★★
New winery in Alexander Valley with 250 acres of VARIETALS making 7,200 cases annually. **Chardonnay**, Cabernet Sauvignon, dry Chenin Blanc, Riesling.

(3) **Almadén.** Santa Clara ★/★★+
One of California's oldest wineries and largest of the premium producers making full range of table, sparkling, and dessert wines; reasonably priced. 6,000 acres in San Benito and Monterey. Charles Le Franc is top line but best values are regular Cabernet, **Merlot**, Gewürztraminer, Gamay Rosé, **Blanc de Blancs** champagne. Good value.

(RW) **Bandiera.** Son. ★★
Small, new winery in northern Sonoma; purchases most grapes for Zinfandel, Cabernet, some whites; plans for good jug wines in future.

(3) **Barengo.** Lodi ★/★★
Large, old winery in central valley making good table reds, Ruby Cabernet, Zinfandel, and port-like dessert wines.

(3) **Bargetto.** S.C.M. ★/★★
Large winery at Soquel known mostly for fruit and berry wines (pomegranate, olallieberry) but also creditable Chardonnay, Riesling; reds less interesting.

(RW) **Beaulieu** (BV). Napa ★★/★★★★★
Classic estate now owned by Heublein famed for premium table wines, especially **Georges de Latour Private Reserve Cabernet**; also Pinot Noir, Sauvignon Blanc, Brut champagne.

(3) **Beringer.** Napa ★★/★★★
One of Napa's oldest wineries owned by Nestlé producing average to good table wines and a good line of jugs, Los Hermanos. Traubengold (slightly sweet Riesling), Fumé Blanc. Good value.

(RW) **Boeger.** Placerville ★★
New, small winery in Gold Rush country (El Dorado County near Amador) making Zinfandel, Sauvignon Blanc, very good **Cabernet**. Good value.

(3) **Brookside.** Cuc.-S.B. ★/★★
Large, old winery making most dessert and fortified wines; table wines from Temecula, Chardonnay, and Sauvignon Blanc; bottled under Assumption Abbey label.

(RW) **Bruce, David.** Santa Clara ★★★
Small winery in northern Santa Cruz range known for intense, full-bodied wines, particularly **Chardonnay** and **Pinot Noir**.

(RW) **Buehler.** Napa ★★+
Growers near Conn Valley now making their own wines—Cabernet, Zinfandel, Pinot Blanc.

(3) **Buena Vista.** Son. ★★/★★+
Oldest winery in Sonoma, founded by Agoston Haraszthy, producing full line of table wines, average to good quality but improving recently, with Cask Cabernet, Fumé Blanc, Riesling.

(RW) **Burgess.** Napa ★★★
On site of the old Souverain winery, about 15,000 cases of top VARIETALS: **Cabernet**, **Chardonnay**, **Zinfandel**, Petite Sirah.

**BV.** Beaulieu Vineyards. See Beaulieu (BV).

(RW) **Cakebread Cellars.** N.V. ★★★
Small winery at Rutherford specializing in Cabernet, **Chardonnay**, and **Sauvignon Blanc**.

(R) **Calera.** S.Ben. ★★+
New, small winery near Hollister making impressive **Pinot Noir** and rather harsh, robust Zinfandel.

(RW) **Callaway.** Tem. ★★
Pioneers in southern California; inky, intense overpowering reds, better whites. Style of wines somewhat controversial. Lightly sweet Fumé Blanc, Chenin Blanc.

(RW) **Carey, Richard.** A.C. ★★
Small winery in San Leandro that purchases grapes for Cabernet, Blanc Fumé, Chardonnay.

(RW) **Carneros Creek.** Napa ★★★
The lone winery in Carneros to date, making excellent home-grown **Pinot Noir**, good Chardonnay, and **Zinfandel** from Amador.

(RW) **Cassayre-Forni.** Napa ★★+
Promising new winery at Rutherford making firm-structured Cabernet and dry, fruity Chenin Blanc.

(RW) **Caymus.** Napa ★★★
Some 70 acres at Rutherford producing estate-bottled **Cabernet** and **Pinot Noir**. Purchased grapes and/or wines form second label, Liberty School, the Cabernets especially good value.

(RW) **Chalone.** Mon. ★★★
Miniscule property in the Gavilan range 2,000 feet above Salinas Valley, noted for Burgundy-style **Pinot Noir** and **Chardonnay**, fine Pinot Blanc, and French Colombard. Chaparral Chardonnay is from younger vines.

(RW) **Chappellet.** Napa ★★★
One of Napa's best mountain vineyards to the east on Pritchard Hill, producing intense, full-bodied wines of vigorous VARIETAL character: **Cabernet**, **Chardonnay**, **Chenin Blanc**, interesting Gamay.

(RW) **Château Chevalier.** Napa ★★+
Old château and estate on Spring Mountain restored in the 1970s, producing good **Cabernet** and **Chardonnay**. Second label from purchased grapes: Mountainside.

(RW) **Château Montelena.** Napa ★★★
Winery in northern Napa at Calistoga with 100 acres plus purchased grapes; noted for **Chardonnay**, J. Riesling, Zinfandel.

(RW) **Château St. Jean.** Son. ★★★+
Growing operation at Kenwood famous for full-blown **Chardonnays** and luscious sweet **Riesling** and **Gewürztraminer** in the Auslese or TBA style (see "The Wines of Germany"). Dry Gewürztraminer also good; from 1979 on, the only red is the intense Wildwood **Cabernet**. Increasing quantities of sparkling wines by méthode champenoise.

(3) **Christian Brothers.** Napa ★★/★★★
Old, established winery run by the religious brotherhood; sound, blended VARIETALS, GENERICS, and fortified wines; some VARIETALS now vintage-dated. Zinfandel, Pinot Noir, Fumé Blanc, and Cabernet are best. Good value.

(RW) **Clos du Bois.** Son. ★★★
New winery in Dry Creek area of northern Sonoma; fine **Chardonnay**, **Cabernet**, Pinot Noir, Gewürztraminer.

(R) **Clos du Val.** Napa ★★★+
Excellent, small French-owned estate making well-structured **Cabernet** and elegant, claret-style Zin; also a tiny amount of **Chardonnay**.

(3) **Concannon.** Alameda ★★/★★★
Founded in 1883 and owned by Irish family of Concannons; but recently sold. Known for very good **Sauvignon Blanc**, **Petite Sirah**, **Zinfandel Rosé**. Good value.

(RW) **Congress Springs.** S.C. ★★+
Very young winery on hillsides near Saratoga, tiny production but plans to grow; good **Sauvignon Blanc**.

(RW) **Conn Creek.** Napa ★★/★★+
Relatively new winery begun by a Napa Valley grower, producing several varieties, good Cabernet, also Riesling and Chardonnay.

(3) **Cresta Blanca.** Men. ★★
One of California's oldest names, originally begun in Livermore Valley, now revived at Ukiah, but owned by Guild of the central valley. Average to good wines, including Petite Sirah. Should be better.

ⓇⓌ **Cuvaison.** Napa ★★★
Medium-sized winery at northern end of Napa, now owned by a Swiss firm; rich, full-bodied **Chardonnay**; big, spicy **Zinfandel**; and forceful Cabernet.

ⓇⓌ **Davis Bynum.** Son. ★★+
Medium-small winery near Healdsburg making several above-average VARIETALS, attractive Pinot Noir.

ⓇⓌ **Dehlinger.** Son. ★★★
Small, new winery in northern Sonoma near Sebastopol, with promising beginning for Cabernet and **Chardonnay**, Pinot Noir, Zinfandel.

Ⓡ **Diamond Creek.** Napa ★★★
Very small vineyards on Diamond Mountain in northern Napa making only **Cabernet** under three excellent appellations: Volcanic Hill, Red Rock Terrace, Gravelly Meadow.

Ⓦ **Domaine Chandon.** Napa ★★★
Glittering new sparkling wine facility at Yountville owned by French firm of Moët-Hennessey. Excellent sparkling wine by true French méthode champenoise: Napa Valley Brut, Blanc de Noirs. Excellent restaurant at the winery. Good value.

ⓇⓌ **Dry Creek.** Son. ★★★
Small, individualistic winery in Dry Creek area of northern Sonoma making quite fine VARIETALS, Cabernet, Chardonnay, Fumé Blanc, Zinfandel, Chenin Blanc.

ⓇⓌ **Durney.** Mon. ★★+
Brand-new winery in Carmel Valley owned by rancher turned wine-grower; 60 acres for well-balanced Cabernet, also Riesling, Gamay Beaujolais, Chenin Blanc.

③ **East-Side.** Lodi ★
Huge central valley winery making full range of table and dessert wines under the Royal Host and Conti Royale labels. Best values: Ruby Cabernet, Grey Riesling, Chenin Blanc, Tinta Port.

ⓇⓌ **Edmeades.** Men. ★★
Very small winery in Anderson Valley west of Ukiah; good Zinfandel, also Cabernet, Gewürztraminer, French Colombard.

**Eleven Cellars.** Brand name for wines of Perelli-Minetti.

ⓇⓌ **Estrella River.** S.L.O. ★★+
Very large property near Paso Robles with 700 acres of vineyards and recently improved VARIETALS like **Chardonnay**, Fumé Blanc, Zinfandel.

ⓇⓌ **Felton-Empire.** S.C.M. ★★
The old Hallcrest winery and vineyards revived in 1976. Mainly white Riesling in the German style; first efforts promising.

③ **Fetzer.** Men. ★★+
Good sized winery making broad range of VARIETALS and GENERICS of somewhat variable quality; good values in Zinfandel, Petite Sirah, Cabernet, Premium Red.

ⓇⓌ **Ficklin.** Madera ★★★
Small family firm producing superb ports, one vintage-dated, another known as Tinta Port. Also limited bottlings of Emerald Riesling and Ruby Cabernet sold only at the winery. Good value.

Ⓦ **Field Stone.** Son. ★★
New winery built into hillside near Healdsburg, specializing in Riesling, Gewürztraminer, also Chenin Blanc and Cabernet Rosé.

③ **Firestone.** S.B. ★★/★★★
Pioneers of the Santa Ynez Valley with 300 acres of VARIETALS planted in 1972. Very good **Riesling**, **Gewürztraminer**, **Pinot Noir**, Merlot, Cabernet, Chardonnay. Bears watching. Good value.

③ **Foppiano.** Son. ★★/★★★
Longtime growers near Healdsburg, recent VARIETALS, including dry **Chenin Blanc**, Fumé Blanc, Cabernet, and Petite Sirah, are of very good value.

*California*

# WHITE TABLE WINE

ALCOHOL 12% BY VOLUME

PRODUCED AND BOTTLED BY

ROBERT MONDAVI WINERY

OAKVILLE, NAPA VALLEY, CALIFORNIA

*A wine for everyday use made entirely of varietal wine grapes. Flavorful and complex in character.*

**WHITE TABLE WINE.** Generic wines such as this one are blended from several grape varieties to a style chosen by the producer. Robert Mondavi's dry White Table Wine shows only a California appellation, which means the grapes may have come from anywhere in the state, including the central valley. Generics come in magnums or multi-liter size bottles, often referred to as "jugs." Other generic wines bear such names as Red Table Wine, Vin Rosé, Burgundy, Mountain Claret, or Chablis.

(RW) **Fortino.** Santa Clara ★/★★
Italian family making Italian-style, robust wines at Gilroy; earthy, full-bodied reds like Zinfandel, Cabernet, Barbera, Petite Sirah.

(RW) **Franciscan.** Napa ★★+
Large winery at Rutherford now under new ownership, known for good-value Cabernet and Chardonnay, also Zinfandel and Riesling.

(3) **Franzia.** S.J.V. ★+
Third largest producer in California, producing table, dessert, and Charmat-process sparkling wines under several brands, all originating from Ripon (near Modesto). Inexpensive, reliable Burgundy.

(RW) **Freemark Abbey.** Napa ★★★+
Medium-size winery at St. Helena specializing in very fine VARIETALS from Napa grapes; notable **Cabernet Bosché, Chardonnay,** sweet Riesling known as **Edelwein,** Pinot Noir.

(3) **Gallo, E. & J.** Modesto ★/★★
World's largest winery, pacesetters for quality jugs like Chablis Blanc, Hearty Burgundy, and recently good, moderate-priced VARIETALS. Best are **Sauvignon Blanc,** Gewürztraminer, Barbera; Cabernet and Chardonnay forthcoming. Good value.

(RW) **Gemello.** Santa Clara ★★
Old family winery, well known for hearty, Italian-style reds: Barbera, Cabernet, Zinfandel, Petite Sirah. Good value.

(3) **Geyser Peak.** Son. ★/★★
Owned by Schlitz Brewing Co. and under new management; keeps trying with moderately good VARIETALS, including Gewürztraminer, Fumé Blanc, and more recently, champagne.

(3) **Giumarra.** S.J.V. ★/★★
Bulk producer of dessert wines at Bakersfield, now also making large quantities of premium and good mid-VARIETALS like French Colombard, Ruby Cabernet, and Petite Sirah. Good value.

(RW) **Grand Cru.** Son. ★★/★★★
Small winery at Glen Ellen making aromatic Gewürztraminer, fresh, fruity Chenin Blanc; also good Cabernet and Zinfandel.

(RW) **Grand Pacific.** Marin ★★

New, small winery at San Rafael in Marin County that purchases grapes to make Merlot, Cabernet, Riesling, and rosés priced rather grandly for good but not distinguished wines.

**Gran Val.** Second label of Cabernet and Zinfandel from Clos du Val. Good value.

(RW) **Grgich Hills.** Napa ★★/★★★

Flowery, fragrant **Riesling** and Chardonnay from this brand-new winery at Rutherford. Reds not yet released.

(3) **Guild.** S.J.V. ★+

Winegrowers' co-op in the central valley; full range of VARIETALS, GENERICS, dessert wines, and brandy. Owns Cresta Blanca, Cribari, Roma; most famous brand is Vino da Tavola and new Winemasters VARIETALS.

(RW) **Gundlach-Bundschu.** Son. ★★/★★★

One of Sonoma's oldest names now revived on original site in the Valley of the Moon. Good **Cabernet**, **Gewürztraminer**, **Chardonnay**, others. One to watch.

(RW) **Hacienda.** Son. ★★/★★★

Immaculate little winery in the town of Sonoma making fine **Chardonnay**, clean, fresh Gewürztraminer, balanced **Cabernet**.

(RW) **Hanzell.** Son. ★★★+

Important pioneer of using oak cooperage for Burgundy-style **Pinot Noir** and **Chardonnay** in the 1950s; both continue to be superb.

(RW) **Harbor Winery.** S.J.V. ★★★

Small operation at Sacramento making small quantities of rich **Chardonnays** from Napa Valley and ripe Amador Zinfandels.

(RW) **Heitz.** Napa ★★/★★★★★

Pacesetter for intensely concentrated Cabernet from **Martha's Vineyard** near Oakville; lush, buttery **Chardonnay**; and an interesting range of other VARIETALS as well as excellent **Angelica** dessert wine.

(RW) **Hoffman Mountain Ranch (HMR).** S.L.O. ★★/★★★

New family-owned estate at Paso Robles making good **Zinfandel**, Chardonnay, and unusual **Pinot Noir** from hill vineyards. One to watch.

(RW) **Hop Kiln.** Son. ★★/★★★

Small producer housed in converted hop kiln in the Russian River Valley near Healdsburg; big Sonoma Zinfandel, good dry **Gewürztraminer**.

(3) **Inglenook.** Napa ★/★★★

One of Napa's oldest wineries now owned by Heublein, making full range of VARIETALS and expanded line of jug wines (Navalle); somewhat variable quality but still excellent **Cask Cabernet**, good Fumé Blanc, delightful **Charbono**. Good value.

(W) **Iron Horse.** Son. ★★★

One of Sonoma's newest wineries in the Russian River Valley; notable first effort at Chablis-like **Chardonnay**, fresh Pinot Noir Blanc; Pinot Noir to come.

(3) **Italian Swiss Colony.** Son.; S.J.V. ★/★★+

Large old winery founded in last century in northern Sonoma, now owned by Heublein with most wines from grapes in the central valley. Good value Chenin Blanc, Zinfandel; wide range of jugs and fortified wines under Lejon label.

(RW) **Jekel.** Mont. ★★/★★★

Quite new winery at Greenfield in Monterey making very promising **Chardonnay**, interesting Riesling. Bears watching.

(RW) **Johnson's Alexander Valley.** Son. ★★

New estate in Alexander Valley with 45 acres planted in **Chenin Blanc**, Zinfandel, and other varieties.

(R) **Jordan.** Son. ★★★

Ambitious new undertaking near Healdsburg modeled after Bordeaux estate and aiming at Bordeaux-style **Cabernet**; first vintage 1976 promising, 1977 better. Limited amount of Chardonnay will be made also.

(RW) **Keenan, Robert.** Napa ★★★

Small estate on Spring Mountain producing excellently balanced **Chardonnay**, good Cabernet, intense Pinot Noir.

(RW) **Kenwood.** Son. ★★/★★★

Located at Kenwood between Sonoma and Santa Rosa; makes full range of VARIETALS, best are **Cabernet** and dry **Chenin Blanc**; also good Zinfandel.

(W) **Korbel.** Son. ★★★

One of earliest producers of good California champagne: Brut, Natural (the driest), and a new Blanc de Noir (all Pinot Noir). Good value.

(W) **Kornell, Hanns.** Napa ★★★

Good sparkling wines in the German style, from Riesling mainly but made by the méthode champenoise. **Extra Dry**, **Sehr Trocken** (driest). Good value.

(3) **Krug, Charles.** Napa ★★+

Founded in the last century at St. Helena, consistently above-average table wines with clean, straightforward VARIETAL character; rarely extraordinary but good Cabernet, Chardonnay, sweet Chenin Blanc. Jug line: CK Mondavi, inexpensive but uninteresting. Good value.

(RW) **Lambert Bridge.** Son. ★★+

Young winery in Dry Creek area of northern Sonoma, attractive **Chardonnay**, Cabernet.

(3) **M. Lamont.** S.J.V. ★

Brand name for wines of Bear Mountain growers' co-op at Bakersfield; now owned by Labatt Brewery. Huge quantities sold also in bulk; decent mid-VARIETALS such as French Colombard, Ruby Cabernet are best values.

(W) **Landmark.** Son. ★★+

New young winery at Windsor in the Russian River Valley specializing in white wines, Chenin Blanc, Chardonnay, Gewürztraminer; also good Cabernet and Zinfandel.

(3) **Lawrence Winery.** S.L.O.

New winery with 900 acres in Edna Valley and plans for producing 36,000 cases of nine VARIETALS, including Sauvignon Blanc, Colombard, Gamay Beaujolais, Cabernet.

(W) **Long Vineyards.** Napa ★★★

Very tiny, very promising **Chardonnay** and **Riesling** from hilltop LATE-HARVEST vineyards on Pritchard Hill; first efforts rich, intense, and well-balanced.

**Los Hermanos.** Beringer's line of GENERIC and VARIETAL jugs.

(R) **Lytton Springs.** Son. ★★★

Tiny property on Lytton Springs Road in Alexander Valley making blockbuster Zinfandel (grapes formerly sold to Ridge) with rich, spicy fruit and aromas.

(RW) **Markham.** Napa ★/★★

New winery in St. Helena with 200 acres in various parts of Napa Valley—Cabernet, Chardonnay, Muscat, Riesling. Wines from bought grapes under Vin Mark label.

(W) **Mark West Vineyards.** Son. ★★+

Russian River Valley estate making good Chardonnay, Gewürztraminer, Pinot Noir Blanc.

(RW) **Martin Ray.** S.C. ★★★+

Small mountaintop property above Saratoga founded by legendary and eccentric wine figure Martin Ray; soil and climate produce intriguing **Cabernet**. Wines now made by Ray's son.

(3) **Martini, Louis.** Napa ★★/★★★

One of Napa's older, most distinguished names with a full range of VARIETALS and GENERICS; good **Cabernet** (Special Selections very fine), Pinot Noir, Zinfandel, Barbera; Mountain jug wines reliable. Luscious **Moscato Amabile**, but very limited availability. Good value.

(RW) **Martini & Prati.** Son. ★★

Large producer of table and GENERIC wines in southern Sonoma, extensive use of redwood cooperage for mostly Italian-style wines.

(3) **Masson, Paul.** Santa Clara ★/★★+

Large premium producer with full line of table, sparkling, and fortified wines, founded by Burgundian Paul Masson and famous for his champagnes. Moderately good VARIETALS and Souzao ports. Top line of vintage-dated wines: Pinnacles Selections. Good Emerald Riesling and sturdy red Baroque.

(W) **Matanzas Creek.** Son. ★★★

Brand new winery in Bennett Valley; small but impressive start with **Gewürztraminer, Pinot Blanc**; reds to come, Cabernet and Merlot planted.

(RW) **Mayacamas.** Napa ★★★+

Small, mountaintop estate in the Mayacamas range making **Cabernet** and **Chardonnay** of big, intense character, very long-lived. Made LATE-HARVEST Zinfandel famous; some Zinfandel occasionally produced.

(RW) **Mill Creek.** Son. ★★★

New, small winery near Healdsburg with good **Cabernet**, Merlot, and **Chardonnay**; worth watching.

(RW) **Mirassou.** Santa Clara ★★/★★★

The fifth generation at Mirassou first produced wines for the family label, formerly large producer of VARIETALS sold to other wineries. Pioneers with mechanical harvesting and field-crushed grapes in Monterey. Good Cabernet, hefty Zinfandel, crisp White Burgundy, and others, also Champagne Nature. Good value.

(3) **Mondavi, Robert.** Napa ★★/★★★★

Dynamic, energetic family winery started from scratch in 1966, now over half a million cases annually. Constant experimentation results in often brilliant wines, but some less so. Outstanding **Cabernet Reserve**, also fine regular Cabernet, **Fumé Blanc, Chardonnay**, sweet **Rieslings**.

(RW) **Monterey Peninsula.** Mon. ★★/★★★

Fruit-jammed **Zinfandel** and **Barbera** and good Cabernet from this winery on the edge of Monterey; also Petite Sirah.

(RW) **Monterey Vineyard, The.** Mon. ★★/★★★

Part of Coca-Cola's Wine Spectrum, a huge facility at Gonzales scaled down from original 1974 projections. Good, sweet **Riesling**, Gamay Beaujolais, Gewürztraminer, and BOTRYTISED **Sauvignon Blanc**.

(RW) **Montevina.** Ama. ★★★

Excellent property in the Shenandoah Valley making passionate **Zinfandel**, potent Sauvignon Blanc, and good Cabernet and Barbera; experimenting with Nebbiolo. Zinfandel Nuevo is a light, fruity treat. Good value.

(R) **J. W. Morris Port Works.** Oakland ★★★

Small operation specializing in very good vintage-dated port and dense, fruity Pinot Noir, Cabernet.

(RW) **Mount Eden.** Santa Clara ★★★+

Formerly part of Martin Ray estate, now owned by multiple partnership. Spectacular vineyard on mountain overlooking Santa Clara Valley above Saratoga gives superb **Pinot Noir** and **Chardonnay**, but succession of owners in recent years leaves it currently in flux. Expensive.

(RW) **Mount Veeder.** Napa ★★★

Tiny mountaintop estate in the Mayacamas range producing intense **Cabernet** from own vineyard; other VARIETALS from purchased grapes.

(RW) **Nichelini.** Napa ★★

Small, family winery in hills east of the valley, with tasting and sales at the winery. Good Chenin Blanc, Sauvignon Vert. Good value.

(R) **Niebaum-Coppola.** Napa

The old Niebaum manor house and Cabernet vineyard purchased from Inglenook by the movie director. 110 acres in vines; mostly Cabernet, some Charbono, Zinfandel, Cabernet Blanc. Ambitious projections, expensive.

**Novitiate of Los Gatos.** Santa Clara ★★
Mostly dessert wines made at this winery run by Jesuits; mostly altar and fortified dessert wines; **Black Muscat, Dry Malvasia.**

(RW) **Obester.** S.C.M. ★★+
Small new operation at Half Moon Bay making VARIETALS from purchased grapes (mostly north coast counties); good Cabernet.

(RW) **Papagni.** Madera ★★+
Sizable grower in the central valley with new winery for VARIETALS, sherry and dessert wines; Barbera, Alicante Bouschet, Zinfandel, excellent **Moscato d'Angelo.** Also bottles Rancho Yerba Buena Cabernet and jugs. Good value.

(RW) **Parducci.** Men. ★★/★★★
Old-style producer at Ukiah known for round, fruity Zinfandel, good Petite Sirah, Chardonnay, moderately priced. Top line is Cellarmaster. Some wines labeled "not aged in wood." Good value.

(RW) **Pecota, Robert.** Napa ★★
Very small vineyard near Calistoga with good Gamay Beaujolais and delicate, spicy Flora, Petite Sirah.

(3) **Pedroncelli.** Son. ★★
Old, family-owned winery at Geyserville producing good standard VARIETALS; earthy, medium-bodied reds; pleasant whites at good value. Zinfandel, Chenin Blanc, Chardonnay. Good value.

(3) **Perelli-Minetti.** San Joaquin ★
Large bulk producers in the central valley, also market own VARIETALS, GENERICS, and brandy under various labels, including Eleven Cellars, Ambassador, Guasti.

(RW) **Phelps, Joseph.** Napa ★★★+
Deluxe small winery in eastern hills above St. Helena; notable **Chardonnay,** late-harvest **Rieslings,** and fine **Gewürztraminer;** powerful reds as well, including Cabernet, Pinot Noir, Syrah. **Insignia** is top-label red; second line of table wines, Le Fleuron.

(RW) **Preston.** Son. ★★★
New small winery at Dry Creek with first-rate **Sauvignon Blanc,** good Cabernet; bears watching.

(R) **Quady. Madera.** ★★★
Small producer in central valley making good vintage-dated port solely from Zinfandel.

(R) **Rafanelli, A.** Son. ★★+
Very small operation in Dry Creek area making good, berryish Zinfandel, Cabernet, and Gamay Beaujolais.

(RW) **Raymond.** Napa ★★★
Newly launched winery at St. Helena with sound, balanced **Cabernet** and Zinfandel, plus Riesling and **Chardonnay.** Promising.

(R) **Ridge.** S.C. ★★★/★★★★
Top-flight winery on ridge of northern Santa Cruz range; pacesetters for Zinfandel in all styles, from smooth, round Coast Range to powerful LATE HARVEST; excellent, intense Cabernet (Monte Bello, York Creek), Petite Sirah, Ruby Cabernet; occasional fine whites.

(3) **River Oaks.** Son. ★★
Large new winery at Healdsburg with extensive vineyards; attractive Chardonnay, Riesling, rosés.

(RW) **Roudon-Smith.** Santa Clara ★★+
Small winery in hills above Santa Cruz, concentrating on powerful Zinfandel, including LATE HARVEST, fruity Cabernet. Best Zinfandel: Chauvet vineyard.

(RW) **Round Hill.** Napa ★★+
Home winemaker now selling commercially from purchased grapes; medium-style Cabernet, Chardonnay, Chenin Blanc at good prices. Good value.

(RW) **Rutherford Hill.** Napa ★★+
New winery owned by valley growers and partners in Freemark Abbey. Good but variable quality, promising Gewürztraminer, Chardonnay.

(RW) **St. Clement.** Napa ★★★
New producer on Spring Mountain with fine, oaky **Chardonnay**, well-balanced classic Cabernet. One to watch.

(RW) **Sanford & Benedict.** S.Barb. ★★★
Young winery and vineyards near Lompoc above Santa Barbara; Pinot Noir, Cabernet, and Merlot packed with extract; intense Chardonnay. Promising, but harsh young reds need time to develop.

(3) **San Martin.** Santa Clara ★★/★★★
Large bulk producer now refurbished and producing very creditable VARIETALS, especially Zinfandel (Amador), attractive Chenin Blanc, also light, low-alcohol whites: soft Chenin Blanc, soft J. Riesling. Good value.

(RW) **San Pasqual Vineyards.** Escondido ★★+
30,000-case winery near San Diego owned by a group of partners growing Napa Gamay, Chenin Blanc, Sauvignon Blanc. Red table wine a blend of Cabernet, Petite Sirah, and Gamay—good value.

(R) **Santa Cruz Mountain Vineyard.** S.C.M. ★★★
Very small property making intense, powerful, hill-grown Pinot Noir and stalwart Cabernet, Petite Sirah from purchased grapes. To watch.

(RW) **Santa Ynez.** S.Barb. ★★/★★★
Promising new winery in the Santa Ynez Valley—lovely 1978 Sauvignon Blanc, fresh Chenin; somewhat vegetal Cabernet so far.

(W) **Schramsberg.** Napa ★★★★
California's finest champagnes, especially fresh Blanc de Blancs, rich **Blanc de Noir**, charming Cuvée de Gamay sparkling rosé; at revived Schramsberg estate in hills near Calistoga.

(3) **Sebastiani.** Son. ★★/★★★
One of the largest family-owned wineries at Sonoma, making full range of table, sparkling, and dessert wines. Good, traditional Italian-style reds and quite fine, well-aged Proprietor's Reserve **Barbera, Cabernet, Pinot Noir,** and **Zinfandel.** Good nonvintage Cabernet and Zinfandel. Gamay Beaujolais Nouveau, Eye of the Swan. Good value.

(3) **Setrakian.** San Joaquin ★
Large producer of bulk wines, plus average table, dessert and sparkling wines.

(R) **Shaw, Charles F.** Napa ★★★
New small producer above St. Helena aiming at cru-style Beaujolais; first effort in 1979 comes very close. Small amount of Zinfandel by 1981.

(R) **Silver Oak.** Napa ★★★
Limited production from small winery at Rutherford. Good Alexander Valley Cabernet to date, given 5 years aging before release.

(3) **Simi.** Son. ★★★
Old winery at Healdsburg now owned by Schieffelin, producing good, sound VARIETALS, especially graceful **Cabernet,** Zinfandel, **Chardonnay, Gewürztraminer.**

(RW) **Smith-Madrone.** Napa ★★+
Small new winery on Spring Mountain making Chardonnay, Cabernet, interesting Auslese-style Riesling (see "The Wines of Germany").

(W) **Smothers.** S.C.M.
Smashing first Gewürztraminer, subsequent wines not as impressive from this producer, in transition from Santa Cruz vineyards to Sonoma near Glen Ellen.

(3) **Sonoma Vineyards.** Son. ★★/★★★
Large, modern winery at Windsor in the Russian River Valley; full range of VARIETALS, GENERICS, good sparkling Brut. Good Chardonnay and Cabernet from estate-owned vineyards, especially **Alexander's Crown Cabernet.** Good value.

(RW) **Sotoyome.** Son.
New small winery at Healdsburg emphasizing unfiltered Cabernet, Petite Sirah, Zinfandel, some Chardonnay.

(RW) **Souverain.** Son. ★★/★★★
Handsome winery in Alexander Valley and an old name revived with sound, attractive VARIETALS, good value Cabernet, French Colombard, Zinfandel, Pinot Noir.

(RW) **Spring Mountain.** Napa ★★★
Showcase estate on Spring Mountain producing very fine **Cabernet**, **Chardonnay**, Sauvignon Blanc, with Pinot Noir in wings.

(RW) **Stag's Leap Wine Cellars.** Napa ★★★/★★★★
Small but growing producer in lower Napa with notable **Cabernet**, very good **Merlot**, good Chardonnay and Riesling; well-made wines that receive meticulous attention.

(R) **Stag's Leap Winery.** Napa ★★+
Longtime grower at estate near the crag known as Stag's Leap, now producing robust, reasonably priced reds like Burgundy, Barboza, Petite Sirah.

(RW) **Sterling.** Napa ★★/★★★★★
Magnificent gleaming winery set on knoll at north end of the valley, now part of The Wine Spectrum of Coca-Cola. Superb **Cabernet**, Merlot, Sauvignon Blanc, **Chardonnay**.

(RW) **Stonegate.** Napa ★★
Small winery in northern Napa, generally attractive but variable quality Sauvignon Blanc, Chenin Blanc, light Pinot Noir.

(W) **Stony Hill.** Napa ★★★★
Notable small estate on top of mountains above St. Helena; very limited quantities of fine, crisp Chardonnay, Riesling, Gewürztraminer, and sweet Sémillon du Soleil. Hard to find, but worth seeking.

(3) **Stony Ridge.** Alameda ★★
Medium-sized winery in Livermore Valley, best known for reds; also fair whites such as Sauvignon Blanc, Chenin Blanc, good dry **Riesling**.

(R) **Sutter Home.** Napa ★★+
Known for stalwart, hearty Zinfandels from Amador; also a fresh, dry white Zinfandel. Good value.

(R) **Swan, Joseph.** Son. ★★★+
Tiny estate at Forestville making very big, rich Pinot Noir and Zinfandel from intense ripe fruit. Most sold out to regulars on mailing list.

(RW) **Trefethen.** Napa ★★★
Large growers at Yountville that sell most of their grapes but now make good, stylish **Chardonnay**, **Cabernet**, and quality table red and white under the Eschcol label.

(RW) **Trentadue.** Son. ★★+
Long-established growers and bulk producers in northern Sonoma, now making recently upgraded VARIETALS like **Zinfandel**, Chenin Blanc, Cabernet, good red GENERICS.

(RW) **Turgeon & Lohr.** Santa Clara ★★/★★★
Small winery in San Jose with sizable holdings in Monterey; wines appear on J. Lohr label, include Chardonnay, aggressive Cabernet, and Gamay Noir.

(RW) **Veedercrest.** Napa ★★+
Winery on Mount Veeder in the Mayacamas range, variable quality reds and whites such as White Riesling, Chardonnay, Chenin Blanc.

(RW) **Ventana.** Monterey ★★+
Very new winery in Soledad with 600 acres, sells most of its grapes; first Chardonnay quite good, further assessments must wait.

(RW) **Villa Mount Eden.** Napa ★★★
Small estate at Oakville making good, elegant **Cabernet**, full, oakish Chardonnay, dry **Chenin Blanc**, elegant Pinot Noir.

(3) **Weibel.** S.C.M. ★
Large, old winery at Mission San Jose making broad range of average wines, both table and dessert; sparkling wines from Sonoma.

(RW) **Wente.** Alameda ★★★
> One of the oldest names in California wine, pioneer with VARIETALS. Best known for fresh, balanced whites like **Chardonnay**, Chenin Blanc, **Sauvignon Blanc**, **Blanc de Blancs**, Grey Riesling; good Petite Sirah, straightforward Pinot Noir. Good value.

(RW) **Wine and the People.** Berkeley ★★★
> Home winemakers' supply company in the heart of Berkeley that also operates like a European village winery, offering small lots of well-made VARIETALS (Cabernet, Zinfandel, **Pinot Noir**) and bulk wines for "bring-your-own" containers. Good value.

(RW) **Yverdon.** Napa
> Still-emerging winery on Spring Mountain; vineyards there and near Calistoga planted to Cabernet, Merlot, Gewürztraminer.

(RW) **Zaca Mesa.** S.Barb. ★★+
> New winery in the Santa Ynez Valley making interesting Zinfandel, **Sauvignon Blanc**; also Cabernet, Chardonnay.

(R) **Z D.** Napa ★★★
> Small winery transplanted from Sonoma to Rutherford in Napa Valley; big, tough **Pinot Noir** promising; good Amador Zinfandel; reasonably good Chardonnay.

# The Pacific Northwest

The vineyards of Washington, Oregon, and Idaho are on the same latitudes as Bordeaux and Burgundy in France, a fact that has fostered a tremendous surge in plantings over the last decade. The state of Washington has the most acreage, most of it in the Yakima Valley 190 miles southeast of Seattle, and some near the Oregon border in Hood River Valley.

Oregon has a sprinkling of small but growing wineries, principally in the Willamette Valley west and south of Portland but also in the Umpqua Valley in southwest Oregon. Idaho's small vineyards lie in the western part of the state between Boise and the Snake River.

A fair amount of Concord grows in the northwest, particularly Washington, but excitement centers on such early-ripening vinifera varieties as Chardonnay, Sauvignon Blanc, Pinot Noir, and Merlot; excellent White Riesling is made in Oregon, also promising for Pinot Noir and Cabernet.

## WINE GUIDE: THE PACIFIC NORTHWEST

**Alhambra.** Large winery (250,000 cases) producing wines from Concord, hybrids, some Pinot Noir near Yakima, Washington. Started after Repeal.

**Amity.** Small winery in southern portion of Oregon's Willamette Valley emphasizing whites and Pinot Noir.

**Associated Vintners.** A group of professors in Seattle whose jointly owned vineyards in Yakima Valley produce notable Gewürztraminer, Sémillon, Chardonnay, and Cabernet Sauvignon.

**Bingen.** Small winery in the Hood River Valley at Bingen, Washington, producing Chenin Blanc, Gewürztraminer, and other varieties.

**Château Ste. Michelle.** Large winery headquartered in Seattle with large vineyards in Yakima Valley. Good Cabernet, Sémillon, Riesling, sweet Chenin Blanc. Sparkling wines from Chardonnay and Pinot Noir grapes are forthcoming.

**Eyrie Vineyards.** Quite small winery and vineyards in the Willamette Valley near Dundee, Oregon, making oak-aged Chardonnay and Pinot Noir and other varieties.

**Hillcrest.** One of the first wineries in the Umpqua Valley at Roseburg, Oregon, emphasizing White Riesling and other white varieties; some Pinot Noir, Zinfandel.

**Hinzerling.** Small winery in the Yakima Valley near Prosser, Washington, making sweet and dry Gewürztraminer, some Cabernet; expansion planned.

**Knudsen-Erath.** Partners in a growing winery at Dundee, Oregon, in the Willamette Valley making interesting Pinot Noir, Chardonnay, some sparkling wines.

**Preston.** Small but growing winery in eastern Yakima Valley near Pasco; quite good Chardonnay, Sauvignon Blanc, Chenin Blanc; also making Cabernet and Merlot.

**Reuters Hill Winery.** Formerly Charles Coury Vineyards in northern Willamette Valley west of Portland (Tualatin Valley) making Riesling, Gewürztraminer, Pinot Noir, and Chardonnay.

**Ste. Chapelle.** Idaho's foremost winery so far, located at Sunny Slope west of Boise; named for the famous Paris chapel and making promising Rieslings, austere Fumé Blanc.

**Sokol Blosser.** Young winery in the Willamette Valley at Dundee, Oregon, making fine Riesling, good Sauvignon Blanc, and big plans for Pinot Noir. One to watch.

**Tualatin.** Growing winery due west of Portland producing excellent Riesling, Gewürztraminer; oak-aged Pinot Noirs beginning to appear. Bears watching.

# New York and Other States

New York and other states east of the Rockies have traditionally produced wines from two types of grapes: (1) those developed from native varieties, such as Concord, Catawba, and Niagara, or (2) from French-American hybrids, crossings of native American grapes with French species bred to survive the colder climates of the Northeast. The native American grapes have a distinct grapiness about them that is quite different from wine grapes grown anywhere else, a flavor sometimes characterized as "foxiness." The French-American hybrids were developed to ameliorate this character; they are much closer in style and flavor to the European grape species *Vitis vinifera* that is grown in wine regions around the world.

New York State's wine industry is the second largest in the nation. Its principal growing regions are the Finger Lakes district west of Albany and toward the Great Lakes, Erie and Ontario; and the Hudson River Valley, a burgeoning region 50 miles north of New York City gaining attention for its hybrid varietals like Seyval Blanc and Chancellor. European varieties are grown in the state's newest region on the eastern tip of Long Island; there is also growing interest for them in the Finger Lakes region.

Important vineyards are also to be found in Ohio, Michigan, Virginia, Maryland, Missouri, Pennsylvania, Arkansas, and Texas.

# GRAPE VARIETIES:
# NEW YORK AND OTHER STATES

**Aurora.** One of the top white French-American hybrids developed by Seibel, producing crisp dry white wines and quite good sparkling ones.

**Baco Noir.** Forceful red French-American hybrid; gives deeply colored wine and is often blended with other red varieties (such as Chancellor) to soften its impact.

**Cascade.** Early-ripening, pale red French-American hybrid used for reds and rosés.

**Catawba.** Native light red grape with strong grapy flavor used to make pink or white wines and a great deal of sparkling wine (New York).

**Cayuga.** A cross between Riesling and Seyval Blanc that makes a soft, fragrant, pleasing white wine.

**Chambourcin.** Increasingly popular French-American hybrid red.

**Chancellor.** French-American hybrid red that produces sound, medium-bodied dry reds.

**Chelois.** French-American hybrid for round, fruity reds of some richness but often hints of native grapiness.

**Concord.** The great American jam grape that produces pungent, usually sweet red wine, or white if juice is pressed leaving color-rich skins behind. Widely planted in New York, strong grapy flavors.

**Cynthiana.** A red grape native to the Ozark Mountains in Arkansas and Missouri; full-bodied, usually sweet, but without the "foxy" flavor.

**De Chaunac.** Good, rich, red French-American hybrid; excellent color and body.

**Delaware.** One of the best of the native white grapes—crisp, clean wine with less of the native grapiness. Dry versions can be quite pleasant.

**Dutchess.** Native grape found mostly in New York, similar to but not quite as good as Delaware.

**Foch (Marechal Foch).** Vigorous French-American hybrid red producing fullish, Burgundy-style wines.

**Isabella.** Deep red native American grape with pronounced grapy flavors; pale juice used in New York sparkling wines.

**Leon Millot.** French-American hybrid producing red wines similar to Foch.

**Niagara.** One of the oldest American grapes used for sweet, grapy whites, sometimes quite pleasant.

**Seyval Blanc.** Possibly the best and certainly most popular of French hybrid whites, making fine, fruity, full-bodied dry wines.

**Verdelet.** Excellent white hybrid producing fragrant, delicate dry white wines; promising future.

# WINE GUIDE:
# NEW YORK AND OTHER STATES

**Benmarl.** Forward-looking property in the Hudson Valley at Marlboro with increasingly good wines from French-American hybrids, notably Marlboro Village White, Red, Seyval Blanc.

**Boordy Vineyards.** Vineyards owned by Philip Wagner who pioneered with French-American hybrids in the United States. Sound red and white table wines from vineyards in Maryland near the Potomac.

**Brotherhood.** One of the oldest wineries in the East (Hudson Valley) with a wide range of mostly sweet table wines, fortified wines, some hybrid VARIETALS such as Chelois, Chancellor.

**Bully Hill.** Small property in the Finger Lakes district of New York making good reds and whites, some sparkling wine from French-American hybrids. Bully Hill Red, Bully Hill White, Chancellor.

**CLINTON VINEYARDS**

HUDSON RIVER REGION

**SEYVAL BLANC**

*A dry white table wine made from 100% Seyval Blanc grapes, using the best traditional practices of small premium estates in Europe and America.*

ESTATE **1978** BOTTLED

GROWN, VINIFIED AND BOTTLED BY
CLINTON VINEYARDS INC.
CLINTON CORNERS, DUTCHESS CO., NEW YORK

11.7% ALCOHOL BY VOLUME

SEYVAL BLANC. This wine is made of 100% Seyval Blanc, one of the French-American hybrid grape varieties that does well in cold climates such as that of New York State. The grapes were grown on the Clinton estate in the Hudson River Region near Poughkeepsie, N.Y., and the wine was made and bottled by the owner.

**Canandaigua.** Old firm in the Finger Lakes region of New York producing under the Virginia Dare label.

**Cascade Mountain.** Small property near Poughkeepsie in the Hudson Valley region of New York producing good dry reds, white, rosé.

**Chateau Grand Travers.** Ambitious producer in Michigan; grows French-American hybrids and imports California vinifera wines.

**Chicama.** Family-owned winery on Martha's Vineyard off Massachusetts, pioneering with vinifera such as Chardonnay, Riesling, Pinot Noir, Zinfandel.

**Clinton Vineyards.** Small but important estate near Poughkeepsie, N.Y., producing superb Seyval Blanc.

**Glassock Vineyards.** Pioneer vineyards in southwest Texas in the Davis Mountains north of Big Bend; grows European varieties such as Chenin Blanc, Pinot Noir, Sauvignon Blanc, Cabernet, Chardonnay, and Zinfandel. Blue Mountain Vineyard wines will be top line. First wines exhibit strong VARIETAL character; an operation to watch.

106

**Glenora.** Young winery in the Finger Lakes region at Dundee, N.Y., producing good hybrid VARIETALS such as Seyval Blanc Cayuga.

**Gold Seal.** Old leading firm in the Finger Lakes region of New York strongly influenced by Frenchman Charles Fournier who encouraged work with vinifera varieties. Best wines: Chardonnay, Charles Fournier Blanc de Blancs champagne.

**Great Western.** Sparkling wine producers of long standing in the Finger Lakes region of New York, now part of Coca-Cola's Wine Spectrum. Reasonably good Seyval Blanc, Great Western Brut.

**Haight Vineyards.** Connecticut's first bonded winery at Litchfield, producing French-American hybrids, prize-winning Riesling.

**Hargrave Vineyards.** Pioneering young winery at Cutchogue on the eastern tip of Long Island, with good Chardonnay, Cabernet-Merlot, Whole Berry Pinot Noir; promising future.

**Heron Hill.** New small winery in the Finger Lakes region at Hammondsport, New York; interesting Riesling, Chardonnay, Seyval Blanc, Delaware.

**Hudson Valley Wine Co.** Winery situated on the bluffs of the Hudson producing mostly native grape wines, some hybrids; good Delaware.

**Johnson Estate.** Small winery near Lake Erie that sells most of its native American grapes and hybrids but makes small amounts of Seyval Blanc, Chancellor, Ives Noir.

**Markko.** Very small property in Ohio near Youngstown producing very fine Chardonnay, good Riesling, some Cabernet. Quantity too small to go very far but quality has far-reaching impact.

**Monarch.** Brooklyn-based producers of the famous Manischewitz kosher wines.

**Montbray.** Carefully tended vineyards of French hybrids and vinifera at Silver Run, Maryland. Good Seyval Blanc, Foch, Chardonnay, Riesling.

**Royal Winery.** Large family-owned winery in the Hudson Valley producing broad range of kosher wines under the Kedem label; also some hybrids.

**Sakonnet.** Small winery making a name in New England for Rhode Island Red and America's Cup White, which is based on French hybrids; some vinifera.

**Tabor Hill.** Well-established winery in Indiana becoming more widely known for its Vidal Blanc, Baco Noir; also some Chardonnay.

**Taylor.** New York State's largest winery with vineyards in the Finger Lakes region and a new line of wines, California Cellars; still produces wines from native grapes, some hybrids for table wines (Lake Country Red, White, Gold), sherries, New York State champagne.

**Vinifera Wine Cellars.** Owned by Dr. Konstantin Frank, pioneer with vinifera wines (Chardonnay, Riesling, Muscat Ottonel) in the Finger Lakes region of New York. Only vinifera VARIETALS.

**Widmer.** Large old firm in the Finger Lakes region producing wide range of table wines from native grapes, hybrids, and vineyards in California. Lake Niagara, Delaware, Cream Sherry.

**Wiederkehr.** The South's largest winery with extensive vineyards in the Ozark Mountains at Altus, Arkansas. Mostly native varieties, including good Cynthiana; earnest experiments with Riesling and other vinifera varieties.

# THE WINES OF AUSTRALIA

I t is only fairly recently that the world has discovered some of the fine wines of Australia. Though the industry got its start about the same time as that of California (wine grapes were planted by the first immigrants in 1788 near Sydney), production and export have increased steadily and impressively in the last 20 years. Credit for the first major plantings of the 1830s goes to a schoolteacher named James Busby, who planted vineyards in the Hunter River Valley of New South Wales. The success of wines from those vineyards encouraged plantings throughout southern Australia, though today they are in widely disparate areas ranging from Perth on the western coast to Coonawarra in the south, and as far north as Roma in Queensland.

Today, Australia has roughly 200,000 acres under vine at latitudes roughly corresponding to the northern coast counties of California around San Francisco (Napa, Sonoma, Santa Clara), as well as those of central Chile. Most of Australia's wine-producing regions are in hot, dry climates that produce full-bodied wines and a large quantity of dessert and fortified wines such as Sherry. The better table wines come from cooler growing regions, such as Hunter Valley in New South Wales, the Barossa Valley of northwestern Victoria, and Coonawarra of South Australia's southernmost portion.

Principal wine grapes were, until recently, the Shiraz for red wines and the Sémillon for white, and they are still the dominant premium varietals. The German Riesling and related varieties have also accounted for many of the lighter, fruitier white wines. In the last decade, however, there has been much interest in such grape varieties as Cabernet Sauvignon and Chardonnay, with the result of many new plantings of these varietals as well as increases for Pinot Noir and Sauvignon Blanc.

Nomenclature is varied and somewhat confusing to those unfamiliar with Australian wines. Many wines are labeled as generics, such as Claret, White Burgundy, or Hermitage (actually considered another name for the Shiraz grape), but varietal names are increasingly used, as in Cabernet Sauvignon, Shiraz, or often a combination of the two, as they are frequently blended. There are numerous proprietary names as well, such as Chateau Tahbilk or McWilliam's Lexia. The most informative labeling, however, gives regional designation and grape variety, as in Watervale Shiraz Cabernet, a red blended from these two varieties from the Watervale district of Southern Australia.

In the last decade tremendous modernization has taken place within the industry. New technology, such as the use of stainless steel fermenting tanks and cold fermentation techniques, has resulted in fresher, more delicate, and fragrant white wines, for example. While Australia has long been known for its robust, full-bodied, and long-lived red wines, it is now producing a great many light fruity reds, increasingly popular for everyday consumption, at very reasonable prices.

Vintages in Australia are rather like those in California since the two climates are relatively similar. Although some years are definitely superior to others such as 1979, which is considered a great year, catastrophes across the board are rare. Poorer vintages in some regions are usually offset in other areas.

# PRINCIPAL WINE REGIONS

## New South Wales (N.S.W.)

**Corowa**  South of Sydney near the Murray River; known chiefly for fortified wines and brandy.

**Hunter Valley**  One of the oldest and most important wine-producing areas for claret-style reds based mostly on Shiraz and dry whites made from Sémillon, also known as Hunter Riesling. Principal areas are Pokolbin and Rothbury, both often seen on labels. Famous individual estates include Lindemans' Ben Ean, Lake's Folly, The Rothbury Estate, Brokenwood, Drayton's Bellevue, and Penfold's Dalwood.

**Mudgee**  Climate similar to Hunter but on higher ground. Principal plantings are Cabernet, Shiraz, Semillon, Rhine Riesling, Chardonnay, and Traminer. Excellent reds are made here.

**Riverina**  Also known as MIA, Murrumbidgee Irrigation Area. Hot, flat country formerly known mostly for fortified wines. Cold fermentation techniques now account for lighter, fruitier table wines, increased emphasis on better varietals.

**Rooty Hill**  Just west of Sydney and best known for its sparkling wines, namely, Minchinbury Champagne.

## Queensland

**Roma**  Australia's northernmost, and warmest, wine region. Mostly fortified and dessert wines made here.

## South Australia (S.A.)

**Barossa Valley** (Eden Valley, Springton)  Famed for fruity whites from the Rhine Riesling, Barossa is Australia's most famous wine region, located about 35 miles north of Adelaide. Settled by German immigrants, the region reflects this heritage in the white wines, cuisine, and music. Most major wineries have vineyards here, including Seppelt's, Lindeman, Penfold, Thomas Hardy, Henschke, Gramp, and the cooperative, Kaiser Stuhl. Also small prestigious producers like Wolf Blass. In addition to fruity whites, Barossa is known for Shiraz and classic reds from Cabernet Sauvignon.

**Coonawarra**  Small but excellent region for red wines based on Cabernet and Shiraz. Aboriginal name means "wild honeysuckle." Coolest and southernmost growing region where grapes ripen slowly and late. Wynns, Redman, and Lindeman are important producers here.

**Keppoch**  Adjacent to Coonawarra on the north, with similar climate and possibilities for future expansion. Reds and whites similar to Coonawarra though perhaps not as intense.

**Southern Vales** (McLaren, Morphett) Langhorne Creek, South of Adelaide Cool regions producing fine reds and whites that are among Australia's best. Hardy's Tintara vineyard is here, Kay Bros. Amery, as well as Reynell, Ryecroft, and Seaview.

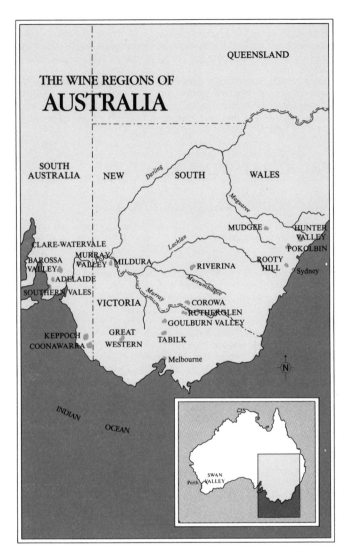

THE WINE REGIONS OF

# AUSTRALIA

QUEENSLAND

SOUTH AUSTRALIA

NEW    SOUTH    WALES

Darling

Macquarie

MUDGEE

HUNTER VALLEY

POKOLBIN

CLARE-WATERVALE

Lachlan

MURRAY VALLEY

MILDURA

BAROSSA VALLEY

ADELAIDE

SOUTHERN VALES

RIVERINA

ROOTY HILL

Sydney

Murrumbidgee

Murray

VICTORIA

COROWA

RUTHERGLEN

GOULBURN VALLEY

KEPPOCH

COONAWARRA

GREAT WESTERN

TABILK

Melbourne

N

INDIAN

OCEAN

SWAN VALLEY

Perth

# Tasmania (Tas.)

**This island** off the southeastern coast is too cool and damp for most varieties, but small experimental vineyards of Chardonnay, Traminer, and Rhine Riesling are under observation.

# Victoria

**Glenrowan-Milawa** (Wangaratta)  Green valley of the Ovens River, producing interesting whites and reds. Leading vineyards are Bailey's Bundarra, Brown Bros.

**Great Western**  Westernmost slopes in Victoria at 1,000 feet above sea level. Known mostly for sparkling wines; dry reds and whites also produced. Seppelt's Arrawatta estate is here and Best's Concongella.

**Goulburn/Tabilk**   Small area north of Melbourne producing good reds, especially from Chateau Tahbilk.

**Mildara** (Merbein, Red Cliffs, Robinvale)   Mostly fortified dessert wines and red/white blending wines here at another district along the Murray River. Crisp dry whites and good reds appear under Mildara Winery label. Robinvale is becoming known for its dryish whites such as McWilliams' Lexia.

**Rutherglen**   South of Corowa on the hot plains of the Murray. Known for Sherries, big, hearty reds from Shiraz, and more recently, lighter table reds and whites.

# Western Australia (W.A.)

**Margaret River**   New region south of Perth showing excellent promise for varietals.

**Swan Valley**   Near Perth, very hot climate producing very robust wines, from Sandalford's and Houghton's.

# PRINCIPAL GRAPE VARIETIES

## Red

**Cabernet Sauvignon.**   Gaining ground rapidly, second only to Shiraz in number of plantings; the two are often blended and prosper similarly in cooler regions. Several 100% Cabernets are extremely good and age well.

**Grenache.**   Fairly widely grown and produces some light wines under the grape name, but mainly used for blending in dry reds.

**Pinot Noir.**   Small acreage as yet but appears promising for cooler regions of Australia.

**Shiraz.**   Of Persian origin and similar to the Syrah of the Rhône Valley in France where it is used in Hermitage and Châteauneuf-du-Pape. In cooler regions of Australia, like Barossa, Coonáwarra, or Mudgee, Shiraz produces big, interesting red wines, though somewhat lighter than those of the Rhône. Wines from the hot plains, however, are much heavier and less distinguished, but often pleasantly robust.

## White

**Chardonnay, Sauvignon blanc, Traminer (Gewürztraminer).**   These varietals are increasingly of interest in Australia, though only small quantities are produced.

**Rhine Riesling.**   The German Riesling. Produces light, aromatic wines, often dry and crisp as Alsatian Rieslings, though just as often fruity or sweet. Best often labeled Moselle, from the Barossa Valley.

**Sémillon.**   Australia's most important grape for dry whites, particularly from Hunter Valley (where it is known, confusingly, as the Hunter Riesling). Produces soft but full-bodied wines labeled by grape variety or as White Burgundy.

**Trebbiano.**   The Italian grape known elsewhere as Ugni Blanc; widely planted for everyday table whites; often blended with white varieties.

# WINE GUIDE

**All Saints.** Vic.

One of Australia's oldest; many vineyards in Rutherglen that produce their Clarets. Lyre Bird Claret, Estate-Bottled Claret, Cabernet Shiraz, Old Liqueur, and Muscat.

**Angove.** S.A.

Mostly blended table wines, a Cabernet Sauvignon and several dessert wines. Fino Sherry, Sauvignon Blanc, and Bookmark Riesling.

**Bailey's.** Vic.

Very old winery whose famous Bundarra vineyard produces long-lived Shiraz and Claret. Also many excellent dessert wines. Bundarra Hermitage, Bundarra Claret, and Muscat Liqueur.

**Berri's.** Vic.

This cooperative in the Murray Valley has Australia's largest winery, producing a full line of table wines, dessert and fortified wines, and Brandy. Rhine Riesling Selected Vineyard, Cabernet Shiraz, and Gordo Moselle.

**Best's.** Vic.

Owners of famous Concongella vineyard in Great Western district of Victoria. St. Andrew's Hermitage Great Western Claret No. 0, producing Claret-style reds, hock, and dessert wines.

**Bilyara, Wolf Blass.** S.A.

Small but outstanding producer of reds in Barossa Valley; also clean fresh whites. Bilyara Individual Vineyard Dry Red (often Langhorne Creek), Bilyara Rhine Riesling.

**Bleasdale.** S.A.

Old family winery in Langhorne Creek district known for quite good dry reds among a full line of table wines and fortified dessert wines. Shiraz, Cabernet Sauvignon, and Verdelho.

**Brand, Eric.** S.A.

Small dedicated winemaker in Coonawarra producing highly respected reds. Cabernet Sauvignon, Laira, and Cabernet-Shiraz.

**Brokenwood.** N.S.W.

Relatively new, small producer of fine reds in Hunter Valley. Hermitage/Cabernet Sauvignon, Cabernet Sauvignon.

**Brown Bros.** Vic.

Family-owned winery of high repute in Milawa producing good table reds and whites; the reds from Milawa are especially good. Milawa Cabernet Sauvignon, Bin Claret, Rhine Riesling, and Mystic Park Dry White.

**Buring, Leo.** S.A.

Large producer of full range of table and dessert wines, Ports, and Sherries in Barossa Valley. Chateau Leonay, Rhine Riesling, and Chateau Leonay Vintage White Burgundy.

**Campbell's.** Vic.

Large producer of full range in Rutherglen, best are whites and dessert wines, including a crisp dry Trebbiano.

**Chateau Tahbilk.** Vic.

Very reputable producer in Tabilk area known mostly for big, well-made reds, some whites. Private Bin Cabernet Sauvignon.

**Chateau Yaldara.** S.A.

Large producer of mostly white wines and good sparkling wines in southern Barossa Valley. Good but not outstanding quaffing wines.

**Craigmoor.** N.S.W.

Sizable winery in Mudgee, producing good table red and white, Port, and Muscat. Cabernet Shiraz, Mudgee Shiraz, Sémillon Chardonnay.

**d'Ahrenberg.** S.A.

Producer of very robust reds in McLaren Vale, as well as some white wine and Port. Aggressive Cabernets, generous full-bodied reds labeled Burgundy.

**De Bortoli.** N.S.W.

Very large producer of over 50 different products, including a line of everyday table wines mostly from the Riverina.

**Drayton.** N.S.W.

Long-established producer in Hunter Valley, owners of famous Bellevue estate. Bellevue Hermitage, Bellevue Riesling.

**Elliott's.** N.S.W.

Quality producer of red and white table wines in Hunter Valley, traditional full-flavored Hunter-style wines. Hunter Valley Riesling Private Bin (Belford) and Dry Red "Tallawanta."

**Gramp's.** S.A.

Large firm in Barossa producing good Rieslings and dry reds under the Orlando label. Best wines contain minute label information. Moorooroo White Burgundy, Miamba Riesling, and Orlando Hermitage.

**Hamilton's.** S.A.

Family-owned winery in south Adelaide producing fresh whites, light reds, and more durable reds from MacLaren Vale and Langhorne Creek. Ewell Vineyards Cabernet, Nildottie Hermitage and Springton Riesling.

**Hardy's.** S.A.

One of Australia's largest wineries with vineyards in Barossa, Hunter Valley, and Southern Vales; best known for reds but produce full line. St. Vincent Chablis, Nottage Hill Claret.

**Henschke.** S.A.

Barossa Valley winery best known for white wines, and one fine red, Hill of Grace; also Rhine Riesling, White Frontignac.

**Hollydene.** N.S.W.

Small new winery in northern Hunter Valley making creditable varietals. Sémillon. Shiraz Cabernet.

**Houghton.** W.A.

Leading producer in the Swan Valley, known for White Burgundy, robust reds, and full-flavored dessert wines.

**Hungerford Hill.** N.S.W.

New Hunter Valley winery, modern, trend-setting with lighter-style reds and fresh, fruity wines. Pokolbin Shiraz and Pokolbin Sémillon.

**Kaiser Stuhl.** S.A.

Large cooperative in Barossa Valley, producing broad range of quite good table wines, mostly white. Individual vineyard selections often outstanding. Rhine Riesling and Special Reserve Bin Claret.

**Karrawirra.** S.A.

Large grower in Barossa who has recently begun to produce and bottle his own wines, good solid reds based on Cabernet and Shiraz.

**Kay Bros.** S.A.

Owners of well-known Amery vineyard in McLaren Vale; good Cabernets and dry whites, especially Amery Rhine Riesling and Sauvignon Blanc.

**Lake's Folly.** N.S.W.

Dr. Max Lake's small winery and vineyards in Hunter Valley produce highly individual reds of interesting complexity and long life. Lake, a retired surgeon, is an influential force in the Australian wine industry. Cabernet Sauvignon, Hunter Valley Estate Dry Red.

**Lindeman.** N.S.W.

Large, old firm with vineyards in most of Australia's wine regions, originally Hunter Valley, site of the famous Ben Ean estate. Full-range production with excellent dry reds and whites. Ben Ean Moselle, Bin 23 Riesling, and Limestone Ridge Coonawarra Shiraz Cabernet.

**McWilliams.** N.S.W.

Large firm in Hunter Valley and Riverina producing full line. Better table wines often given such names as Ann or Elizabeth Riesling, Philip Hermitage. Private bin wines generally quite good. Rhine Riesling, Robinvale Lexia, and Riverina Cabernet Sauvignon.

**Mildara.** Vic.

Producer of dessert and fortified wines in the Murray River Valley but well known for its Reserve Bin Cabernets and Shiraz; many now from Coonawarra.

**Morris.** Vic.

Full-spectrum producers in Rutherglen. Blue Imperial Dry Red, Cabernet Shiraz.

**Norman's.** S.A.

Medium-sized producer of sound reds and whites. Angle Vale Claret, Angle Vale Gewürztraminer.

**Orlando.** See Gramp's.

**Penfold's.** S.A.

Another of the largest wineries in Australia, with vineyards everywhere; wines from various regions often blended. Outstanding reds and whites, very good dessert wines. Autumn Riesling, Grange Hermitage, Coonawarra Claret, St. Henri Claret, and Grandfather Port.

**Pokolbin Estate.** N.S.W.

New small winery in Hunter Valley using modern techniques for quality red wines. Gold Medal Hermitage, Cabernet Sauvignon.

**Quelltaler.** S.A.

One of oldest wineries in Clare-Watervalle region above Adelaide. Best known for Sherries, Ports, and German-style whites; some sparkling wines. Granfiesta Sherry, Hock Bin 65.

**Redman.** S.A.

Winemaker Owen Redman makes outstanding Coonawarra Claret (from Shiraz and Cabernet Sauvignon).

**Reynell.** S.A.

The House of Reynell, famed for its Reynella line of reds and whites, is now owned by Hungerford Hill but still produces under its own label. Chateau Reynella Claret, Rhine Riesling, White Burgundy, and Alicante Flor Sherry.

**Rothbury Estate, The.** N.S.W.

New modern winery in Hunter Valley whose aim is French-style classic red and white wines, with special lots of individual vineyard wines.

**Ryecroft.** S.A.

Producer of agreeable table and sparkling wines; emphasis on big, full-bodied reds from Shiraz and Cabernet. McLaren Vale Hermitage.

**Saltram.** S.A.

Barossa Valley producer of aromatic reds and good quality ports and sherries. Mamre Brook Cabernet and Rhine Riesling.

**Sandelford.** W.A.

New winery near Perth making interesting varietals from newly-developed Margaret River area.

**Seaview.** S.A.

A large old winery in the Southern Vales, noted for white wines, some sparkling, and an excellent Cabernet Sauvignon.

**Seppelt.** S.A.

Headquartered in Barossa, this huge firm has vineyards in all wine-producing regions for its full line of table wines, champagne, and dessert wines, some of which are outstanding, such as the 1972 Cabernet Sauvignon. Widely exported. Great Western Brut Champagne, Moyston Claret, and Arrawatta Riesling.

**Southern Vales.** S.A.

Cooperative marketing large range of reasonably priced whites, reds, and fortified wines. Certain lots of best wines are set aside from each vintage that is specifically labeled (such as Tatchilla Cabernet Shiraz or Langhorne Creek Dry Red); generally worth looking for.

**Stanley.** S.A.

Producers of good, sturdy reds in the Clare-Leasingham district west of Adelaide.

**Stonyfell.** S.A.

Sturdy, full-flavored reds from the Barossa Valley, several private bin

Clarets and Burgundy made from Shiraz and/or Cabernet Sauvignon.

**Tolley.** S.A.
Old firm known mostly for dessert and sparkling wines but recently producing very good Cabernet. Pedare Cabernet Sauvignon, Pedare Rhine Riesling, and Pedare Red Hermitage.

**Tulloch.** N.S.W.
Old Hunter Valley firm notable for its fine reds and Hunter Rieslings (Semillon). Pokolbin Dry Red and Pokolbin White Label.

**Tyrell.** N.S.W.
Important Hunter Valley producer of long standing, known for good reds and whites; best given special vat numbers. Recently making Chardonnay and Pinot Noir.

**Wynns.** S.A.
Large, widespread producer, especially in Coonawarra, probably the first to bring that region into prominence back in the 1950s. Coonawarra Claret, Huntersfield Riesling, Coonawarra Estate Hermitage.

**Yalumba.** S.A.
Large producer in Barossa with full range of table wines, dessert and sparkling wines. Some good Cabernet and Shiraz. Galway Vintage Claret and Pewsey Vale Hock.

# New Zealand

The two islands of New Zealand lie on the same latitudes in the southern hemisphere as Bordeaux and Burgundy in the northern hemisphere, thus the country's future for wine production is being considered with interest. Very little wine is exported as yet, but expanded plantings on both islands, particularly in Chardonnay, Cabernet Sauvignon, and Pinot Noir, seem promising. Principal growing regions on the north island are at Hawkes' Bay, Henderson/Auckland, and, more recently Gisborne and Waikato. The northern part of the southern island at Blenheim has a high quantity of sunshine hours and is becoming known for dry, fruity whites.

Six companies dominate production: Cook's, Corbans, Glenvale, McWilliams, Montana, and Penfolds.

## WHITE WINES

**Chardonnay, Gewürztraminer.** New plantings from these European varietals promising but only small quantities so far.

**Chasselas.** Mostly sweet whites from this lesser grape.

**Palomino Hock.** Light, pleasant semidry whites from the Palomino grape.

**Riesling-Sylvaner.** Dominant white wine, actually from Müller-Thurgau, cross between Sylvaner and Riesling; both dry and sweet wines.

## RED WINES

**Cabernet Sauvignon.** Among New Zealand's oldest reds, especially those of Hawkes' Bay.

**Hermitage (Shiraz).** Medium-bodied reds from the Shiraz grape. Also Pinotage, cross between Hermitage and Pinot Noir.

**Pinot Noir.** Experimental but promising for future on south island.

# THE WINES OF

# SOUTH AFRICA

**S**outh Africa's wine industry dates to the seventeenth century when the land was settled by the Dutch. Her famed sweet wine, Groot Constantia, a rich and noble muscat, was well known to Europeans in the 1800s, as her fine sherries and ports came to be later on and are still today.

New technology and modern equipment, including stainless steel cold fermentation, are making a big difference in the quality of table wines, particularly the white wines, and the move to good varietals is growing rapidly. In 1972 the government set up controls for Wines of Origin and certified wines bear neck seals guaranteeing origin, vintage date, and grape variety.

Wines are made in the southernmost Cape Province in such districts as Constantia, Stellenbosch, Tulbagh, and Paarl; the coastal belt near Capetown; the drier, warmer region of the Little Karoo (Klein Karoo); and to the north, Piquetberg and the Olifants River area.

## WINE GUIDE

**Alto.** A leading estate in the Stellenbosch region noted for sturdy reds, Cabernet, and Alto Rouge.

**Backsberg.** Large estate between Stellenbosch and Paarl with recently upgraded wines, especially reds.

**Bergkelder.** Large commercial firm distributing several major brand lines such as Fleur du Cap, estate wines of Hazendahl and Meerendahl, Grunberger Steen.

**Boberg.** A regional designation for sherries and other dessert wines of Tulbagh and Paarl.

**Cabernet Sauvignon.** South Africa's best reds are made from this Bordeaux variety.

**Cinsaut.** Formerly known as Hermitage, a Rhône grape now made as a sound red varietal or blended with Cabernet.

**Colombard.** The white variety of French Colombard producing light fruity whites similar to those of California.

**Constantia.** Southernmost growing region below Capetown, known earlier for sweet muscat wines, today producing good varietals.

**Drostdy.** Large growers' co-op in the Tulbagh area producing wide range of table wines, sherries.

**Groot Constantia.** Famed estate outside of Capetown renowned for its sweet muscat of the nineteenth century; now state-owned and producing Cabernet and other very good reds.

**Kanonkop.** Private registered estate north of Stellenbosch note for good Cabernet Pinotage.

**Klein Karoo.** Growing area to the east on warm, dry plains between the Drakenstein and Swartberg mountains, producing mostly fortified dessert wines and bulk wines for distilling into spirits.

**K.W.V.** South Africa's largest producers, a cooperative at Paarl making wide range of table and dessert wines of good quality. Better lines include Cape Cavendish and Paarlsack sherries, Landskroon ports, Roodeberg Red, and varietals such as Cinsaut and Cabernet.

**Montagne.** New large estate in Stellenbosch region making impact with varietals like Cabernet, Chenin Blanc, and Riesling.

**Montpellier.** One of South Africa's old famous estates near Tulbagh, best known for varietal whites such as Riesling, Chenin Blanc, Gewürztraminer; also méthode champenoise sparkling wines.

**Muratie.** Old family estate near Stellenbosch producing solid red varietals, especially Pinot Noir plus Steen and Riesling.

**Nederburg.** Famous estate in Stellenbosch now owned by the Stellenbosch Farmers' Winery. Early producers of estate Cabernet and other fine wines; latest innovation: a sweet Botrytised Edelkeur Riesling.

**Olifanstrivier.** Northern section of the Cape Province, a warm, dry climate producing wines mostly for distillation but some table wines of late.

**Paarl.** Wine capital of South Africa and center for several co-operative producers known mostly for white wines and fortified wines, especially sherry.

**Pinotage.** A hybrid red varietal made from a cross of Pinot Noir and Cinsaut, increasingly a South African specialty for round, full-bodied reds that age well.

**Roodeberg.** A sound, blended red from K.W.V. producers.

**Rustenberg.** Estate-style red wines from Cabernet and Cinsaut, among South Africa's best, in Stellenbosch.

**Schoongezicht.** Registered estate in Stellenbosch region making popular Steen, Riesling, and other whites.

**Simonsvlei.** Large co-operative estate near Paarl noted for good reds and whites.

**Steen.** The name for Chenin Blanc in South Africa making both sweet and dry white wines; the country's leading white grape.

**Stellenbosch.** Town and region noted for excellent table wines, especially reds from Cabernet, Pinotage, Cinsaut.

**Stellenbosch Farmers' Winery.** Famous co-op with extensive estates and vineyards producing a wide range of good wines, including Chateau Libertas Cabernet, La Gratitude (white), Nederburg Cabernet and Steen, Oude Libertas Muscat, Tassenberg (red).

**Superior.** Government-regulated standard of quality for superior wines.

**Theuniskraal.** Famous estate in Tulbagh known for well-made whites from Riesling, Steen, Gewürztraminer, Sémillon.

**Tulbagh.** Important growing region for white wines north of Paarl.

**Twee Jongegezellen.** Very old famed estate at Tulbagh known for white wines made from Riesling, Steen, Sémillon; more recently, ambitious efforts with Cabernet Sauvignon.

**Verdun.** Registered estate near Stellenbosch producing good Gamay.

**Zonnebloem.** Brand name for a line of good varietals (Pinotage, Steen, Cabernet) from the Stellenbosch Farmers' Winery.

# THE WINES OF

# SOUTH AMERICA

 he best known wine-producers of Latin America are Chile and Argentina, both of whom are dilligently working to expand and improve vineyard plantings in their respective wine regions. Experiments with varieties like Chardonnay, Chenin Blanc, and Pinot Noir are promising but of small scale as yet. In both countries the best reds are based on Cabernet Sauvignon. Though the wine regions of Chile and Argentina lie only 150 miles apart, they are separated by the Andes, with different soils, climates, and approach to winemaking.

## Argentina

Argentina jockeys with Russia for fourth place in wine production. Most of it stays in Argentina, however, for the country's per capita consumption is almost on a par with those of France and Italy. Most of Argentina's wines come from Mendoza, from vast flat plateaus that back up against the Andes. Glacial melt irrigates the hot, arid plains of vineyards, which are about the same distance from the equator as the vineyards of North Africa.

The Argentines like robust, full-bodied wines that go well with the hearty beef dishes that are the focal point of their cuisine. Modern techniques and equipment in recent years have improved the quality of the wines based on such varietals as Cabernet Sauvignon, Malbec, Merlot, Pinot Noir, Chardonnay, and Chenin Blanc. The whites especially are fresher and fruitier than before, though ripe, well-aged, rather heavy whites are still popular locally.

## WINE GUIDE: ARGENTINA

**Andean.** Brand name for the wines of five growers in Mendoza carefully developed for international markets; good Chardonnay, Chenin Blanc, and Cabernet Sauvignon.

**Arizu, Bodegas.** Large producer with wineries and vineyards in Mendoza planted principally in Cabernet, Merlot, Chardonnay, and Sauvignon. Also méthode champenoise Champagene Arizu.

**Bianchi, Bodegas.** One of the best-known producers of sound varietals, including Don Valentín, a robust red, Lacrado, and Bianchi 1887 (based on Cabernet and Merlot).

**La Caroyense Cooperativa.** Co-op with vineyards in Cordoba, best known for the robust red Vasija Mayor made from Pinot Noir.

**Carrodilla.** Red and white table wines based on Cabernet, Malbec, Pinot Blanc; also bottle-fermented sparkling wine from Pinot Blanc and Pinot Noir.

**Crillon, Bodegas.** Sparkling wine producer producing tank-fermented wines under the Crillon, Monitor, and Frederic Bastiat labels.

**Etchart.** Well-known producer in the Salta region north of Mendoza with popular line of table wines udner the Etchart Privado label.

**Flichman, Bodegas y Vinedos.** Large Mendoza producer of several varietals, including the popular Caballero de la Cepa, a blend of Cabernet and Syrah.

**Furlotti, Angel.** Well-known and widely exported wines from Cabernet and Merlot among reds, whites from Riesling and Pinot Blanc.

**Greco Hermanos.** Large growers in eastern and central Mendoz producing reds from Malbec and Lambrusco, dry, full-bodied whites from Sémillon.

**Lopez, Bodegas.** Old, family-owned winery well known for its full and long-lived Cabernet, Chateau Montchenot.

**Peñaflor.** Giant producer of mostly fortified and dessert wines, including the well-known Tio Quinto, a medium sweet sherry.

**Santa Ana.** Mendoza producer with vineyards planted mostly in Italian red varieties such as Barbera and Pinot Blanc. Best-known dry white is White Pinot; also Santa Ana Burgundy (red).

**Suter, Bodegas.** Highly regarded firm producing sound reds and whites, including the popular Etiquetta Marron, dry white from Pinot Blanc, and Reserva reds.

**Toso, Pascual.** One of Argentina's best-known producers of Cabernet, Riesling, and sparkling wines.

**Trapiche.** Family-owned firm high in Mendoza producing good Cabernet, Malbec, Pinot Blanc, and Montana table wines in liters.

# Chile

Chile's best reds are very good indeed—Cabernets and Merlots handled in the Bordeaux style, a holdover from earlier days when Bordeaux vintners, fleeing the ravages of phylloxera in the vineyards of Bordeaux, came to Chile. The little bug that dines on vine roots never made it across the Andes. Chile's climate in the central valleys of the Aconcagua, Maipo, Cachapoal, and Maule rivers is ideal for Bordeaux varieties, including Sauvignon Blanc and Sémillon among the whites. Riesling also makes fruity, flavorful whites. If Chile can emerge from political difficulties long enough to organize her wine industry for export, we should see more of her good wines in the near future.

# WINE GUIDE: CHILE

**Aconcagua Valley.** Region north of Valparaiso and Santiago in central Chile with some of the best Cabernet and Merlot vineyards.

**Canepa, Jose.** One of Chile's modern, forward-looking firms with vineyards in the Maipo basin south of Santiago. Excellent Cabernet in the Bordeaux style and dry Sémillon.

**Concha y Toro.** Large old firm with wineries at Pirque and San Miguel in the Maipo River Valley; very good Cabernet, especially Casillero del Diablo Tinto and Sauvignon Blanc.

**Cousiño-Macul.** One of the oldest and most distinguished estates in the Maipo basin near Santiago; vineyards planted with cuttings from Pauillac and Graves. Excellent reserve Cabernet aged in French oak. Also good Sémillon and Chardonnay.

**Maipo River Valley.** Leading region south of Santiago for top varietals, such as Cabernet, Merlot, Chardonnay, and Riesling; several of the top wineries located here.

**San Pedro.** One of Chile's oldest producers in the Talca Province of the Maipo district. Claret-style Cabernet quite fine.

**Santa Carolina.** Popular reds and whites ranging from light, fruity style to aged, more mature Cabernet Estrella de Oro; Gran Porton red has more fruit and charm, is better value.

**Santa Rita.** Winery in the Maipo basin just south of Santiago with popular light reds and a good Casa Real Cabernet.

**Undurraga.** Large firm in Santa Ana, west of Santiago, producing Cabernet, Riesling, generic burgundy, and Pinot Noir. Sporadically exported to the United States.

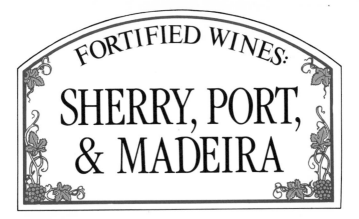

# FORTIFIED WINES:
# SHERRY, PORT, & MADEIRA

ortified wines are those to which brandy is added, bringing their level of alcohol to between 18 and 20%. Both dry and sweet versions are made, the dry ones popular as aperitifs and the sweet ones as dessert or after-dinner wines.

The unique style of sherries from Spain, Porto from Portugal, and madeiras from Madeira, the island in the Atlantic off the northern coast of Africa, is imitated in many wine-producing countries around the world, including the United States, South Africa, Argentina, Australia, and Cyprus. None, however, has as yet managed to achieve the distinctive character and finesse of the prototypes, steeped in centuries-old traditions of their respective countries.

The various types of ports, sherries, and madeiras are described in the Wine Guide that follows. The guide includes brief notes on the leading firms that produce them and the names of their best wines. Vintage years are those declared for vintage port.

## WINE GUIDE

**Amontillado.** A medium-dry, amber-colored sherry, richer and more full-bodied than fino or manzanilla but only slightly less dry. Name means "in the style of Montilla," a town and its wine near Cordoba.

**Amoroso.** A name occasionally used for sweet oloroso sherries.

**Barbeito.** Madeira shippers exporting under the Crown label—Malmsey, Rainwater, Bual.

**Bertola.** Sherry shippers owned by the conglomerate Rumasa, exporting mainly to the United Kingdom.

**Blandy.** Old firm of Madeira shippers at Funchal, principal city and port of Madeira. Duke of Clarence Malmsey.

**Bual.** Medium-sweet sherry, rich and dark but not as sweet as Malmsey.

**Calém.** 77 75 63 60 58 55 48 47 35
Family-owned firm of Portuguese port shippers that has recently widened exports. Full line of ports.

**Cockburn.** 77 75 70 67 63 60 55
A leading shipper of fine ports (British-owned), including a very good Special Reserve Ruby.

**Cossart Gordon.** One of the oldest shipping firms in Madeira; good, dry Rainwater Madeira and No. 92 Crown Bual.

**Cream Sherry.** An oloroso sherry blended with sweet wines made from Pedro Ximenes or Moscatel; can be richly dark or mellow amber in color.

**Croft's.** 77 75 70 66 63 60 55
Distinguished shippers of port and sherry; one of the oldest firms in Oporto now owned by Gilbey's. Croft's Distinction (Particular in Great Britain) is fine old tawny.

**Crusted port.** Port blended from two or more vintages but bottled within a few years; as it matures a "crust" of sediments forms in the bottle; like vintage port, it requires decanting.

**Delaforce.** 77 75 70 66 63 60 58 55
Port shippers with expanding world market. His Eminence's Choice is excellent tawny.

**Domecq, Pedro.** One of the largest sherry shippers, still family-owned. La Ina, excellent fino; Celebration Cream. Now also making Rioja under Domecq Domain label.

**Dow.** 77 75 72 70 66 63 60 55
Vintage port sold mostly in England, the name retained when Dow merged with Portuguese firm of Silva & Cosens.

**Dry Sack.** Popular amontillado marketed by Williams & Humbert.

**Duff Gordon.** Old firm of sherry shippers now owned by Osborne. El Cid amontillado, Santa Maria Cream.

**Fino.** Lightest and driest of sherries, usually 15 to 16% alcohol. Bone dry, crisp, distinctive almond aromas; a superb aperitif that should be served chilled.

**Flor.** A unique yeast that forms on the surface of certain sherries as they develop, giving the wines a particular character and aroma that set them apart as finos.

**Fonseca.** 77 75 70 66 63 60 55 48
Port shippers with an excellent range of ports, particularly fine ruby, Bin 27, and dark, full-bodied vintage port.

**Garvey.** Very old sherry storage and shipping firm in Jerez, several sherries and brandies. Fino San Patricio, Tio Guillermo Amontillado.

**Gonzalez Byass.** One of the largest, oldest shipping firms in Jerez, with one of the best finos, Tio Pepe; also a very good Alfonso Dry Oloroso, La Concha Amontillado.

**Graham.** 77 75 70 66 63 60 55 48
Best known for vintage ports popular in England and Scotland, also late-bottled vintage.

**Harvey's.** Widely known sherry shippers in Bristol, England; famous Bristol Dry, Bristol Milk, and Bristol Cream sherries. Also port shippers, good Ruby and Directors' Bin Tawny.

**Henriques & Henriques.** Shippers of fine madeiras, mostly to Europe.

**Jerez de la Frontera.** Center of sherry production in Spain near Cadiz. The name sherry derives from the town name that is pronounced "Hereth." Most of the leading *bodegas*, or storage and shipping warehouses, are located here and open to tourists.

**Kopke.** 77 70 66 63 60 55 48
Said to be the oldest port shipper, founded in 1630s.

**Late-bottled vintage (LBV).** Port of a single vintage kept in wood beyond the two-year limit for vintage port. Matures faster and is ready to drink sooner, often the equal of some vintage ports.

**Leacock.** One of the oldest and best-known Madeira shippers; excellent dry Sercial, rich Malmsey.

**Malmsey.** The sweetest madeira, rich, dark, luscious but finely balanced. The word is a corruption of Malvasia, one of the grapes that is used to make it.

**Manzanilla.** Dry fino-style sherry that is sent to seaside town of Sanlucar de Barrameda on the Spanish coast where it picks up a certain tang from the salt-sea air. A connoisseur's favorite. La Gitana is one of the best known.

**Martinez.** 77 75 70 67 63 60 58 55
Old, distinguished port shippers now owned by Harvey's.

**Niepoort.** Dutch-owned port shippers, still family-owned. Good Ruby.

**Offley Forester.** 77 75 72 70 67 66 63 62 60
One of the oldest port shippers, famous for vintage ports from the estate Quinta Boa Vista.

**Oloroso.** Dark, rich sherry, more full-bodied than fino or amontillado with a distinctive nutty aroma; completely dry but sweetened for cream sherries; dry oloroso also popular.

**Palo Cortado.** Dark-colored dry sherry, lighter than oloroso but richer in body than amontillado, appealing fragrance; serve chilled.

**Palomino.** Well-known sherry shippers best known for Palomino Cream, now owned by Rumasa.

**Port of the vintage.** Wood-aged port (usually tawny) mostly of a single vintage; not the power and character of vintage port as name implies.

**Puerto de Santa Maria.** Coastal town near Jerez with a number of important sherry shippers.

**P.X.** Abbreviation for Pedro Ximenez grapes that are dried in the sun to intense sweetness; used to sweeten olorosos, occasionally made into very sweet wine on its own.

**Quinta do Noval.** 77 75 70 67 66 63 60 58 55 31
One of the great port estates famed for its vintage ports, particularly the 1931.

**Rainwater.** A style of madeira similar to Verdelho but a bit drier; seen mostly in the United States and Canada.

**Rebello Valente.** 77 75 70 67 66 63 60 55
The vintage ports of the shipping firm of Robertson's, now owned by Sandeman.

**Robertson.** Port shippers now owned by Sandeman. Rebello Valente vintage ports, also a pleasant tawny called Dry Humour.

**Rozés.** Port shippers formerly owned by a French firm, now with Domecq; medium-quality white, ruby, tawny ports.

**Ruby.** Youngest style of port aged 2 or 3 years in wood; rich red color; bold, fruity character, some richness at best; lesser ones harsh, thin.

**Rutherford & Miles.** Old shipping firm in Madeira with famous Old Trinity Bual, good Malmsey, Rainwater.

**Sandeman.** 77 75 70 67 66 63 62 60 58 57 55
Huge concern with large shipping houses for both port and sherry. Partners' Port is an excellent tawny, also big, full-bodied long-lived vintage ports. Excellent sherries such as Dry Don Amontillado, Apitiv, Armada Cream. Recently sold to Seagram's.

**Sanlucar de Barrameda.** Seaside town on the Andalusian coast of Spain where manzanilla is aged.

**Sercial.** Driest of the madeiras and an excellent aperitif; serve chilled.

**Solera.** A system used for aging and blending sherries and madeiras to maintain quality and consistency of style. A number of barrels containing wines of various ages are grouped together; as wines are drawn from the oldest level, the barrels are topped up with younger wines. Average solera age is usually up to 20 years.

**Tawny.** Port aged a number of years in wood until it becomes tawny in color, though some lesser ones are mixed with white port. The best aged 8 to 15 years or more in wood are mellow, rich, and very fine.

**Taylor, Fladgate.** 77 75 70 66 63 60 55; LBV 72
One of the great port houses best known for its very full-bodied vintage ports, intense ruby and No. 10 tawny.

**Tio Pepe.** Well-known fino sherry from Gonzalez Byass.

**Verdelho.** Semidry style of madeira, best when chilled and served as an aperitif; often sold as Rainwater in Canada and the United States.

**Vintage port.** The best port of a single vintage, bottled after 2 years in wood to mature in bottle. Powerful, intense, sweet, and extremely long-lived, requiring at least a decade to mature, often two. Throws heavy sediment and must be decanted. Vintages declared only when quality of grapes merits it. Important old vintages are 48 45 35 34 27 20 12 11 08 04 1900.

**Warre.** 77 75 70 66 63 60 55

One of the more distinguished port shippers and one of the oldest; long-lived vintage port, excellent Warrior Ruby, Nimrod Tawny, LBV '69.

**Wood port.** Port aged in wood (rubies and tawnies) rather than bottle (vintage).

# WINE & FOOD

A strict code of rules for what wine goes with what food is out of place today. Most people feel free to choose according to personal preference. There are those who prefer to drink white wine with everything; others feel that a serious dinner without red wine is somehow incomplete. Certain time-honored pairings, however, that have evolved over the last century or so indicate how specific wines bring out the best in a particular dish, or vice versa. They are well worth investigating, if only to see whether or not you agree.

Wines should be avoided with certain foods. Foods that are overly spicy and pungent may overwhelm even the sturdiest wine, especially such condiments as pickles, chilis, citrus, mustard, Worcestershire or Tabasco sauce, and vinegar. Try using dry white wine or cognac in salad dressing instead of vinegar. Chocolate also throws off the taste of sweet wine, so save the mousse to serve with coffee.

## APÉRITIF

One of the most delightful choices to precede the meal is champagne or other sparkling wine. A glass or two sets things off on just the right note and it's a marvelous icebreaker. Wines that are too sweet will dull rather than stimulate the appetite, but lightly sweet ones such as German Moselle, California Chenin Blanc or Blanc de Pinot Noir, or Gewürztraminer are very good choices. Chilled Fino Sherry is a classic apéritif wine and goes particularly well with salty or smoked hors d'oeuvres.

The following suggestions are intended only as a general guide to traditional combinations and a few recommendations that have particularly interested me on occasion. There are so many wines available to us today that any number of substitutions can be made, so I urge you to be adventurous and extend your taste horizons with discoveries of your own.

## HORS D'OEUVRES AND FIRST COURSES

**Antipasto.** Crisp, dry white such as Pinot Grigio or Tocai; light, Italian red Chianti, Valpolicella, Côte du Rhône.

**Asparagus.** Saint-Véran, California Chardonnay.

**Avocado.** Stuffed with shellfish: Johannisberg Riesling; Grey or Emerald Riesling.

**Caviar.** Champagne, iced vodka.

**Crudités.** Dry white such as Sancerre or Sauvignon Blanc or light red such as Côte du Rhône, Gamay, Bardolino.

**Eggplant, stuffed.** Robust red such as Zinfandel, Barbera, Dão.

**Escargots.** White Burgundy or Rhône such as Hermitage (white).

**Fish, smoked (salmon, sturgeon).** Fino Sherry, Manzanilla, dry sparkling wine from California or Saumur, Kriter.

**Foie gras.** Sauternes is preferred in Bordeaux; champagne or dry Gewürztraminer also good.

**Pasta.** With fish or cream sauce, Pinot Bianco, Soave; with meat or vegetables Chianti Classico, Carema, Valtellina, Charbono, Beaujolais.

**Pâté.** Dry white such as Mâcon-Villages, Chardonnay, Sauvignon Blanc, Seyval Blanc.

**Pizza.** Inexpensive Chianti, Zinfandel, Sicilian red, Barbera.

**Prosciutto and melon.** Dry fruity white such as Mâcon, Pinot Blanc; or just off-dry Sylvaner, Mosel, Grüner Veltliner.

**Quiche.** Light red from the Rhône, Chinon, Cabernet, Chancellor.

**Salami, cold cuts.** Dry rosé like Tavel, Roditys, Zinfandel.

**Terrine.** Light red from the Côte de Beaune, Pinot Noir, Corbières.

# FISH

**Bass, striped.** White Burgundy such as Puligny-Montrachet if baked or poached with sauce, or California Chardonnay. If grilled: dry Chenin Blanc, Rhine Kabinett.

**Blue fish.** Full-bodied dry white or medium-bodied red such as Volnay, or other Côte de Beaune; Rioja.

**Salmon.** Full-bodied dry white or medium-bodied red Côte de Beaune.

**Shellfish.** Crisp, dry, tart white; mussels with Muscadet; oysters with Chablis Grand Cru; crab, lobster with Chardonnay; shrimp, scallops with Sauvignon Blanc, Gros Plant, Gavi di Cortese.

**Sole.** Same as striped bass.

**Trout.** Delicate white such as Mosel, Chenin Blanc, Lugana.

# MEAT

**Beef, roast.** Full-bodied Cabernet, Merlot, Hermitage, Shiraz, Dôle, Egri Bikavér, Chianti Classico, Gattinara, Rioja, Taurasi.

**Beef stew.** Hearty red such as Côte Rotie, Spanna, Zinfandel, Dão, Barolo, Vino Nobile di Montepulciano.

**Chicken, roast.** Medium-bodied Cabernet, Merlot, Rhône, Chianti, Rioja, claret-style Zinfandel.

**Chicken, sautéed, Provençal, etc.** Dry, full-bodied white or medium red such as Crozes-Hermitage, Perequita, Inferno.

**Chicken, white sauce.** Full-bodied dry white Graves, white Burgundy, Chardonnay.

**Chinese food.** Crisp or spicy white such as Tocai, Grüner Veltliner, Gewürztraminer, generic chablis.

**Curry.** Same as Chinese food; or beer.

**Duck, goose.** Rhine Spätlese, Alsatian Gewürztraminer; Bordeaux or red Burgundy.

**Game.** Sturdy red such as Côte de Nuits Burgundy, Côte Rotie, Vino Nobile, Barolo, Brunello di Montalchino, Napa Valley Cabernet.

**Ham.** Fresh dry white or rosé, light red; California champagne.

**Hamburger.** Beaujolais-Villages, Champigny, Napa Gamay, Zinfandel.

**Lamb.** Fine Bordeaux or California Cabernet, Merlot; Sassicaia, Australian Cabernet-Shiraz.

**Liver, kidney, sweetbreads.** Light to medium-bodied red Bordeaux or Cabernet from California, Chile, Australia.

**Paella.** Rioja, Gran Coronas.

**Pork, roast.** Medium-bodied red from Rhône, Barbaresco, Barbera. Riesling Spätlese from Rheingau or Rheinpfalz; Alsatian Gewürztraminer.

**Steak.** Firm, sturdy red such as young Cabernet, Hermitage, Shiraz, Gattinara, Chianti Riserva.

**Stews, cassoulet.** Hearty, robust red such as Zinfandel, Châteauneuf-du-Pape, Spanna, Barbaresco, Amarone, Fitou, or Cahors.

**Veal.** Smooth, light to medium-bodied red for chops and scallops; in cream sauce, white Burgundy or Chardonnay.

# CHEESE

**Blues.** Medium-full red with Oregon, gorgonzola, and other light blues, such as Barbera, Valtellina, Nebbiolo d'Alba. Roquefort and Danish Blue need very big, full-flavored wines like late-harvest Zinfandel, Amarone, or sweet fortified wines.

**Creams, brie, camembert.** Mature Bordeaux or Cabernet; medium-bodied Rhônes.

**Cheddar.** Substantial, full-bodied red, especially Cabernet; also Corvo, Rhône, Dôle, Shiraz.

**Cheshire, Stilton, or other English cheeses.** Good ruby or tawny port; big reds such as Amarone, late-harvest Zinfandel.

**Goat cheeses.** Crisp, dry whites such as Sancerre, Sauvignon Blanc, Pinot Grigio; fine, mature Médoc or Côte de Nuits Burgundy, Gattinara.

**Parmesan.** Wines of the Piedmont: Barolo, Barbaresco, Fara, Ghemme.

**Souffles.** Warm, medium-bodied reds like Moulin-à-Vent, Crozes-Hermitages, Corvo, Pinot Noir.

# DESSERTS

**Cakes.** German Auslese, Sauternes, Hungarian Tokay Aszu; Bual Maderia; Asti Spumante.

**Chocolate.** No wine goes with it.

**Creams, custards, puddings.** Barsac, sweet Vouvray, or other sweet white from the Loire.

**Fruit Bavarians, bombes.** Sauternes, Beerenauslesen (BAs); sweet Muscats.

**Fruit, fresh.** Pears or sweet apples paired with cheese can take red wines, but citrus or other acid fruits are difficult unless they are cooked in cakes or custard.

**Nuts.** Tawny port, vintage port, dry Oloroso sherry, Bual Madeira, or Verdelho Madeira.

**Sorbets, ice cream.** Liqueurs instead of wine.

**Strawberries, whipped cream.** Sauternes, late-harvest Rieslings, Gewürztraminer

**Souffles.** Sauternes, Beerenauslese (BA); Tokay Aszu; late-harvest Riesling.

**Note:** A glass of fine, sweet wine is often a perfect choice served by itself instead of, or after, dessert.

# STORING &
# SERVING ADVICE

## STORAGE

Improper storage can damage or destroy a wine, depriving you of the pleasure of fully enjoying what you paid for. Wines should be stored on their sides, for example, so that the cork will stay moist and firmly in place to keep air from getting to the wine. When wines are left upright for a couple of weeks or more, the cork will dry out and shrink, allowing air to reach the wine and spoil it. Heat and vibration can also be injurious to wine.

The most important things to consider in storing wines is to place them in a stable atmosphere, free of vibration, fluctuations in temperature and away from light. The cellars of old houses were ideal in many respects, but today they are often the site of the boiler, washer, and dryer. Cool temperatures are best for wines—the ideal cellar temperature of yore was around 55° to 57°F (13° to 14°C). Normal household temperatures of 68° to 72°F (20° to 22°C) will not harm wines, as long as those temperatures are fairly constant year-round. In warmer atmospheres, however, the wines will tend to age faster, so keep that in mind.

It is useful to have a space to store wines so that you can stock what you need without having to rush out at the last minute to the wine shop or be caught short at a dinner party. Having a "cellar," even a small one, also allows you to take advantage of sales and special offers. After Christmas, for instance, odd lots of wines sometimes become available at special prices as close-outs for incomplete case-lots. It is also nice to be able to acquire wines that tend to disappear from the market soon after they appear—and often save money by doing so. Certain highly prized Cabernets from California are snapped up quickly or escalate in price within a few months. This is sometimes true of great Bordeaux and Burgundies, though consultation with a reliable wine merchant is your best guide here. You should get to know your wine merchant anyway and let him or her know the kinds of things you like. A good wine merchant will be quick to let you know about good buys that would interest you.

There is also the enjoyment one gets in being able to select a favorite wine at a moment's notice or contemplate the pleasures that lie ahead as good wines mature. Whether your storage space is large of small—the corner of an apartment, a closet, or a whole room—try to organize it by category so that you can find what you want easily. Keeping a cellarbook, or log, is also useful. It will enable you to know what you drank and when and what you need to replenish.

# Space for Storing

Storing wines can be done attractively in a variety of styles. Criss-cross bins can be constructed to hold as much as two cases each (all the same kinds of course, so you just remove the bottle on top as needed). Rectangular compartments can serve just as well, though perhaps should be smaller to hold fewer bottles so that they don't roll around. They can be built to your own design or specific space needs, or you can purchase ready-made wine racks that come in wide-ranging styles and sizes. Stackable racks that hold anywhere from eight to sixteen bottles allow you to expand your "cellar" at exactly the rate your wine collection grows.

# SERVING

**Glasses.** Wine glasses come in a variety of sizes and shapes. The all-purpose glass of nine or ten ounces will suit most situations admirably. It should be made of clear, unetched glass (so you can enjoy the wine's appearance), preferably with no lip at the rim. Avoid glasses of less than eight ounces—there isn't room to swirl the wine to open up its bouquet and flavors. Fill each glass only half full so that you have plenty of room for swirling the wine about. Using glasses of different sizes is useful when you are serving two or more wines—it helps people keep them separate and it looks attractive and more festive.

**Temperature.** Room temperature, the traditional recommendation for red wines, can be a bit warm these days. I try to set my red wines in a cool place the day I plan to serve them so that they are around 65°F (19°C). Light reds such as Beaujolais-Villages, Gamay, or Côte du Rhône, even the lighter Zinfandels, are often enhanced by cooling—it makes them fresher. A half hour in the refrigerator puts them at a pleasing temperature. Fine white wines should not be overchilled or it will rob them of flavor, particularly white Burgundy and good California Chardonnays or Rieslings. About three hours in the refrigerator is sufficient for most, or 20 minutes in an ice bucket (half ice, half water—ice alone won't do the job) is best of all. Lesser white wines may benefit from more chilling, as the cold will mask certain deficiencies or overbearing flavors.

**Breathing.** Wines "breathe" when they come into contact with the air. Oxygen opens them up and releases flavors and aromas. Pulling the cork and letting the bottle stand for an hour has virtually no effect on the wine. If you want to aerate wine quickly, pour it into a carafe. Or, once the cork is pulled, immediately pour the wine into glasses and allow it to breathe in the glass.

**Decanting.** Decanting a wine is nothing more than pouring it from the bottle into another container. Any vessel—a carafe, pitcher, or crystal decanter—will serve the purpose. Wines, generally only red, are decanted for two reasons:

1. To separate the wine from sediments that have formed during maturation. This is a natural occurence, and most red wines over eight years old will have "thrown" some sediment; even younger ones occasionally will. The steps for decanting off sediment are illustrated below.
2. To aerate a young wine and loosen it up more quickly for pleasurable drinking.

STORING AND SERVING ADVICE

# Glasses

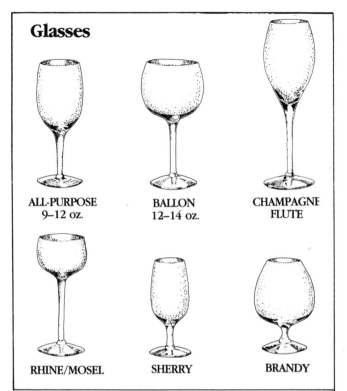

**ALL-PURPOSE**
**9–12 oz.**

**BALLON**
**12–14 oz.**

**CHAMPAGNE**
**FLUTE**

**RHINE/MOSEL**

**SHERRY**

**BRANDY**

# Decanting

Decanting a red wine off its sediment can be done in three simple steps, leaving the wine crystal clear for your enjoyment.

1. Stand the wine upright for several hours or a day to allow the sediment to collect in the bottom of the bottle.

2. Place a candle or other source of bright light near the decanter so that you can see the sediment move toward the neck of the bottle.

3. Pour in one continuous motion from bottle to decanter. When you see the dark shadow of sediment appear in the neck, stop pouring. An inch or two of cloudy wine will remain in the bottle, and the wine that you drink will be clear and free of grit that would spoil its texture.

131

# ACKNOWLEDGMENTS

Numerous people and organizations have been helpful to me in the course of preparing this book. I want to thank the following in particular:

Sam Aaron
Gerald Asher
Martin Bamford
Phillip di Bellardino
Bordeaux Wine Information
    Bureau
Dr. Lucio Caputo
Champagne Information Bureau
Darrell Corti
Michael Coultas, Australian
    Trade Commissioner
Neil Empson
German Wine Information
    Bureau
The Marquis de Goulaine
Louis Iacucci
Italian Wine Promotion
    Center, NY
Edmond Maudières

Daniel Mirassou
Robert Mondavi
Laurenz Moser
Kenneth L. Onish
Dr. Richard Peterson
Bruno Prats
Rioja Wine Promotion Bureau
The Marquis de Roussy de Sales
Jean Sauvion
Sherry Institute of Spain
Steven Spurrier
Andre Tchelistcheff
Alfred G. Tesseron
Byron Tosi
Trade Commission of the
    Government of South Africa
Frederick Wildman & Sons
Wine Institute, San Francisco